SPANISH ROME, 1500–1700

SPANISH ROME
1500–1700

THOMAS JAMES DANDELET

YALE UNIVERSITY PRESS NEW HAVEN & LONDON

Published with assistance from the Program for Cultural Cooperation Between Spain's Ministry of Education, Culture and Sports and United States Universities, and from the foundation established in memory of Philip Hamilton McMillan of the Class of 1894, Yale College.

Designed by James Johnson and set in Monotype Dante types by Tseng Information Systems, Durham, North Carolina. Printed in the United States of America by R. R. Donnelley & Sons, Harrisonburg, Virginia.

Library of Congress Cataloging-in-Publication Data
Dandelet, Thomas James, 1960–

Spanish Rome, 1500–1700 / Thomas James Dandelet.
p. cm.
Includes bibliographical references and index.
ISBN 0–300–08956–2 (alk. paper)

1. Rome (Italy)—History—1420–1798.   2. Papal States—Politics and government.
3. Catholic Church—Foreign relations—Spain.   4. Spain—Foreign relations—Catholic Church.   I. Title.
DG797.8.D36   2001
945'.63207—dc21   2001002544

A catalogue record for this book is available from the British Library.

The paper in this book meets the guidelines for permanence and durability of the Committee on Production Guidelines for Book Longevity of the Council on Library Resources.

10   9   8   7   6   5   4   3   2   1

To Robert and Felicia for their generosity, and to Gloria, Sophia, and Lucas for their love and inspiration

CONTENTS

MAPS

ACKNOWLEDGMENTS

The generosity of many people and institutions made this work possible. First and foremost, colleagues at the University of California, Berkeley, Randolph Starn and Gene Brucker, gave me a great deal of critical advice, time, and encouragement from the earliest stages of the work. Thomas Brady, Theodore Rabb, Charles Faulhaber, Peter Sahlins, and Carla Hesse also offered helpful suggestions. So, too, did Anthony Grafton and John H. Elliott, who both read early versions of the text. I am grateful for a Fulbright fellowship and a fellowship from the Andrew W. Mellon Foundation that financed the initial years of research in Spain and Italy, as did grants from the University of California and the Program for Cultural Cooperation Between Spain's Ministry of Education, Culture and Sports and United States Universities. A year at the American Academy in Rome made the final revisions possible and even enjoyable.

A NOTE ON CURRENCY

The three primary monetary units that were central to the financial transactions between the Spanish Empire and the Papal State in the sixteenth and seventeenth centuries were the Spanish ducat, the Spanish escudo, and the Roman scudo. In the late sixteenth century the value of the Spanish ducat declined slightly in relation to the escudo, but by 1600 the ducat was a stable unit of account worth 375 maravedis, while the gold escudo coin stabilized at 440 maravedis after 1609. See John Lynch, *The Hispanic World in Crisis and Change* (Cambridge: Cambridge University Press, 1992), appendix 1. Exchange rates between Rome and Spain fluctuated little during this period, and the Spanish ducat was worth roughly 1.3 Roman gold scudi. See Antonio Calabria, *The Cost of Empire* (Cambridge: Cambridge University Press, 1989), p. xiii, for exchange rates between Spain and Naples and between Naples and Rome in this period. For the complex details of the broader implications of Spanish monetary policy in Italy, including questions of inflation and exchange fluctuations, see especially Fernand Braudel, *The Mediterranean and the Mediterranean World in the Age of Philip II* (New York: Harper and Row, 1972) vol. 1, pp. 418–542.

INTRODUCTION

I N the Jubilee year of 1500, with the Italian Renaissance in full bloom, two events took place in Rome that served as omens of a fundamental transformation that would occur in the city over the next two centuries. As was often the case with Renaissance omens, the events were not without their ambiguity and contradiction: one signaled the arrival of a powerful and generous new patron while the other spoke of a potentially destructive new force on the Roman scene. Both came from the same distant shore.

To begin with the bright omen, it was in 1500 that Pope Alexander VI Borgia (1492–1503) traveled to the outskirts of Rome, just inside the Aurelian walls, to dedicate the new church and convent of San Pietro in Montorio. Set upon the Janiculum Hill, overlooking the neighborhood of Trastevere, the old church and adjoining Franciscan convent had been rebuilt during the previous two decades through the generous patronage of Spain's Catholic Kings, Ferdinand and Isabella.[1]

In 1480 the monarchs had answered the pleas of the Spanish Franciscan Father Amadeo to become patrons of the convent and church, which were held by some to be built on the location of the crucifixion of Saint Peter. Initially, Ferdinand gave 2,000 gold ducats for the project.[2] In 1488 he pledged annual contributions of 500 gold ducats until the church was finished and wrote to the agent of the bishop of Cefalu in Sicily commanding him to provide 2,000 more toward the cause. In 1493 Ferdinand wrote to his Sicilian viceroy commanding him to send 1,000 ducats to Rome for the church.[3] The Roman church and convent were subsequently rebuilt almost entirely from the revenues of churches under the king's royal authority in the Kingdom of Sicily.[4]

FIG. I   SAN PIETRO IN MONTORIO
(AUTHOR'S PHOTO)

For the king, being the patron of San Pietro in Montorio was an important matter that, in his words, "greatly affects my reputation."[5] Indeed, augmenting the good standing of the Spanish monarchy in Rome
was at the heart of his patronage. For the young Ferdinand and Isabella,
still insecure and less than a decade into their reign, the papacy was an
important potential ally for increasing their authority both internationally and at home. Moreover, all their successors to the Spanish throne
seemed to agree that money spent in Rome was a good investment in
both Roman public relations and internal ecclesiastical affairs. Spanish
rulers continued to send funds to the church and monastery regularly
for maintenance and repair.[6] A plaque in the sacristy of the church reminded later generations of the generosity of the Spanish monarchs and
the corresponding obligations of the friars to pray for their souls.[7] Similarly, an inscription in Bramante's famous Tempietto next to the church

paid homage to the Catholic Kings as benefactors of that jewel of Renaissance architecture, begun in 1502.[8]

The decision by Ferdinand and Isabella to become the patrons of the Franciscan convent and church, as well as of one of Rome's most famous Renaissance architects, established a Spanish royal tradition of patronage in the city that continued for two hundred years. Spanish rule in Sicily, and after 1504 in Naples, brought the monarchy into ever closer contact with the Papal State, and money from those realms was consistently used as a source of royal patronage. It was a good omen, indeed, of the Spanish largess that would help build early modern Rome.

The deepening Spanish involvement in Roman affairs via Sicily and Naples came with a cost, however, as was most clearly demonstrated by the choice of pope presiding at the dedication of the new church of San Pietro in Montorio. Rodrigo Borja—Alexander VI—had originally come to Italy as a child at the urging of his uncle, the Spanish cardinal Alonso de Borja, who later became Pope Calixtus III (1455–1458). The elder Borja belonged to the court of King Alfonso the Magnanimous of Aragon, Ferdinand's uncle, who had conquered the kingdom of Naples in 1442 and created a flourishing Renaissance court there. His rule established the subsequent claims of the Spanish monarchs to Naples. He also brought the Borja family to Italy. The Aragonese monarchy in Naples and the Borja family in Rome became the major factors in the growing Spanish presence in that city in the late fifteenth century.[9]

The brief pontificate of Calixtus III had little lasting impact on Rome, however, and contributed little to the Spanish presence there, with one major exception: after the election of Calixtus, Rodrigo, who had been educated in Rome and Bologna, quickly rose to prominence and was made a cardinal at the age of twenty-six. Although many of the Catalans brought to Rome with Calixtus had been driven from the city upon his death, Cardinal Borja (whose family name was increasingly given as the Italianized Borgia) flourished. By 1492 he was one of the wealthiest and most powerful cardinals in the city. When he was elevated to the papal throne in that year, a crowd of five thousand Romans shouted, "Spain, Spain, and long live Pope Alexander the Roman!"[10]

It became clear early on in his pontificate, however, that this Spanish pope also brought with him the threat of violence and of submission to both foreign soldiers and cultural traditions. No one person embodied this threat better than the pope's son and primary military commander,

Cesare Borgia, who was the focus of the second event of 1500, which constituted the darker omen of the Spanish presence.

On June 24, the feast of Saint John the Baptist, Cesare hosted a bull-fight in the piazza in front of Saint Peter's basilica. Together with a number of other men, Cesare fought a total of six bulls, attacking first on horseback with a long lance, as was the usual tradition among nobles. Cesare chose to fight the last bull on foot, however. Taking a short sword, he cut off the bull's head with one epic blow, making a great impression on the crowd.[11]

Far more than a sporting event, the bullfight embodied the ruthless reputation of not only Cesare Borgia but the thousands of Spanish soldiers under him, a notoriety that had been well established in Rome and the rest of Italy by 1500. In April 1495, for instance, an estimated two thousand Spanish soldiers had surrounded sixty Swiss soldiers in the same piazza where the bullfight was held. Hated for their collaboration with the occupying French army of Charles VIII in January, the Swiss were attempting to leave the city when the Spaniards under Cesare's control attacked them, killing sixteen, among them a woman, and robbing and beating the others.[12] By 1500 many Romans, too, had been killed or exiled at Cesare's orders, including numerous members of Rome's most powerful noble families. In the historian Leopold von Ranke's memorable phrase, "How did Rome tremble at his name."[13]

Even after the death of Alexander VI in 1503 and the fall of Cesare Borgia, the threat of wandering Spanish soldiers remained. According to Francesco Guicciardini's not entirely accurate lament referring to the soldiers of this period, "The Spaniards were the first to begin in Italy to live wholly upon the substance of the people, giving as the reason—and perhaps necessity—for their licentiousness the fact that they were poorly paid by their kings who lacked funds."[14] This was precisely the case in 1527, when Spanish soldiers, together with Germans and a variety of others in the imperial army of Charles V, sacked Rome. Moreover, with tens of thousands of Spanish soldiers serving in the presidios of Naples and Milan in the years to come, their potential threat to Rome was always very real: in 1557 Spanish troops under the duke of Alba massed on the Neapolitan border during the brief war between Philip II and Paul IV; and in the late 1580s and the 1630s Spanish military action against Rome was once more a possibility.

The contrasting images of the early Spanish presence in Rome pre-

FIG. 2   DONATO BRAMANTE,
TEMPIETTO, SAN PIETRO IN MONTORIO
(AUTHOR'S PHOTO)

sented by the patronage of the Catholic Kings on the one hand and
the violence of the Borgias and their soldiers on the other reveal some
basic truths about Spain's position in Rome at this early stage. First, it
included both beneficent patronage and military domination. Both aspects of Spain's involvement were rooted in historical facts and embodied
in economic, political, and social structures. Both reshaped the urban
landscape of Rome. They were the two early faces of Spanish Rome and
Spanish imperialism: generous patron and conquistador. What is equally
clear is that Rome, the traditional center of European empire, was central to the aims and aspirations of the Spanish monarchs, and by 1500 it
was already coming under the shadow of their growing empire.

   This book tells the history of this meeting between Rome and the
Spanish Empire. In the sixteenth and seventeenth centuries Rome was
an old but vigorous remnant of its ancient imperial glory, living out
the final chapter of Gibbon's epic history. Spain was a rising giant that
would become the world's first modern global empire. Papal Rome was
rich in religious authority, the artistic and intellectual trappings of imperial power, and historical memory; Spain in New World gold, a large

navy, and Europe's best soldiers. Each had treasures the other needed and wanted.

Between 1500 and 1700, this combination of necessity and desire drew the old and new empires closely together. Rome played the wise but demanding parent trying to shape Spanish policy and practice on a local and global scale while at the same time asking for increasing levels of support. Spain claimed the role of dutiful son, defending the Papal State with its ships and soldiers and pouring a large amount of money into the old family home, the city of Rome. In return the Spanish monarchs demanded favored-son status not only in Christian Europe but in the eternal city itself.

Rome was transformed as it was drawn into the orbit of Spain. It became Spanish Rome. In the period of Italian history known as the age of the Spanish preponderance, the Papal State was a vital player in the Spanish Empire. Although it formally remained an autonomous monarchy, by the middle of the sixteenth century the Spanish monarchs looked upon it almost as a part of their own state. Rome became the center of Spain's Italian diplomacy and international imperial politics.

It was also the center of Spanish imperial religion. The Spanish monarchs relied upon the papacy to support their ecclesiastical agenda throughout the empire. In turn they fashioned themselves as faithful defenders of papal authority. Spanish absolutism and papal absolutism went hand in hand, and the Catholic Reformation of the late sixteenth and early seventeenth centuries, spearheaded by the papacy and the Spanish monarchy, took on a distinctly Spanish face. In Rome, Spanish churchmen, charities, and saints increased in number and visibility, while in Iberia and other parts of the empire a Catholicism emerged that shared more with traditional universal Roman Catholicism than with any local Spanish Catholicism.

This book explores the history of Spanish Rome, beginning with its foundations. This was the Rome of the Borgia family, whose memory and images are still painted on the walls of the Vatican apartments that take their names. But it was also the city that benefited from Spanish patronage and a growing military alliance with the Catholic Kings. It was with these shrewd and dynamic monarchs that the rough outlines of a political policy and set of practices toward Rome emerged that remained intact for two centuries. By setting an example of generous patronage and political alliance, Ferdinand and Isabella began a policy that was repeated over and over again. Their conquest of Naples in 1504, moreover, established them as Rome's most powerful neighbor and created a strong motive for Spaniards to travel to southern Italy and Rome.

The deepening Spanish contact with the city also led to the creation of a distinctly Spanish myth of Rome during the reign of Charles V, the Holy Roman emperor and king of Spain. The grandson of Ferdinand and Isabella, Charles was the most powerful ruler of his day. Over the forty years of his reign, Spanish soldiers and statesmen increased their presence in Rome, and Spanish humanists began to devise a literary picture of the historical relationship between Spain and Rome. Renaissance Spain met Renaissance Rome more closely during these decades.

This picture was deeply connected to the politics and piety of the time, and it revealed a great deal about the Spanish imperial imagination and mentality toward the old center of European empire. Golden Age literature produced by a range of Spanish novelists, political satirists, historians, religious essayists, poets, playwrights, and pilgrims helped create and reflect a distinctly Spanish idea of Rome. They provided the images and metaphors that informed and shaped the lives and thoughts of Spaniards toward and in Rome. For the monarchs, these works helped justify their roles as patrons and military defenders (or dominators) of the city.

Patron — and military defender — were roles Charles V played with great effectiveness in Rome and other parts of Italy as he succeeded in adding Milan to the Italian possessions of his son and successor, Philip II. Thus, by the time Philip ascended the throne in 1557, Spain was the dominant power in Italy, and Spanish political and economic influence in Rome had expanded substantially. Building on the policies and successes of his predecessors, Philip claimed the role of Rome's primary foreign patron and defender. More than any other prince or pope, he defined and shaped the Roman and Mediterranean world in his lifetime.

As the diplomatic center of Europe and the seat of Roman Catholicism and religious authority, Rome was crucial to the Spanish monarchy's international reputation, expansionist agenda, internal authority, and financial control of the church. The popes, for their part, together with Roman cardinals, clerics, and laity, all benefited from Spanish pensions, gifts, grain, and religious charity on a large scale. No other European power played the patron and protector of Rome in this period as Philip did. In military matters as well, he fashioned himself as the principal defender of the church and provided the military backbone for Italian defenses against the Turkish threat for forty years. In short, Spanish imperialism and the Spanish hegemony in Rome after 1559 was a largely beneficent imperialism that helped build the city into the center of Catholic Reformation Europe.

But the establishment of the Spanish hegemony did not happen without resistance and struggle. Like many Renaissance dynastic struggles, Spain's desire to claim a dominant role in papal Rome and European Christendom was seen as an attempt by a junior sibling to usurp the role traditionally held by the older siblings, France and the Holy Roman Empire. The papacy, fearful of a political and religious breach with France and aspiring to its own independence, frequently resisted Spanish attempts to influence Roman affairs. Indeed, it took more than eighty years for Spain to defeat France and forge a lasting alliance with papal Rome in which it was the dominant partner. In an age that has often been noted for the rise of the nation state, this was a victory of the Spanish Empire over the French nation state. Moreover, it was a victory that revealed the rise of modern imperialism as the dominant political development in Europe and the Mediterranean world in this time. And it was the development upon which the parallel rise of the nation state ultimately depended.

At the same time, the Spanish Empire's success in Rome and Italy represented a victory of a modern global empire over another old Mediterranean empire, that of the Ottomans. Although the Ottoman naval threat constantly hung over the Papal State—indeed, over all Italy—throughout the late fifteenth and early sixteenth centuries, by the late sixteenth century a Spanish navy of roughly a hundred ships dominated the Mediterranean Sea. The Spanish Empire's role as military protector of the Papal State against the Ottomans pushed the Papal State further into the Spanish embrace and cemented the alliance. Again, a growing supply of gold from the colonies to build ships and pay soldiers was critical to the Spanish success.

Thus the great-grandson of Ferdinand and Isabella, Philip II, became the most powerful monarch of the sixteenth century and the major foreign patron of Rome. His image, carved in marble and bronze, painted in oil and fresco, took its place in the churches and palaces of the city. While Roman humanists, musicians, and theologians dedicated their works to the Spanish monarch, the king sent increasing amounts of Spanish gold to help rebuild churches, such as the new Saint Peter's, Santa Maria Maggiore, San Pietro in Montorio, and many more.

Along with the monarch, Spanish cardinals and churchmen took on a new prominence, sometimes welcome and sometimes not. Certainly, the reign and legacy of the Borgia family were not universally applauded. And yet Borgias played a central role in Rome for much of the sixteenth and seventeenth centuries as the only Spanish papal family. They intermarried with the Italian nobility, built and maintained Roman palaces, became leading Jesuits in the city, and held high offices in the papal Curia.

And they were far from alone. Tens of thousands of Spaniards subsequently traveled to Rome and made it their home. Ambassadors, soldiers, courtiers, priests, and painters, they were the new players in town, the most powerful foreign faction, and crucial to Spanish imperial politics and political culture. They were colonizers for a form of Spanish imperialism that is largely unexamined in the historical literature: "soft," or informal, imperialism.[15] This is their history as much as it is that of the monarchs and popes, for they too reshaped the politics, economy, culture, and urban landscape of Rome in ways large and small. By the late sixteenth century, at least one source had them comprising nearly a third of the city's population.

The power and presence of the Spaniards in sixteenth- and seventeenth-century Rome did not go unnoticed by contemporary visitors. On December 2, 1580, when Michel de Montaigne finally reached Rome after the long journey from France, he rented rooms "at the house of a Spaniard, opposite Santa Lucia della Tinta."[16] Indeed, Montaigne had seen large numbers of Spaniards in many Italian cities, and Rome was no exception. His journal is spotted with references to the many Spaniards in Roman colleges and to "the Spanish pomp" where "they fired a salvo of guns at the Castle of S. Angelo, and the ambassador was escorted to the palace by the Pope's trumpeters, drummers, and archers."[17] Gregory Martin, an Englishman visiting Rome at the same time, also noted the strong presence of the Spaniards and declared after visiting the Spanish church of Santiago (Saint James, also known as San Giacomo degli Spagnoli), "In al things that pertaine to Religion, this Nation is of al Strangers the cheefe."[18]

Among these "strangers" were wealthy businessmen like the Fonsecas and famous musicians like Tomas Luís della Vittoria, who came to

Rome to study with Palestrina and to direct the choir in the church of Santiago in the Piazza Navona. Powerful Spanish ambassadors like the count of Olivares maneuvered for political influence in Rome, while other, less powerful figures like Miguel de Cervantes made their way to Rome in search of a patron and perhaps inspiration. So, too, did some of Spain's most important Golden Age painters, including José Ribera and Diego Velázquez, who left behind as a reminder of his stay one of seventeenth-century Rome's greatest portraits, that of Pope Innocent X.

A small sample of the Spaniards present in Rome between 1500 and 1700, these men and many more reveal the interwoven histories of the Spanish Empire and Rome. For politicians, poets, and painters alike, Rome was an essential center of activity and inspiration that animated the Spanish Empire. At the same time, as the "most important non-Italian 'nation'" residing in the city and the one that was "richest in men," Spaniards revitalized Rome.[19]

One of the major institutions that brought Spaniards together in Rome was the Spanish Confraternity of the Most Holy Resurrection. After its founding in 1579, this association quickly grew to include more than a thousand members, one of the largest confraternities in a city of roughly a hundred thousand.[20] As a place where Spanish identity and communal ties were cultivated and encouraged, the confraternity became a locus of Spanish power, patronage, religious display, and charity in Rome together with the clerics who served in the national church of Santiago. Ambassadors, cardinals, clergy, Spanish courtiers, tradesmen, merchants, and wealthy noblewomen resident in Rome all belonged to the confraternity, and as a "nation" the Spaniards were well aware of their importance to the interests of the Spanish crown.

Like the monarchs, these Spaniards were eager to stake a claim to Rome through their self-proclaimed role as pious patrons. Manifestations of Spanish piety in Rome included large-scale charitable giving in the form of bequests to Roman churches, orphanages, hospitals, convents, and monasteries. Hundreds of wills preserved in the archive of the Spanish church and the State Archive reveal much about the Spaniards' relationship to the broader Roman population and the development of their own religious sensibilities.

In addition to their charitable giving, the Spaniards made a religious claim to the city through their ritual life. In a city that revolved around ritual and display — in Europe's quintessential theater society — the Spaniards proved themselves masters of the game. As early as 1574 they began celebrating Easter with a large procession at dawn in the Piazza Navona. By 1597 the event had become so huge that public laws were passed regulating traffic and attendance at the ritual. In short, the Easter ceremony and other Spanish rituals, such as the annual dowry presentations, the feast of Corpus Domini, the triumphs ordered for Spanish military victories, and the masses and festivities celebrating the births and marriages of Spanish royalty, were all part of the Spaniards' attempt to present themselves to the city and the world as the most devout people of Christendom and the leaders of the Roman Catholic world. These festivals were their way of imposing a master myth on Rome, and outdoing the Romans at their own game.

In anthropological terms, the Spanish proved themselves masters of turning traditional religious structures or social "texts" such as processions, ritualized charity, and saint-making into a Spanish text. At one and the same time they both embraced and entered into the traditional Roman world and transformed it into a noticeably Spanish version of the earlier model. This was done not only by the force of literary constructions or ritualized claims to the city but also by the political and economic coercion common to most empires. The Spanish Empire thus reproduced and transformed the religious and social structures of Rome; Spaniards entered into the *longue durée* of Roman society and religion only to leave it something quite different. Moreover, the process of religious Romanization that had begun in Spain centuries before was reinforced and deepened. Thus, both the local culture and the new empire were changed and transformed by the encounter. In the process, a common southern-Mediterranean religious culture emerged that would continue throughout the early modern and modern periods.

One culminating example of the Spanish drive to gain religious honor, reputation, and ultimately power in Rome focuses on the successful attempts by the Spanish monarchs and religious congregations to have Spaniards canonized as Roman Catholic saints. Beginning in 1560, Philip II kept ecclesiastical lawyers permanently in Rome lobbying the papacy to canonize the fifteenth-century Franciscan Diego of Alcalá. Finally, in 1588 Diego became the first saint of the Counter-Reformation as well as the first person canonized in sixty years.

He was not the last, however, and between 1588 and 1690, twenty-seven new saints were added to the Roman calendar; of these thirteen

were Spanish and two came from realms of the Spanish Empire.[21] This is
a dramatic sign of the transformation of Roman Catholicism during the
Catholic Reformation to a Catholicism with a Spanish face, a transformation that is largely unexamined but that had a decisive influence on
the city of Rome and Roman Catholicism in the late sixteenth and early
seventeenth centuries. Moreover, it was this particular success on the part
of the Spaniards that may have been the most permanent victory they
would achieve in Rome. Long after their political, economic, and military power had waned, their saints remained firmly in place as the heroes
of early modern Roman Catholicism and the Catholic Reformation.

What is perhaps most remarkable about the Spanish imperial agenda
toward Rome that was set in motion by Ferdinand and Isabella, furthered
by Charles V, and brought to its height by Philip II is that it continued
to be effective throughout the seventeenth century. During the ill-fated
reigns of Philip IV and Charles II, punctuated by the diminishment of
Spanish power in much of the rest of the Spanish Empire, the monarchs
and Spanish community in Rome retained their presence and influence,
albeit not without periods of serious weakness. Their resilience revealed
the effectiveness of the particular form of Spanish imperialism that flourished in Rome and that constituted one of the great successes of the Spanish Empire.

To approach the history of early modern Rome from the perspective of
the Spanish Empire, as this work does, is to depart from traditional historical themes and theoretical approaches. Historians of 1500–1700 Rome
have most often focused on Renaissance humanism, the growth of the
baroque city, the religious development of Tridentine Catholicism, or
Rome's greatest popes: Pius V, Gregory XIII, Sixtus V, Clement VIII,
Paul V, and Urban VIII. These are all important topics and valid approaches to the history of the city, but they nonetheless present a somewhat fragmented picture of Rome. In short, most recent social, cultural,
and intellectual histories of early modern Rome or on Roman topics have
been disconnected from the key political reality of the period: Spanish
imperial domination.

It is this theme that provides the general theoretical orientation of
this work; but it is important to distinguish from the outset that Spanish imperial domination in Rome was something quite different from
Spanish imperialism in other parts of the empire. The Spanish shadow

touched all aspects of life in early modern Rome, but Spain's imperialism did not take the form of domination that is most familiar to students of the empire. Unlike the direct, heavy-handed military rule from Madrid — formal imperial rule — that characterized other parts of the Spanish Empire, Rome experienced a form of imperialism known to sociologists of empire as informal imperialism. Simply stated, Spanish informal imperialism in Rome acknowledged the political independence of papal Rome and the Papal State. At the same time, however, Spanish monarchs sought successfully to establish authority indirectly through the control and collaboration of various groups in Rome, and by establishing a de facto colony to do their bidding.[22]

This form of Spanish imperialism is not well known or studied in the broader literature on the Spanish Empire. Yet it is critical to an understanding of Spanish Rome and the Spanish Empire itself. The complexity of informal imperialism defies a simple or tightly unified theoretical approach or a focus on a particular group or institution. Rather, it requires a synthetic approach to the problem that draws on a variety of methodological techniques and tools provided by recent works in political anthropology, sociology, cultural studies, religious studies, social history, and political-economic history.

More specifically, in this study I shall incorporate such familiar and disparate topics as confraternities, saints, humanism, patronage, papal politics, charity, Spanish diplomatic history, and Roman urbanism. But the uniting thread loosely connecting all these themes will be informal Spanish imperialism. The large array of topics and the broad chronological span depart from recent tendencies in early modern European history toward more narrowly focused microhistories. Yet this approach has the advantage of making connections between often unconnected topics in cultural and social history by placing them within the interpretive framework of the Spanish Empire. It also has the advantage of restoring the international context and political importance of Rome to a scholarly field that has tended to focus on local and specialized themes in recent years.

From another vantage point, the emphasis on Spanish imperialism within Europe also promises to complicate and alter the prevailing emphasis in early modern history on the rise of the nation state. As the case of the Spanish Empire in Rome and the broader Mediterranean world makes clear, it was the rise of this modern global empire that was the dominant political development of the sixteenth and early seventeenth centuries. Nation states and ideas of national identity developed along-side—and often in response to—the needs and challenges of empire.

The history of Spanish Rome is thus critical for an understanding of papal Rome, Spanish Italy, and the Mediterranean world. It is also central to the broader themes of European imperialism, absolutism, the devel-opment of national and religious identity, and the Catholic Reformation. Why, then, has it remained largely unwritten?

The primary explanation is the historical antipathy toward the Span-ish presence in Italy, a distaste that occasionally includes literal attempts to destroy the memory of that presence. In 1580, when Montaigne first viewed the ruins of ancient Rome, he was moved to reflect on the cause of their destruction and noted in his journal that "the world, hostile to its long domination, had first broken and shattered all the parts of this wonderful body; and because, even though quite dead, overthrown, and disfigured, it still terrified the world, the world had buried its very ruin."[23]

Some three hundred years later, another humanist observer of Ro-man ruins, the prolific epigrapher Vincenzo Forcella, reflected on the "ruins" of a more modern Roman temple, the fifteenth-century Span-ish national church of Santiago. Dismayed at the level of vandalism and destruction, he wrote:

> Rich with so many magnificent works of art, great on account of its many illustrious and celebrated countrymen who had chosen it as their last resting place, at the beginning of our century it was plundered, abandoned, and humiliated by vile service. Reduced to a ruinous state and threatening to collapse, it was buttressed and all the precious ob-jects were transported to the church of Santa Maria de Montserrat, where the hospital was also transferred. I don't remember an example of similar vandalism or equal savagery.[24]

Although the remains of the Spanish ruins had escaped the literal burial that was the fate of most of imperial Rome, their ignominious treatment at the turn of the nineteenth century was born of an anti-imperialist sen-timent not unlike that described by Montaigne.

Fifty years after Forcella's lament over the condition of the church of Santiago, Benedetto Croce turned his attention to the general topic of the Spaniards in Italy and thereby gave impetus to a new generation of scholarship, particularly on Spanish Naples. But it was a very national-ist impetus. In his book *La Spagna nella vita italiana* (1922), Croce tellingly entitles one of his chapters "The Protest of Italian Culture Against the Barbaric Spanish Invasion" and makes no effort to hide his own distaste for the interlopers.[25] Although he had originally planned a book that would have covered the Spanish presence in Italy from the Middle Ages to the eighteenth century, he dropped the idea, returning to a much shortened version of the Spanish project twenty years later. The result is that his work, including a chapter devoted to the Spanish influence in Rome, limits itself to the fifteenth and early sixteenth centuries. It is a brief analysis that covers only the initial incursion of Aragonese immigrants in the fifteenth century, and the impact of the Spanish Borgia popes Calixtus III, and Alexander VI, essentially where my study begins.

It is perhaps understandable that Croce and other Italian scholars were reluctant to invest much time and effort on a chapter of Italian history that their generation found inherently distasteful. Even some contemporary Spanish scholars hesitate to write about a topic that may appear at first sight to celebrate Spanish imperialism or to be part of a triumphalist historiographical tradition. It is undeniable that Spanish Rome constituted one of the jewels of the Spanish Empire and its history was often written about in triumphal terms. The history that follows, however, is an analysis of the success and its historical implications, not a celebration of it. Although the purpose of this work is first and foremost to explore a vital chapter in European history, as an American historian writing in the age of American empire, I found that the topic provoked reflection on the character and consequences of informal empire more generally. I hope that it will do the same for citizens and subjects of empire today.

CHAPTER 1

FOUNDATIONS

L ong before Alexander VI was elected pope in 1492, Ferdinand and Isabella had been consolidating their power in southern Italy and insinuating themselves into the political life of Naples and Rome. More specifically, from 1480, the time they began supporting the church of San Pietro in Montorio, the young monarchs were also creating an image of themselves as strong allies of Naples and defenders of Rome.

That year the Turkish threat to Rhodes and southern Italy helped establish the primary overlap between the interests of the Catholic Kings and those of Italy and the popes. Ferdinand wanted to protect his realm of Sicily and the interests of his family in Naples, where his sister Juana was queen. In addition, he and Isabella started to represent themselves as loyal protectors of the church. It was important to them that the policies of their court were seen as adhering to those of Rome. Stability in southern Italy and strong relations with Rome went hand in hand.

The idea of an Italian league that bound the papacy and the Spanish monarchy as allies, a feature of Spanish policy throughout the two centuries that followed, was already under way by 1481. In that year Ferdinand and Isabella sent two squadrons of ships, one from Castile and one from Aragon, to aid in a naval battle against the Turks. The Battle of Otranto was actually won before the Spanish ships arrived, but the point of Spanish support for papal Mediterranean policy was made. A letter from Ferdinand written immediately before the battle summed up his idealized dedication to the defense of Rome. Sending instructions to his ambassador, Cardinal Luís Juan de Milá, he emphasized that all Christendom had cause to be concerned by the threat of a Turkish invasion of Italy since Rome as well as Naples was thereby endangered. The archbishop

FIG. 3   RAPHAEL, *FERDINAND, THE CATHOLIC
KING*, SALA DELL'INCENDIO, VATICAN
(MONUMENTI MUSEI E GALLERIE PONTIFICIE,
CITTÀ DEL VATICANO)

of Toledo himself had pledged to go to Rome with other Spaniards to
help protect the city, according to the king.[1]

Similarly, Ferdinand made it clear from early in his reign that he also
considered himself responsible for the defense of Naples. He went so far
as to write to his sister the queen, stating that he considered their kingdoms "to be one" and that he would continue to work in their defense as
though they were "his own."[2] This brotherly love may not have moved
the queen or her husband, King Ferrante, as much as Ferdinand hoped,
but it was a clear and honest expression of the Spanish monarch's attitude
toward Naples. He already saw it as part of his own kingdom and was
ready to fight for it. Indeed, Ferdinand appears never to have completely
accepted King Alfonso's earlier decision to divide the Aragonese king-

MAP I   ITALY, 1494 (WILLIAM L. NELSON)

doms and give the Kingdom of Naples to Ferdinand's cousin Ferrante upon Alfonso's death in 1458.[3]

Given their desire to have both Rome and Naples as strong allies, Ferdinand and Isabella also sought to avoid the constant threat that the interests of the two would collide. Even more ominous was the possibility that the pope would ally himself with the French, thereby opening the way for an invasion of Naples by the Most Christian King, who had his own claims to the kingdom. Active and persistent diplomacy was essential. Ferdinand made a point of sending envoys and ambassadors constantly shuttling around Iberia, Naples, Sicily, and Rome. He subsequently became a critical player on the Italian scene in the last decades of the fifteenth century, with Rome as the center of his diplomacy.

In 1482, for example, he helped mediate a peace treaty between Naples and the papacy. Writing to his special ambassador, Juan de Margarit, following the treaty, he urged him to go to Pope Sixtus IV, the cardinals, and the people of Rome and assure them that it was the desire of his court to support the papacy. Moreover, the ambassador was to kiss the pope's feet both as a sign of the king's filial obedience and in thanks for the love, trust, and honor that the pope had bestowed on the Spanish monarchs.[4]

In 1485, Ferdinand was again compelled by political interests to intervene between a pope and his brother-in-law. Pope Innocent VIII Cibo and King Ferrante had clashed when the new pope challenged the Aragonese right to Naples and encouraged a revolt of the nobility there.[5] Since the right of Aragonese succession was also a particularly delicate matter for Ferdinand, he sought the intervention of Cardinal Rodrigo Borgia as intermediary. Rodrigo successfully helped to negotiate a peace between the two powers in 1486.[6]

With these smaller interventions serving as a prelude, in the early years of the reign of Alexander VI the Spanish monarchs made their most important moves into Roman and Neapolitan affairs through a number of treaties and alliances. In 1493 Ferdinand and Alexander signed the Treaty of Barcelona, which granted the pope's sons Cesare and Juan the bishopric of Valencia and title of duke of Gandia, respectively. In exchange, the pope promised to refuse to acknowledge the French king's claims to Naples and to ally himself with the kings of Naples and Spain against any such encroachments.[7] This last condition became a traditional element of Spanish policy in Rome, and it underlined the intertwined nature of Roman and Neapolitan political strategies.

The French threat proved real in late 1494, when Charles VIII of France surprised virtually all Italy with the famous invasion that Guicciardini later condemned as the beginning of the end of an Italian Golden Age. While this last claim was largely rhetorical (particularly in the case of Rome), the conflict did initiate a series of wars between the French and Spanish monarchs for control of Italy that lasted for the next sixty-five years. It also led to a formal alliance, the Holy League of 1495, between

FIG. 4   PINTURICCHIO, *ALEXANDER VI*, DETAIL
FROM *THE RESURRECTION*, BORGIA APARTMENTS,
VATICAN (MONUMENTI MUSEI E GALLERIE
PONTIFICIE, CITTÀ DEL VATICANO)

the papacy, Spanish monarchs, Emperor Maximilian, and Venice. The
success of the league in driving Charles VIII out of Italy almost as quickly
as he had entered gave Ferdinand and Isabella a leading role in Italian
affairs for the first time. It also allowed the Spanish monarchs to gain a
military foothold in Naples and deepen their claim as critical protectors
of the papacy. At the same time, it provided the first extensive military
experience of a holy league binding Spanish monarchs and the papacy.[8]

All was not bliss, however, between the Spanish monarchs and Alexander VI. Rather, Pietro Martire's dire prediction about the danger of
Alexander's love of his family above all else proved true: in 1499 the pope
happily agreed to a marriage between his son Cesare, who had given
up religious life, and the sister of the king of Navarre, a marriage spon-

sored by the king of France. The military implications of the marriage were clear: the new king of France, Louis XII, would become allied to the papacy, and the two would support each other's claims in Italy. This action predictably enraged Ferdinand and Isabella, leading to a vehement exchange of insults between their ambassador, Garcilaso de la Vega, and the pope.[9]

Eventually, the ever shrewd and skillful Alexander VI worked out a series of appeasements that gave the Spanish monarchs widespread economic powers over the church in their realms. And in 1500 a treaty was negotiated that led to the partitioning of Naples between France and Spain.[10] In short, the Borgia pope and his son had succeeded in playing the two major European powers off against each other while gaining advantages from both. This gave them a good degree of autonomy—not to mention wealth and military power—which they used to make their imprint on the city of Rome. Although it was a dynastic imprint above all else, it was a distinctly Spanish dynastic imprint, and it set a precedent for inscribing Spain and Spaniards into the myth of Rome, a precedent that would have long-lasting implications.

ALEXANDER VI AND THE ROME OF THE BORGIAS

A wealthy, well-educated, and sophisticated Renaissance patron, Cardinal Rodrigo Borgia had already built a fine palace in Rome before he was elected pope. Although relatively little is known about his household during his long period as cardinal, it is clear that his wealth from the revenue of his Spanish churches made him increasingly prominent in the court of Rome in the 1470s and 1480s. Self-conscious and proud of its role as the center of classical antiquity, Christian and pagan, by the 1490s papal Rome rivaled Florence as the urban center of cultural and intellectual production. Rome, in short, had embraced the Renaissance ideal of renewal to the extent that by 1500 it had become "the undisputed queen of literary and intellectual life in Europe."[11]

This was Cardinal Rodrigo Borgia's Rome, and, not surprisingly, as soon as he became pope he began working to have his family woven into the historical and artistic fabric of Europe's greatest city. A patron of artists and men of letters, he thus contributed to a tradition of writing and painting Spain into the history of Rome both past and present that would increase over the centuries with the Spanish monarchs. This was a

well-established Roman tradition by the time of Alexander VI, and most
of the oldest Roman noble families, such as the Colonnas and Orsinis,
claimed an ancient Roman lineage. For such families, to celebrate and
memorialize Roman antiquity was to celebrate themselves.[12]

For the Borgia family, however, this meant going even deeper into the
Roman past than the period of the republic, empire, or Christian empire.
Rather, Alexander, whose ties to the city were more recent and tenuous,
required excavations and literary evocations of the ancient heroes and
giants who had made their way to Italy and Spain from Egypt. This was
the period in which Renaissance scholars enamored of Egypt "rediscov-
ered" Italian and Spanish foundations. Foremost among such scholars in
the Borgia court was Annius of Viterbo.

A Dominican priest known for his knowledge of ancient languages,
theology, and archaeology, Giovanni Nanni, or Annius of Viterbo (1432–
1502) as he came to be known, was made a Master of the Sacred Palace by
Alexander sometime in the 1490s.[13] As a courtier valued for his "scholarship," Annius, more than any other writer, provided the raw materials for
the creation of a Borgia family myth that gave Alexander VI an ancient
lineage worthy of a Renaissance prince.[14]

Annius's best-known work was a set of commentaries on supposedly
ancient texts published under the patronage of the Spanish ambassador in
Rome, Garcilaso de la Vega, father of the famous poet of the same name.
It was dedicated to the Catholic Kings in 1498 with the papal stamp of
approval.[15] The *Commentaria super opera diversorum auctorum de antiquitatibus* was, in fact, based largely on Annius's own forgeries. Foremost
among these was a text attributed to the ancient Babylonian historian
Berosus of Chaldea.

Drawing on the authority of this priest and other "sources," Annius
constructed a history of Europe that began with Noah and his sons. The
Commentaries thus had as much in common with the sacred histories of
the Middle Ages as with new Renaissance commentaries based on au-
thentic classical texts. Unlike medieval chronicles, however, the *Commentaries* was a polytheistic sacred history that took the Egyptian gods seriously. Thus Osiris, Isis, the bull Apis, and Hercules join Noah and his sons
as central players in Europe's history.

The "history" created by Annius provided Alexander VI with a largely
symbolic link to the foundational period of sacred and heroic begin-
nings in Europe. More specifically, the Borgia family found its genealogi-

FIG. 5   PINTURICCHIO, *LUCREZIA AND CESARE BORGIA*,
DETAIL FROM *THE RESURRECTION*, BORGIA APARTMENTS,
VATICAN (MONUMENTI MUSEI E GALLERIE PONTIFICIE,
CITTÀ DEL VATICANO)

cal connection to antiquity through the myth of Noah, Isis, Osiris, and
Apis. As recounted by Annius, the myth provided an irresistible symbolic
match with the heraldic image of the bull that had been a part of the
Borgia coat of arms for at least two centuries.[16]

   To recall the central aspects of the myth as told by Annius, Osiris was
the son of the biblical Noah, also known as Janus. Having made his way
to Italy from Egypt with his son Hercules, Osiris succeeded in civiliz-
ing the tribes inhabiting Italy before he returned to Egypt. Back home,
Osiris was killed by his brother Typhon, but was resurrected as the bull
Apis. Meanwhile, Hercules and his mother, Isis, defeated Typhon, and
Hercules went on to wage war against Typhon's followers and various
others in North Africa and Europe.[17]

FIG. 6 PINTURICCHIO AND WORKSHOP, *STORY OF ISIS, OSIRIS, AND APIS*, BORGIA APARTMENTS, VATICAN (MONUMENTI MUSEI E GALLERIE PONTIFICIE, CITTÀ DEL VATICANO)

Significantly for Spanish and Italian connections, Hercules became king of Spain, succeeding his uncle Tubal, another son of Noah and the first king of Spain. He then moved on to Italy to make various conquests there. In the Annian scheme of things, the kings of Spain thus traced their lineage to Tubal and Hercules and were related to the founder of the Borgia line, Osiris. This clearly made the Borgia branch part of the family tree of the Spanish monarchy. Just as the pope had sought a marriage alliance between his son Juan and a cousin of the Catholic Kings in 1493, so too did Annius forge a marriage of family myths. The myth of Osiris, Apis, and Hercules accomplished this perfectly, as did the history of the Spanish monarchy that he included in his *Commentaries*.[18] To add one more sacred connection, Noah, or Janus, was also credited with first settling the Janiculum Hill in Rome, thus prefiguring the popes and presumably providing yet another reason for Spanish patronage on the hill.[19]

The degree to which this wild merging of biblical, Egyptian, and European creation stories was actually believed and incorporated into either the Borgia family history or the history of the Spanish monarchs is impossible to determine. The idea that Noah's son Tubal was the first king of Spain was already a part of earlier Spanish chronicles, such as that of Isabella's courtier Diego de Valera (1482). But Annius does appear as a source for various other later Spanish histories, as we shall see in chapters to come. Still, whether Annius ever made a literary genealogy for the Borgias that overtly stated these connections is simply not known.

It is widely held by art historians, however, that the Osiris origin myth of the Borgia family was immortalized in a painted genealogy created by one of Alexander's most famous court painters, Pinturicchio. Presumably using the Annian "history" as the basis for the artistic program he chose for the decoration of the Borgia apartments of the Vatican palace, Pinturicchio created a syncretic swirl of Egyptian and Christian stories that covers the walls and ceiling of the Vatican room known as the Sala dei Santi.[20]

One of the centrally located reception rooms in the six-room Borgia apartment, the Sala dei Santi takes its name from the wall paintings, which depict lives of the saints. But the room clearly was meant to celebrate the life of Rodrigo Borgia as much as that of any of the saints, a fact driven home by the hundreds of images of the heraldic bull of the Borgia family found in the room. Images of the bull are carved repeatedly in the decorative marble frieze that rings the room; bulls are painted into the background scenes of the saints' lives; and, most noticeably, Apis appears twice as a central figure in the frescoed ceiling, which is decorated with a succession of scenes depicting the myth of Osiris.[21]

The ceiling is remarkable for the prominence that the pagan myth takes in a room dedicated to Christian saints. Indeed, this expansive collection of scenes embodied the bold religious and artistic syncretism that marked the High Renaissance of Pico and Ficino as well as that of Alexander and Annius. The striking allegorical message of the relation between the Spanish noble family and the divine heroes of both Christian and pagan antiquity was made abundantly clear by the pervasive presence of the heraldic symbols of the Borgias. A literary genealogy could hardly have done it better.[22]

Beyond their genealogical function, the frescoes of Pinturicchio did for Alexander VI what Bramante's Tempietto and the church of San Pietro in Montorio did for Ferdinand and Isabella: they established a lasting locus of Spanish patronage at the heart of papal Rome. Moreover, even after Alexander's death in 1503 and the expulsion of his son Cesare from Italy, Borgia cardinals would continue to appear in Rome as major personalities in the Spanish community. The Borgia apartments reminded succeeding generations that theirs was a Spanish papal family, and like their Roman counterparts, future Borgias parlayed this heritage into a lasting claim to Roman prestige and the highest ecclesiastical office.

Another way Alexander staked a claim to Rome was by developing a sizable Spanish community in the city. Although the pope had lived for decades in Rome, he filled his court with Spanish soldiers and courtiers, perhaps because he believed them to be more loyal. No existing census from the period allows us to measure the community with any certainty, but based upon scattered reports concerning one group or another, it probably numbered in the thousands.

We know, for example, that in 1500 Cesare Borgia commanded two thousand Spanish soldiers. By 1503 he was estimated to have seven thousand under his command in Rome, but how many of these soldiers were from Iberia is not clear.[23] Notable among the military class was Don Micheletto Corella, Cesare's closest and most feared henchman. More professional and less murderous in their roles, perhaps, were Bernardino Algas, the *castelano* (commander) of the fortress in Rome's port city, Civitavecchia, and Giovanni Marrades, who served in the same capacity in the fortress of the papal city of Viterbo, as did Juan Carmona in another city of the Papal State. Playing the part of a medieval Spanish fighting bishop, Martino Zappata, the bishop of Sessa, served as a soldier (*condottiero*) of the pope in 1503, and Ugo de Moncada and Pedro de Oviedo held the lesser rank of captain in the papal army.[24]

Spaniards also held other important positions in the Papal State during Alexander's twelve-year reign, including that of governor. Both Jaime Serra, a maternal cousin of the pope's, and Garcilaso de la Vega were governors of Rome, and Don Ramiro de Lorqua, a Spanish nobleman, was governor of the Romagna. Not surprisingly, numerous Spaniards held lower offices in the papal Curia: secretary, notary, and canon lawyer. This was the case with Gaspare Pou, Pedro Caranza, Alfonso de Lerma, and Ferdinando Guttierez, to name a few.[25]

Closer still to the pope were a variety of Spanish courtiers, including Pedro de Aranda, the bishop of Calahorra, who served as the pope's

majordomo until he was imprisoned for Judaizing in 1498. Diego de Valdés y Porres, the bishop of Salamanca and Zamora, replaced him in that
important role. Finally, Pedro de Rapolla, a Catalan, served as the pope's
doctor, while another Catalan, Antonio Bret, was one of his personal
chaplains.[26]

Perhaps the most prominent and visible Spaniards surrounding the
pope were the cardinals. By 1504 they numbered eight, or close to 20 percent of the College of Cardinals, and included two Borgias, Remolino and
Pedro Ludovico. This was a large increase from the two Spanish cardinals
found in previous decades, and it bred resentment. As early as 1497 a report from a visiting dignitary noted that the pope's tendency to surround
himself with Spanish cardinals and courtiers was making him extremely
unpopular.[27]

Another group of Iberians worth noting here was the merchants,
primarily Catalan, who established a lucrative trading business between
Iberia and the Papal State. They were numerous enough to institute a *con-
sultat,* or type of trading guild, to protect and control their business interests, and they built homes and warehouses along the banks of the Tiber
in the neighborhood of Trastevere to store their merchandise. Together
with other Catalans in the city, and with the blessing of Alexander VI,
they had built the new church of Santa Maria de Montserrat, where they
also had a small confraternity.[28]

The great irony of the pontificate of Alexander VI is that while the
Spanish community was more numerous and influential than it had ever
been before, its success and the deepening hatred of the pope by the
people of Rome left it socially stigmatized and vulnerable to retribution.
In 1499, for example, Spaniards were required to stay in their houses during Carnivale, a social quarantine that was credited with keeping the
festivities from becoming violent.[29]

When Alexander died, however, in August 1503, nothing could keep
violence from breaking out. Initially, according to Guicciardini, "all of
Rome went to view the dead body of Alexander with great joy," happy
to see the "serpent" responsible for so many examples of cruelty lying
dead.[30] While the masses were apparently satisfied to see the "black" and
"very ugly" body of the poisoned pope, this was not enough for the Roman nobles who had been treated harshly by the Borgias. With Cesare
Borgia sick but safely shut up in the Vatican palace, the bitter hatred
of the Orsini and Colonna families turned against the broader Spanish

community. Entering Rome with 1,200 men, the Orsinis burned an estimated one hundred Spanish houses and warehouses and killed at least
three Spaniards who had not had the good sense to flee Rome.[31] Fabio
Orsini, whose father had been strangled by Cesare's order, was not content until he had "washed his face and hands in the blood of a murdered
Borgia."[32]

Alexander VI and his son Cesare were thus primarily responsible for
the strong backlash against Spaniards that undermined the stability of the
community and the ability of the Spanish monarchy to influence Roman
affairs. Although Alexander's reign left a few permanent iconographic
reminders of the Spanish presence, it failed to establish a lasting or influential Spanish community. Rather, it was left to Ferdinand to rebuild ties
with the new pope and try to repair the image of the Spanish in Rome.

FERDINAND, KING OF NAPLES AND
ROME, 1504–1516

Ferdinand was probably relieved when he received news of the death
of Alexander VI. It was true that the Catholic King had succeeded in
acquiring many privileges over the church in his realms thanks to various
negotiations with the Borgia pope. Among the most notable, he and his
queen had enhanced their international reputation by winning for themselves and their successors the title of Catholic Kings, an honorific rivaling
that of Most Christian King, which was given to the king of France. Of
greater economic and political benefit, the monarchs had been granted
the *patronato real* over the entire church in the newly conquered kingdom of Granada, not to mention title to the great majority of the New
World.[33] This gave the monarch exclusive rights of appointment to ecclesiastical offices and greater control of ecclesiastical income in Iberia, as
well as setting the precedent for the same rights over the church in the
New World.

In Italian affairs, however, Alexander and Cesare had been far less
cooperative as allies, if not outright opponents of Ferdinand's political
designs, particularly in Naples. It was no surprise, then, that the prince
whom Machiavelli estimated to be the most powerful in Christendom
would move against Cesare Borgia and attempt to extend his power in
Naples.

The year 1504 represented a watershed in Spanish and Roman relations. It was then that Ferdinand or, more precisely, his military chief, the Great Captain, Gonzalvo de Córdoba, succeeded in accomplishing those tasks.[34] The defeat of the French and Louis XII's renunciation of his claims to Naples in 1505 signaled the beginning of the Spanish domination of southern Italy.[35] The Spanish Empire now shared a long common border with the Papal State, and because the papacy claimed the ancient right of holding Naples as its fief, political relations with Rome subsequently became more pressing and more complex. The papacy, in short, was the key to the stability of Spanish Naples, a fact well understood by both king and pope. Increasingly, Rome became the center of the world, or *plaza del mundo,* in Ferdinand's mind, as well as the center of Spanish international diplomacy.[36]

From the Roman perspective, Europe's most powerful king was now its closest neighbor and the ascending power in Italy. As an ally, Spain could be Rome's greatest military asset; as an enemy, its greatest threat. For Pope Julius II Rovere (1503–1513), a pontiff determined to preserve and expand the Papal State, managing relations with the Spanish monarch therefore took on a new importance and urgency.

The central business dominating the decade of Julius's reign was Ferdinand's continued attempt to win investiture as king of Naples and the pope's obsession with expansion of the Papal State in the north. These agendas became tightly bound together, and they eventually led to a military alliance between the two powers that gave Ferdinand the role he had been seeking since 1480. But the pope was not quick to give up such a valuable prize — or to alienate the French.[37]

Rather, Julius backed out of an early agreement to present the investiture in 1504 and refused to move on the issue throughout two years of persistent prodding by the king's ambassador in Rome, Jerónimo Vich. In 1507, during his sojourn in Naples, Ferdinand increased the diplomatic pressure. In a series of letters to his ambassadors focusing on the investiture and a variety of related issues, he presented a concise synthesis of the various concessions and rights that he desired from the papacy over the church and kingdom of Naples. At the same time he instructed the ambassadors to "respond very sweetly" to any suggestion of "a very strong and perpetual union" between Rome and Spain made by the pope, and to assure him that the king desired "to be very united with his Holiness."[38]

For all Ferdinand's sweet talk, Julius continued to withhold the investiture. Ferdinand, in response, refused to make a promised visit to

Rome that Julius had desired and instead sailed directly back to Spain. The marriage was being stalled because the parties were haggling over the dowry.

In fact, not until mutually beneficial military necessity required their union did the monarch and the pope draw closer. In 1508 the challenge of Italy's other great power, Venice, provided the motive that pushed Ferdinand and Julius into a formal alliance, along with a number of other European powers, including France and the Holy Roman Empire. Both Ferdinand and Julius believed that the Venetians had usurped territories that were rightfully theirs: the pope claimed Ravenna, Rimini, Faenza, and Cercia as his own, while Ferdinand claimed a number of lesser port towns on the Adriatic coast. With both the king of France and the Holy Roman emperor eager to make their own claims, Europe's strongest powers allied themselves against La Serenissima (Venice) in the League of Cambrai in 1508.[39]

The league was yet another step forward for Spanish and Roman relations. It brought papal and Spanish troops together, demonstrated to Julius how important Ferdinand was for his own military ambitions, and set the stage for the investiture that the new king of Naples desired. From Ferdinand's perspective, this was the beginning of a series of alliances with the pope that illustrated his role as the primary defender of the church. It was a position he would masterfully exploit to his benefit: in 1508 he was also granted the *patronato real* over the church in the Indies.[40]

In 1510 the pope again needed a defensive alliance: the League of Cambrai had dissolved, and the French had emerged as the new threat to Italian stability. He proposed three possible alliances to the Spanish ambassador, two of which included other powers. Ferdinand wrote to his ambassador, making it clear that he preferred the third option, a confederation between only himself and the pope. Making the most explicit connection yet between his established role as king of Naples and his self-proclaimed role as protector of Rome, he acknowledged that "on account of the kingdom of Naples I am more obliged to help His Holiness and the Church than any other prince and His Holiness me." Moreover, Ferdinand stipulated to his ambassador that "before or at the same time" the confederation was proclaimed, the pope would have to put into the ambassador's hands the sealed bull granting the king and his successors the investiture of Naples.[41] Julius agreed to the general conditions, and in

July, Ferdinand received for himself and his successors the prize of formal papal investiture to the fief of Naples. It was an event that would shape the future not only of Naples but of Rome and the rest of Italy as well.

Although the pope needed military assistance throughout 1510, it was not until 1511 that a formal alliance between Spain and Rome was declared that included the Venetians. France had become the new threat to an Italian balance of power, so much so that Ferdinand had convinced the Spanish grandees and Cardinal Ximenes to send the Spanish army, then fighting in Africa, to Italy.[42] Again the old king used the alliance with the papacy to domestic advantage. Fighting at that time with Louis XII for control of the kingdom of Navarre, he secured a bull of excommunication against all those who supported the French. And in 1511, at a solemn ceremony in the cathedral in Burgos, the bishop of Oviedo preached a sermon proclaiming Louis XII the principal foe of the Catholic church.[43]

Although initially defeated by the French at the grim Battle of Ravenna on Easter Sunday 1512, the Holy League won the war with a decisive victory at Pavia in June. France lost all its possessions in Italy, most noticeably Milan; the papacy recovered many of its territories including Bologna; and the Spanish were left as the dominant power in the peninsula and Europe.

When Julius II died in 1513, Ferdinand was without question the most accomplished and feared political figure in Europe. Although he seems to have had little influence in the conclave that elected the next pope, Leo X Medici (1513–1521), he clearly considered it his right and duty to advise the young pope as a father figure. In a remarkable letter shortly after the election, Ferdinand advised the pope in a pedagogical tone to refrain from showing enmity toward any obedient prince or disturbing the peace of the Christian republic. Moreover, he admonished Leo to govern all his subjects in peace and justice and not show partiality toward anyone.[44]

At this late point in his career, Ferdinand had obviously accepted his self-appointed role as the leader of Christendom to the point of dictating instructions to the new pope. By 1514 he had achieved an extraordinary consolidation and extension of power in Iberia, the New World, and Italy, and his attitude toward Rome reflected this exalted position. The old monarch was also speaking of Spain's relationship to Rome when he proclaimed in 1514: "For over 700 years the Crown of Spain has not been as great or as resplendent as it is now, both in the west and the east, and all, after God, by my work and labor."[45]

By the time of Ferdinand's death in 1516 many of the foundations for the relationship between the Spanish Empire and the Papal State that would be built upon in the sixteenth century had been established. Even before Naples had been conquered and annexed as a part of the Spanish Empire in 1504, a tradition of formal alliance with the papacy in an Italian league was in place. The league of 1481 and especially the Holy Leagues of 1495, 1508, and 1511 became a fixture in Spanish-papal relations throughout much of the sixteenth and seventeenth centuries. Moreover, the ideal of the Spanish monarchs to be the greatest defenders and propagators of the *international* Catholic faith became a central part of their identity and the identity of the empire from that time forward. It was an ideal embodied in their new title of Catholic Kings. Spain, in short, was no longer fighting a local fight. The Catholic Kings had gone global, and their political aspirations matched the universal religious aspirations of their papal counterparts.

At the same time, Ferdinand established himself as a visible local patron in Rome through his donations to the church of San Pietro in Montorio, where he also began the long tradition of diverting funds from his southern kingdoms to Rome. Similarly, by establishing his first permanent ambassador in Rome, the Catholic King had created an important base of political patronage and knowledge that would continue throughout the early modern period. Ferdinand was perhaps the first of the Iberian monarchs to fully realize the political necessity and benefit of close, constant ties with the papacy, and his new Italian possessions made these even more essential. At the same time, Ferdinand and Isabella were the first Iberian monarchs to understand the importance of the Spanish church and clerics of Santiago in the Piazza Navona as a base of contact and influence in the Roman court second only after the ambassadors.

Ironically, it was the presence of a Spanish pope, Alexander VI, that temporarily undermined Spanish reputation and the power of the Spanish community in Rome, and his death in 1503 brought on backlash against this community that limited its power and influence for several years. Still, it is apparent from the census of 1527 that in the years between the death of Alexander and the census, the community of Iberians grew into a considerable foreign presence, largely because of business interests fostered by the presence of the Catalan commercial guild that controlled trade with the Papal State.

And the Borgias, for all the damage they did, also established Spain's only papal family in Rome. Borgia cardinals would continue to play a role in the papal court throughout the period, and the tradition fostered by Alexander's court of painting and writing Spaniards into the myth and iconography of Rome had begun in earnest.

Thus, by the time Ferdinand's grandson Charles V, Holy Roman emperor and king of Spain, came to power in 1517, the foundations of Spanish influence and control in Rome had been established. What is most remarkable about Ferdinand's success is that his political model, based on a delicate balance of military alliance and beneficent patronage, would provide a formula for Spanish success in Rome that was repeated for the next two centuries. With a few noticeable exceptions, his lessons led to a decline in the heavy-handed domination characteristic of the Borgias, and his model dominated future Spanish political policies and practices in Rome.

CHAPTER 2

CHARLES V AND THE SPANISH MYTH OF ROME

HEN the young grandson of Ferdinand and Isabella, Charles I of Spain and Charles V of Germany, came to power in 1516, he and his ministers pursued a policy toward Naples and Rome that sought to preserve the victories and alliances won by the Catholic Kings. During the four long decades of his rule, however, there was no distinctly Spanish agenda toward Rome but rather an imperial policy in which Spain took part. Charles, who gained the title of Holy Roman emperor in 1530, ruled an empire that included territories in Germany, the Netherlands, Burgundy, Italy, and the New World. As perhaps the most important part of this empire, Spain provided diplomats, soldiers, and money for imperial pursuits in Rome and elsewhere.

This was an unusual and novel role for the Iberian kingdoms that complicated their political relations with the rest of Europe, including Rome. More important in the Italian context, it was a role that provided Spaniards with an experience of empire that further sparked their own imaginations and ambitions. Rome, as the old center of empire, increasingly became a common topos, or theme, in early modern Spanish writing. This anticipated the related development of the new topos, or place, Spanish Rome, as the home of thousands of Iberians in the second half of the century.[1]

As an important part of the Roman Empire and the birthplace of two of Rome's greatest emperors, Trajan and Hadrian, Spain was dotted with visible reminders of its ancient relationship with the city in the form of aqueducts, amphitheaters, and various other ruins.[2] This past, combined with the experience of empire under Charles, was a potent inspiration for playwrights, political theorists, historians, and poets, who made Rome the subject of their work and a major point of comparison and contrast with Spain.³ Over time, they created a distinctly Spanish myth of Rome that was shaped by, and reflected, the deepening political and social relations between Spain and Rome.

ALLIANCE AND ENMITY, 1516–1527

U nfortunately for Charles and Spain, relations with Rome were anything but smooth during the first decade of his reign. Not surprisingly, the main source of the troubles was again the French challenge in Italy and the wildly vacillating alliances and policies of the Medici popes, Leo X and Clement VII (1523–1534).

At the beginning of the new king's reign, there was the appearance of continuity with the policies of Ferdinand. Charles had entered into a formal alliance with the pope and Henry VIII of England in 1516,⁴ and in 1517 Leo X confirmed the title of Catholic King upon the young monarch.⁵ More important, a treaty dealing specifically with Italian affairs had been drawn up in 1521 that brought Spain and the papacy together in an alliance against France and Venice. The details of that agreement read like a close copy of the earlier Spanish-papal leagues: the French were to be driven out of Milan, which Francis I had taken in 1515; the pope would get Parma, Piacenza, and Ferrara; and Charles would be crowned king of Naples by the pope in Italy.⁶

The death of Leo X in 1521 briefly interrupted the alliance as the new pope, Adrian VI (1521–1523), Charles's former tutor, sought to bring the Christian princes together in a league against the Turks. By 1523, however, imperial pressure, combined with Francis I's decision to cut off all funding to Rome, led Adrian to embrace a new Holy League with Charles, Florence, Milan, Genoa, Venice, and others against France. The political status quo of the previous decade continued.⁷

Yet this seemingly secure alliance took an unexpected and abrupt turn for the worse after the election of the next pope, Clement VII Medici. Ironically, the former Cardinal Giulio de' Medici was one of Charles's most loyal servants in Italy; Giulio was indebted to the king for restoring his family to power in Florence. In fact, the young monarch had given instructions to the duke of Sessa, his ambassador in Rome, to push for Giulio's election in the conclave. This was one of the first overt and well-documented cases of a Spanish monarch sending a great deal of gold to

Rome during the papal election season; it was not the last. Rather, it set a precedent for every future king of Spain into the eighteenth century.[8]

Still, in the case of Clement VII, it was a waste of money. Wanting to pacify France and fearful of Charles's growing power, Clement refused to renew the Holy League of 1523. Then in 1525, and again in 1526, the pope entered into an alliance with the French that was formalized in the League of Cologne of 1526.[9] Charles was enraged, and the stage was set for another grim drama that had Spanish soldiers spilling blood on the streets of Rome. All Italy was at war by summer, and the dark side of the Spanish presence in Rome reappeared with consequences that made even the memory of Cesare Borgia fade into the background.

THE SACK OF ROME

The twisted and torturous path that led to the sack of Rome in 1527 has been studied in great detail.[10] Perhaps no other event more deeply affected Spanish relations with Rome, Spanish attitudes toward the city, Italian attitudes toward Spain, and the Spanish presence in Rome for the generation that followed the tragedy. It represented both a great interruption in the deepening relations between Spain and Rome and a transformation of their future.

Like the reign of the Borgias, the sack of 1527 underlined the fact that in the early sixteenth century Spanish soldiers were far from being a disciplined army under the strict control of the king. On the contrary, like Cesare Borgia and his followers, they were often loose cannons whose thirst for personal gain and the booty of war overshadowed any loftier aims.

This was clearly the case in May 1527, when a large imperial army under the command of Charles of Bourbon marched on Rome. Shortly after Clement had joined the League of Cologne, Charles V's enemies, led by his French nemesis Francis I, had taken Milan and Genoa and set their sights on Naples. By the spring of 1527, however, the imperial army, composed primarily of German and Spanish soldiers, had taken back Milan and was winning the war. As was common practice in these campaigns, the soldiers had not been paid for eight months. Tragically, they looked to the Papal State and the treasures of Rome as the most obvious place to take their reimbursement.[11]

The sack of Rome began on May 6, when roughly twenty thousand

soldiers attacked the city. When Charles of Bourbon was killed early in
the battle, the imperial army was left without leadership or discipline. Yet
they were far superior in number and strength to the defenders of Rome
and defeated them in a matter of hours. Before the day ended, crowds
of soldiers and their followers were shouting, "Empire, Spain, Victory,"
throughout the burning city.[12]

By virtually all contemporary accounts, the pillaging, looting, and
rape that followed were epic in scale. Palaces, churches, convents, monasteries, and their occupants were all despoiled. Only Clement and the
people who made it into the Castel Sant'Angelo were safe. Even Spanish
and German residents of Rome suffered from the rampaging soldiers,
who ignored a prohibition against looting proclaimed by the new leaders
after the third day of the sack.[13]

Although this last point underlines the lack of any "national" or ethnic
unity on the part of invading Spanish soldiers and Spaniards residing
in Rome, contemporary Italian authors tended to paint "the Spaniards"
with the same dark rhetorical brush in their accounts. They depicted the
Spaniards as the most cruel of all the soldiers.[14] Luigi Guicciardini, for example, claimed that as soon as the Spanish soldiers entered the city they
began yelling, "Spain! Spain! Kill! Kill!" Moreover, "even though those
who were being tortured cried out continually for death, the cruel and
greedy Spaniards kept them alive."[15] The humanist Pietro Corsi, who was
himself robbed by the imperial troops, added the sin of rape to the image
of Spanish brutality in his treatise *Romae urbis excidium*. On All Saints'
Day, no less, he reports that Spanish troops raped a young girl in public
after taking her from her mother's arms in a church.[16]

Cruel, greedy, murdering, raping, blaspheming barbarians: this was
the Italian literary portrait of "the Spaniards" that arose primarily from
the events of 1527. Thus, the sack, more than any other historical moment,
gave birth to an Italian "black legend" of the Spanish that had long-lasting
implications for their reputation in Rome and Italy. It took many decades
and quantities of Spanish gold to repair the damage.

The Rhetoric of Reform

On a more immediate level, however, the sack—and the Italian descriptions of it—generated a Spanish rhetorical response that created a
very different picture. Politically, the sack was a disaster for Charles V,

who was in Valladolid celebrating the birth of his son, the future king
Philip II, when he received the grim news. Many high-ranking Spaniards,
including the archbishop of Toledo and the duke of Alba, expressed their
dismay at the events, and it was crucial for the emperor to create a history that placed the blame elsewhere and bolstered his reputation as a
pillar of the church.[17]

The task fell to a Franciscan friar, Charles's humanist secretary for
Italian affairs Alfonso de Valdés, who was called upon to compose a justification of the sack by the emperor's chancellor, Mercurino Gattinara.
As the architect of Charles's Italian policy, Gattinara drafted a speech in
1523 for the emperor to deliver to the Cortes of Castile (parliament) concerning Italy. In need of money to further the Italian campaign, Gattinara
flattered the Spanish as the first people of both the empire and Christendom, who had implicit obligations in Italy, specifically Rome. Credited
with drawing the lesser nobility into greater sympathy with the world-
governing role of their king, the speech appealed to religious pride in its
readers.[18]

Confronted with the obvious contradiction between the defender of
the church and the sacker of the Holy City and with the anger of Spanish nobles and clergy, Gattinara needed an eloquent and convincing response. More specifically, Gattinara instructed Valdés to "draw the moral
that henceforth war in Christendom must be stopped, a general council must be called, and the Church reformed."[19] The result was the most
expansive and clearly official Spanish view of the sack, the *Diálogo de las
cosas ocurridas en Roma,* otherwise known as the *Dialogue of Lactancio.*

True to Erasmian form, Valdés constructed a treatise that took the
form of a fictional dialogue between a soldier, Lactancio, and an archdeacon who had gone to Rome as a soldier, witnessed the sack, and returned to Spain.[20] The purpose and argument are not subtly woven into
the treatise but overtly stated at the beginning: "In the first part, Lactancio shows the archdeacon how the emperor has no fault for it [the sack],
and in the second how God has permitted everything for the good of
Christendom."[21]

The dialogue begins with the archdeacon recalling the barbarity of
the sack and asking how such things can happen — more particularly, how
they can occur at the hands of Spain and its monarch. In the course of
his lament, the idealized relationship that was supposed to exist between
Rome and Spain emerges: "Was this the honor that Spain hoped for from

its most powerful King? Was this the glory, was this the defense that the Holy See hoped for from its defender? . . . For this his grandparents acquired the title of the Catholic [Kings]?"[22]

According to this view, Charles was first and foremost king of Spain, and although it was primarily as Holy Roman emperor that he had claimed the position of protector of Rome, the author here emphasized and connected the roles of king of Spain, Catholic King, and protector of Rome. Clearly, Valdés understood the part that Ferdinand and Isabel had so carefully constructed for themselves and wished to stress that historical lesson in his text. But he also moved past that lesson.

The responsibilities of the king go beyond simple defense, according to Lactancio, as the dialogue moves into an exploration of the responsibility of the king not only to protect but also to castigate if necessary. Responding to the rhetorical questions of the deacon, Lactancio claims that the deacon has been badly informed if he thinks that the emperor has done anything wrong in allowing the sack. Rather, the real purpose behind it was to deliver the just punishment of God on the city for its great sins. The sack was the "clear judgment of God, to castigate that city, where with great disgrace for the Christian religion all the vices that man could invent reigned, and with that punishment to awaken the Christian community."[23]

Although he supports the Franciscan in calling Rome *sancta,* and in acknowledging the dignity and place of the pope, whom God has given to humans as their teacher, the soldier's main point is that under Clement VII the rightful role of the papacy has been corrupted. Here Valdés adopts the Erasmian rhetoric of criticism and reform so common to the age. The rightful place of the pope, he explains, is to interpret Scripture, to teach doctrine with both word and example, to convert and absolve, and to procure peace among Christians. Instead the pope has broken his treaty with Charles and sown discord by taking up arms against him. In fact, Valdés goes so far as to say that since the popes have not listened to the honest criticisms of Erasmus or to the dishonest insults of Luther, then God was forced to find another way to convert the city.

Thus, Lactancio tells the deacon, God "did with your sons," the soldiers, what the others have not been able to, and allowed the city to be brutally destroyed so that it cannot return to its former vices.[24] The Spaniards are conveniently absolved from guilt. They become instead God's agents of justice; and the king of Spain, in addition to acting as the defender (and now castigator) of Rome, becomes God's instrument for the reform of the church: "Jesus Christ formed the church and the Emperor Charles V restored it."[25]

The importance of this revisionist view in forming the attitude of the Spanish political and intellectual elite is hard to overestimate. The dialogue circulated widely in humanist circles in the universities and at court.[26] Moreover, it was this accepted version of events that transformed the sack from a tragedy to a divine sign of a new age of renewal of Christianity and Rome in which Spain would play a central role.[27]

The Costs and Benefits of the Sack

Although Spanish political and religious rhetoric at home claimed an exalted position for Spain, the short-term impact of the sack on the Spanish community in Rome was quite the contrary. Just as the menacing character and often-murderous nature of the Borgia rule a generation earlier had led to a backlash against the community, so too did the events of 1527.

The census had just been completed on the eve of the sack, and we know from that document that 210 heads of household out of a total of 9,328 were identified as being Spanish (*spagnolo*).[28] This means that, based on an average of five people per household, there was probably a community of roughly a thousand Spaniards. Unfortunately, the impact of the sack was as negative on documents as it was on people, and a great many records for the early decades of the sixteenth century were destroyed during the rampage. Similarly, the decline in the general population, estimated to have been roughly 50 percent, together with the lack of documentation in the two or three decades immediately following the catastrophe, make it difficult to judge the size of the community during that period.

What is clear from surviving letters written by Spaniards in Rome is that the social climate had turned dangerous. The Spanish ambassador to the city summed up the situation in a letter to Charles V in 1529 when he warned of "the great danger that all of the Spaniards and other good servants of your majesty [are] in here."[29] The remaining Spaniards suffered from their association with the conquering army, which occupied Rome for almost a year and then threatened the city from its base in Naples. In addition, imperial troops continued to occupy the nearby papal cities of Ostia and Civitavecchia in early 1529.[30]

Clearly, it would take the entire city—and specifically the Spanish community—a long time to recover from the damage. Charles and his wayward army may have won the battle of 1527, but the sack was a social setback in the larger contest for Rome, and it was central to the struggle between France, the papacy, and Spain for control of Italy. Unlike Ferdinand, Charles was slow to learn that patronage worked far better than war in conquering Rome.

Still, the emperor used his position of strength after the victory of 1527 to obtain many concessions from the papacy that shaped relations between the two for most of the next three decades. At the heart of these was the reestablishment of their alliance. In May 1529, Clement decided to send his nuncio to Barcelona to negotiate a new agreement with the emperor. In June the Treaty of Barcelona was signed, which established many of the central features of imperial-papal political relations that would remain in place for the rest of Charles's reign and beyond.[31]

More specifically, the agreement of 1529 created an alliance against the Turks that included an increase in the amount of the *cruzada,* or indulgence revenue aimed at the crusade against Islam, and gave to Charles 25 percent of the ecclesiastical income of the churches in his realms to help defray the cost of the war. It also confirmed Charles as king of Naples, with the feudal dues owed the pope set at the low sum of 7,000 ducats and a white horse, and gave to Charles and his successors the right to appoint an additional twenty-four bishops in Naples. Imperial armies were given the right of passage through the Papal State, and all excommunications issued because of the sack were lifted. In return for all this, the emperor agreed to support the restoration of the Medici family in Florence and help win back the papal cities of Ravenna, Modena, Ferrara, and Reggio for the pope.[32]

The agreement of 1529, together with the Treaty of Cambrai reached between the empire and France later that year, set the stage for Charles's great victory tour to Italy in 1530. Having negotiated his imperial coronation by the pope in the Barcelona treaty, Charles traveled to Bologna to receive the papal blessing. The emperor entered the city with a great following of Spanish grandees, demonstrating to all assembled that his was the new preeminent power in Italy and Europe. For some modern historians this was the moment when the Italian states first came under the subjection of the "alien Spaniard."[33]

While this last sentiment was certainly an overstatement—German, French, and Italian subjects of the emperor had played an equal role in the wars—it was true that the victories of the late 1520s were decisive in establishing the political conditions that eventually made Philip II the most powerful prince in Italy. Besides his papal gains Charles also set the stage for claiming Milan by reducing that important state to a condition of virtual fiefdom through the establishment of an imperial army in one of the main fortresses of the city.[34] Genoa, Siena, Florence, Ferrara, and Mantua also fell under the imperial umbrella and were for the most part weak and dependent allies of Spain in the following century.

In the case of Milan, it was the death of Duke Francesco Sforza without heir in November 1536 that left Charles in sole control of the city. Despite repeated French challenges over the next decades, the emperor held Milan as his own, and in 1540 he named his son Philip duke of Milan. Kings of Spain held the title throughout the sixteenth and seventeenth centuries.[35]

The monarchy's new position as both king of Naples and duke of Milan had important implications for Spanish relations with Rome, for it put the city and the Papal State literally in the middle of Spanish-ruled territories. Spanish soldiers, statesmen, and others moved with greater frequency between the two kingdoms via Rome, and Charles V and his son increasingly thought of the city and state as part of their Italian kingdoms.

Charles V voiced this idea most clearly in an instructional letter or political testament written to his son sometime between 1545 and 1558. Now preserved in Philip II's library in the Escorial, an Italian version of the letter reveals Charles's bold claim that "the states of the church are in the center of Italy, but [they are] surrounded by ours in such a way that one can say that they form one kingdom."[36]

The idea that the Papal States were a de facto part of the Spanish kingdoms of Italy where soldiers could be recruited, funds for war raised, and ports freely used for Spanish galleys was established by Charles V. It was possibly the most important contribution of the emperor to future Spanish political policy and attitudes toward Rome. Regardless of the continuing sovereignty of the pope as prince of the Papal State and official Spanish recognition of papal rule, the real political attitude toward

Rome and the papacy was that they were there to be subjugated and as-similated into the Spanish Italian kingdoms. This attitude represented a new stage in the Spanish program toward Rome, a stage of more overt domination, and it was accompanied by a further important rhetorical development that helped reflect and shape this change.

THE RHETORIC OF HISTORICAL CONQUEST

Within the contemporary sack literature, a theme that occasionally emerged but generally remained unexamined was Rome as the historical center of the Roman Empire. Although Rome as a Christian center, or rather, a corrupted Christian center, dominated such litera-ture, Spanish historians during the reign of Charles V also took up the subject of classical Rome or, more specifically, of the place of classical Rome in Spain's ancient past and vice versa.

Historical production in Golden Age Spain was vast, but two authors in particular, Florián de Ocampo and Ambrosio Morales, serve to illus-trate the officially sanctioned historical view of Spain's early relationship with Rome. Both wrote with the official title of royal historian, Ocampo for Charles V and Morales for Philip II, and together they produced one of the most widely published histories of Spain in the sixteenth century, the *Crónica de España*.[37] This text was reprinted ten times between 1541 and 1604, in Medina del Campo, Zamora, Alcalá, Valladolid, and Cor-dova, albeit only portions were printed before 1574, when the composite work of the two authors was published as one text.[38] Although technical information on the Spanish printing trade is in short supply, it has been estimated that in the early sixteenth century each press run averaged a thousand copies, indicating that there were substantial numbers of these works circulating.[39]

When Ocampo began to write his history in 1526, he was twenty-seven years old, and he continued to work on the *Crónica* until his death in 1555.[40] As a student of the great humanist Antonio de Nebrija at Alcalá de Henares, he was a product of the full flowering of Spanish Renais-sance humanism. He had studied Greek, Latin, and Hebrew, and dem-onstrated his linguistic talents in the *Crónica* wherever possible. In 1539 he was named royal chronicler of Charles V and in 1541 published the first five books of his history.[41]

As a work dedicated to the "Emperador de Roma, Rey de España, de

Allemania, y delas Indias," Ocampo's *Crónica* was intended to serve as an instruction to Charles concerning the previous princes of Spain, their line of succession, and their notable deeds and conquests.[42] Although called a chronicle, the text crossed the literary line into narrative; from the beginning it was clear that it contained a controlling political agenda that gave it narrative unity.[43] The history clearly existed to serve and legitimate royal authority, while also deriving its own authority from the king.[44] Ocampo stated early on that the work "will be more highly valued and esteemed" because it enjoyed the patronage of Charles's "greatness."[45]

In Ocampo's text, "our Spanish nation" (*nuestra nación española*) was the dominant geographical and social unit that served as the focus of the history. Rather than placing Spain in the context of the other major European "nations" of Germany, France, Italy, and Greece, the author was primarily concerned with establishing Spain's place in the classical past with respect to the Greek and especially the Roman empire.[46]

Thus, Ocampo was true to Nebrija and early Italian Renaissance histories in his desire to connect Spain to the classical past. Unlike the Italians, however, Ocampo strove to make Roman and Greek culture dependent upon Spanish antecedents. The most dramatic example of this was his treatment of the story of the founding of Rome. After dismissing the traditional story of Romulus and Remus as a myth, Ocampo claimed that probably Rome had been named for Romi, the daughter of the Spanish king Atlante. This king was credited with founding many other cities on the Italian peninsula and with ruling over Italy as well as Spain. Although Ocampo did not pretend to know with certainty whether the story of Romi was true, he nonetheless claimed that when one weighed all the stories concerning ancient Rome, "finally they come to agreement in that it was Spaniards that founded it and conserved it."[47]

This was an extraordinary statement. Indeed, in all the histories of the Roman Empire that appear during the Renaissance, only Ocampo and the later Portuguese historian Manuel de Faria y Sousa (1590–1649) claimed "national origins" for the founding of Rome. Yet the rhetorical motive for the move resembles that of Annius of Viterbo in creating his history of the Spanish kings and the Borgia origins: they both seek to claim a place for their people in the history of Rome. In fact, Annius has been identified by later scholars as the source for Ocampo's own claims, and both authors do ascribe to certain aspects of the ancient myths of the Spanish kings.[48]

Indeed, Ocampo's imaginative interpretation of "the evidence" about Rome serves both to claim credit for its very existence and to establish the historical precedent and justification for Spanish domination of Italian affairs in his own day. The exploits of the fifteenth and sixteenth kings of Spain, Sicano and Siceleo, are further examples of this preoccupation. Sicano is praised for his conquests in Sicily, and his son Siceleo is credited with continuing the many victories and accomplishments "against the Italians and in favor of the Spanish nation" (*la nación española*).[49] Soon thereafter King Siculo is also noted for his many conquests in Sicily and for honoring "the Spanish nation [*la nación española*] with these favors and victories."[50] According to Ocampo, this early domination—dated to the time the Jews left Egypt—prefigured the second occasion the island would be returned to "spanish lords" (*señorios españoles*) under King Ferdinand.[51]

Like Annius of Viterbo's history of the first twenty kings of Spain, Ocampo's history thus served as a justification for Spanish rule in Italy. But Ocampo went even further in constructing a rationale for claiming a historical place and even precedence in Rome. This was an important step in the construction of a Spanish myth of Rome that was used in later histories as well, and it clearly carried the royal seal of approval. Ocampo's work was thus infused with contemporary political meaning and closely connected to the political ideology of Charles and Philip II.

IMPERIAL PATRONAGE AND POLITICS IN ROME, 1534–1555

This expansion of the language of historical connection and conquest between Spain and Rome was accompanied by a deepening of political and economic relations in the 1530s and 1540s. When Pope Paul III Farnese (1534–1548) was elected in 1534, he honored most of the concessions made to the emperor by his predecessor, Clement VII, and supported Charles V with three papal galleys in a new crusade against the Turks.[52] More substantially, the pope also granted the emperor an increased subsidy from the Spanish clergy in the amount of 252,000 ducats to build twenty-one new galleys for the war.[53] The renewal of the cruzada was also confirmed, and a report from 1536 noted that it had brought 400,000 Spanish ducats into the royal coffers.[54]

Although not formally joined in a holy league, pope and emperor were nonetheless allies in the war against the Ottomans that contributed to the expansion of imperial power and to one of the emperor's greatest accomplishments up to that time, namely the conquest of Tunis. At the age of thirty-five, Charles V personally fought at Tunis against the scourge of the Mediterranean, Khayr ad-Din Barbarossa. As an ally of the Ottoman sultan Suleiman, Barbarossa had been raiding the Italian coast for years. His defeat in July 1535 subsequently carried great symbolic weight and increased the reputation of Charles as the chief defender of Christendom. Te Deums were sung in Rome as soon as news of the victory arrived. When the emperor returned to Italy shortly after the battle, it was as a conquering hero and the most powerful prince in Italy.[55]

Landing first in Sicily, Charles was honored with pageants in Palermo and processions modeled on ancient Roman victory parades in Messina. So, too, were there fetes in Naples when Ferdinand and Isabella's grandson traveled through his Italian kingdoms for the first time. Carefully watching the imperial march, Pope Paul III sent his son to Naples with an invitation for the emperor to visit Rome. It was a shrewd move on the pope's part, but also a dangerous one, underlining Rome's continuing fear of the imperial army. As late as January 1536 the pope still anticipated a possible repeat of the sack of 1527 by the emperor, and he had levied troops and prepared the Castel Sant'Angelo for an attack.[56]

Charles had no such thing in mind, however, and instead used the visit to Rome as an opportunity to cement his reputation as defender of the church and loyal son of the papacy. When the emperor finally arrived in Rome in April 1536, he was accompanied by four thousand well-disciplined troops and a crowd of Spanish grandees, Roman nobles, and various other dignitaries. As Roman emperors of old had often done, the procession marched down the Appian Way, through the arches of Constantine and Titus, and along the Via Triumphalis in the Roman Forum. After this, Charles slowly made his way to the Campo dei Fiori, across the Tiber near Castel Sant'Angelo, and finally through the Borgo to the basilica of Saint Peter's, where he was met by Paul III.[57] The weeks spent in Rome, which included the Holy Week and Easter celebrations, were marked by tours of the city and meetings with the papal court. They included a notable speech by Charles in Spanish to the assembled cardinals, pope, and ambassadors, and numerous displays of goodwill and an exchange of gifts between pope and emperor. Perhaps greatest among the gifts were those promised to the son and grandsons of the pope: rich

FIG. 7   TITIAN, *CHARLES V* (PRADO MUSEUM)

bishoprics and states in Spain and Naples. In exchange, the prize desired by Charles V was papal support, or at least neutrality, in his impending war with France. This he achieved. The formidable imperial minister Nicholas Granvelle summed up the achievement of the visit with the comment that the pope had become an imperialist.[58]

This was not entirely accurate — the old Farnese pope was a Roman patriarch above all else — but 1536 marked a decisive stage in the improvement of papal-imperial relations. Charles V proved that he could be a generous patron during his visit, and he appeared to have learned the lesson of his grandfather that gifts, Spanish pensions, and Neapolitan or Sicilian land was the surest way to win supporters and influence in the Roman court. During the following decades the imperial faction in Rome grew steadily as Roman nobles and cardinals began writing to Charles requesting offices for themselves and their families.[59]

More immediately, the imperial victory over the French in the Italian wars of 1536 underlined the power of the emperor, and the continuing Turkish threat made the papacy ever more reliant on him for military defense. Early in 1538, the republic of Venice, Paul III, Ferdinand I of Hungary and Bohemia, and Charles V entered into a formal holy league against the Ottoman Empire with Charles's empire providing the majority of the troops. The sixty-thousand–man force included thirty thousand Germans, fifteen thousand Spaniards, and fifteen thousand Italians. Of these half of the Germans and the Spaniards were under the command of Charles V, the Italians and the rest of the Germans were paid for and commanded by Venice and the papacy.[60] To help pay the emperor's share, the pope granted a five-year renewal of the cruzada and other grants from the Spanish churches worth an estimated 2 million ducats.[61]

Three primary aspects of the pattern of give-and-take established in papal and imperial finances just noted are of special importance: the increasing dependence of the papacy on the empire for military defense against the Ottoman threat; the dependence of the empire on Spanish ecclesiastical revenues for military financing; and the increasing level of imperial patronage in the papal court in the form of Spanish or Neapolitan pensions. These were all central elements of imperial-papal relations that the Spanish Empire would assume after Philip II came to power in the 1550s, and they continued throughout the sixteenth and seventeenth centuries.

Perhaps most important of these political practices for the long-term development of strong Spanish influence in Rome was the increased cultivation of ties and influence with Roman clergy and members of the nobility. Starting at the top of the social hierarchy, in 1538 Charles V had agreed to marry his natural daughter, Margaret of Austria, to the pope's grandson, Ottavio Farnese. Although this turned out to be less than a blissful marriage, it established a bond of blood that linked the Farnese family to the Spanish crown for decades to come.[62] It did not eliminate the possibility of political relations turning sour between the two powers—in fact, they did for a time in the 1540s—but it did create a precedent that in-clined the increasingly powerful cardinal Alessandro Farnese, in particu-lar, toward the Spanish faction of cardinals in Rome. This was especially important in the second half of the sixteenth century.

But even more than the Farneses, it was with the Colonnas, one of Rome's oldest noble families, that Charles V most closely allied himself. With many lands in the Kingdom of Naples, the Colonnas were subjects of the emperor as well as the pope, and in the crisis days of 1526–1527 and after, they had clearly sided with Charles. As late as the 1540s they still held lands and fortresses in the Papal State claimed by the pope, such as Rocca di Papa in the hill towns south of Rome. The conflict reached a peak in 1541, when Paul III ordered his Spanish military commander to move against the head of the family, Ascanio Colonna.[63]

This was a particularly delicate situation for the emperor since the Colonnas had been counted among his most reliable allies. Yet his over-riding concern was tranquil relations with the pope, and he instructed his ambassador, the marquis of Aguilar, to intercede with the family. When Ascanio Colonna agreed to move his soldiers and the family belongings to the Colonna estates in the Kingdom of Naples, it was a strong sign to both the Roman nobility and the pope that the old rules of political contest among Roman families was changing. The active intervention of Charles as king of Naples and lord of the Colonnas was one of the first major examples of this kind of political influence. To make the message even clearer, the ambassador emphasized to the pope that "his majesty wants all of his subjects to have all reverence toward Your Holiness."[64]

The unspoken message, however, was that the king of Naples con-trolled some of the most powerful Roman nobles. This was one of the biggest favors the kings of Naples could do for the popes, because the old Roman nobles most threatened papal rule on a local level. With the emperor and future Spanish kings usually controlling the Orsini and Colonna families, in large part because of their estates in Naples, the pope's political stability increased. But it was a stability dependent upon the Spanish monarchs. As part of the imperial and Spanish faction, these nobles could also be used against the pope in the event of serious differ-ences or outright hostilities.

Indeed, more hostilities were in the near future, and for all the vari-ous alliances formed between the papacy and empire in the 1530s and 1540s, there was a deep and continuing lack of trust between the two.

This became most apparent in 1546, when war broke out in Germany. Although Rome and the empire entered into yet another holy league, this time against the Schmalkaldic League of Protestant princes, the pope's troops quickly withdrew from the battle. Charles felt that he had been tricked into a costly war and bitterly complained to his ambassador in Venice, Don Diego de Mendoza, that the pope had meant all along "to entangle us in this snare and then desert us."[65]

A continuing desire to diminish imperial power in Italy and to see Milan in the hands of a weaker Italian prince or a Farnese was at the root of much of the tension between pope and emperor. So, too, were major differences over the reform of the church, the stalled Council of Trent, and the question of the pope's role in church finances and the control of benefices. A letter from Charles V to his ambassador Juan de la Vega in 1545 emphasized the long list of issues that needed to be addressed, which included all of the problems above and the added thorny issue of the *Pragmatica*.[66]

The *Pragmatica,* issued by the Cortes in 1542, prohibited any foreigner from holding a benefice from a Spanish church. This deeply affected the College of Cardinals and other members of the court, who frequently sought substantial pensions from Spain. It also directly infringed on papal prerogative since the pope held the right to give out many of the benefices to whomever he pleased. The issue of Spanish ecclesiastical funding for the Roman court, which had just begun to emerge as a major issue at this time, was to be one of the most critical, long-lasting political controversies between Rome and Spain. How the pope and the king would share the presentation rights of lucrative church pensions was a constant point of negotiation, tension, and debate.

In the case of 1543, a serious rupture was avoided by the use of the *naturaleza,* the granting of a form of naturalization to foreigners that allowed them to hold benefices. This was a right reserved to the kings of Spain, and it substantially increased their patronage power and influence in Rome. And members of the papal court requested this favor with increasing frequency. Paul III did not like the arrangement very much, but it was one of the first issues Prince Philip addressed when writing to the pope as acting regent after his father officially named him heir in 1543. In a long letter to the pope in 1544, Philip pointed out that the kings of Castile had always granted naturaleza to foreigners who wanted a benefice, but only after they had proved with words and deeds that they were worthy of it.[67]

The imperious tone of Philip's letter could not have been pleasing to the pope, but it accurately revealed the Spanish monarch's lofty view of his role as the primary patron of Spanish church finances. Such a view only fueled the fires of resentment in Rome against growing Spanish power, a resentment that Spanish ministers in Italy felt strongly in the late 1540s. Their warnings of the dangers faced by Spaniards in Rome surpassed even those of the period after the sack. Don Diego Mendoza, writing in 1547, went so far as to claim that there was a plot in Rome to murder all Spaniards and then blame it on mob fury.[68] Much of this tension was temporarily diffused by the death of Paul III in 1549 and the election of the pro-imperial pope Julius III (1550–1555). His short pontificate, which coincided with the last years of Charles V's reign, afforded the old emperor some peace from, or at least cooperation with, the papacy. The two powers were again allies in an Italian campaign against Henry II of France, and once more the French were beaten back. In the midst of this, the emperor financed a papal campaign against Parma with 100,000 Spanish ducats, which he sent to Rome as a sign of "the affection and devotion we have for you," and the pope wrote a warm letter of thanks blaming the French for all their troubles.[69]

THE LESSONS AND LEGACY OF
CHARLES V IN ROME

These good relations notwithstanding, the early 1550s were also a time for Charles to reflect on the future of Spanish-Roman affairs for the benefit of Philip. In a long political testament that included strong advice on Italian affairs, the emperor stressed to his son the importance of Italy as the key to "all your power." Moreover, it was the papacy and papal court, first and foremost, that were to receive his devotion and care. Philip was instructed to be quick to come to the protection and defense of Rome and to be attentive to the cardinals, bishops, and other high-ranking clerics. He should court them with pensions and benefices, and use the greatest liberality in granting the court concessions "from all your states."[70]

This advice helped set the political tone of Philip II's attitude toward the papal court, and it also revealed just how central Rome and Italy had become for the Holy Roman Empire, and how much they would be for the Spanish Empire. Indeed, while the critical place of Italy and Rome in the Spanish Empire is often overlooked or understated by contemporary historians, it was obvious to both Charles V and Philip II. At the same time, Charles had learned the important lesson that the best way to gain favor and cooperation from the papacy was to play the generous patron and devoted son. The emperor came into his reign like a lion, but he exited like a lamb.

This lesson may have come too little too late as far as the Spanish community in Rome was concerned. Their fear of Roman loathing was hard on Spaniards living in the city. Not until the reign of Philip II would the strength and prominence of the Spanish community in Rome reflect the political influence of their monarch. The problem, in short, was that the generosity of the emperor's old age did not erase the lingering bitterness many in Rome felt toward the empire or their anxiety when confronted with the power of the new Spanish monarch. The old dream, or more accurately, fantasy, of driving the Spanish out of Italy lingered on for yet a while longer.

The short reign of Julius III proved to be only a temporary respite from conflict with the empire and more potential violence in Rome. No sooner had the tired, gout-ridden Charles V formally abdicated power to his son in 1555 and retired to a Spanish monastery in Yuste than a new pope, Paul IV Caraffa (1555–1559), was elected. A Neapolitan who harbored deep anti-Spanish sentiments, he precipitated the first crisis of Philip II's reign.

CHAPTER 3

THE ROMAN WORLD
IN THE AGE OF
PHILIP II

J UST as Charles V had faced a war against the pope early in his reign, so too did Philip II. The so-called Caraffa War, named after the Caraffa pope Paul IV (1555–1559), was far more important in establishing the Spanish hegemony in Rome than any earlier event had been, including the sack of 1527. Ironically, it has received little historical attention, perhaps because it was quick and quiet and left the city unscathed physically. Nonetheless, it led to the increasing Spanish domination of Rome over the next sixty years.

Again it was the pope who precipitated the war. Paul IV had no sooner assumed power than he entered into a secret treaty with Henry II of France to drive the Spanish out of Italy and give the Kingdom of Naples to the French.[1] Thus, for Philip II, the warnings of the old emperor about the importance of Rome to Spanish power in Italy proved all too accurate in the very first year of his reign. As though the lesson needed to be taught again, the war brought home to Philip that the papacy was the linchpin to stability or instability on the eastern front of the Spanish dominions.[2]

The Kingdom of Naples had become an increasingly important source of Spanish revenue and military recruits by the middle of the sixteenth century, and as a Neapolitan, Paul IV resented Spanish governance and the exploitation of his native land.[3] Resentment, in fact, is too weak a term. Contemporary reports eloquently summed up by Leopold von Ranke claimed that the pope "would sit for long hours over the black thick fiery wine of Naples . . . and pour forth torrents of stormy eloquence against those schismatics and heretics, those accursed of God, that evil generation of Jews and Moors, that scum of the world, and other titles equally complimentary, bestowed with unsparing liberality on everything Spanish."[4]

How unfortunate, then, for Spain that this man was the cornerstone and arbiter of Italian internal affairs, a fact that was clear to an anonymous Spanish agent who in 1556 addressed two treatises on the troubles of Italy to the king. Identifying himself only as a medical doctor, the writer claimed that as a man trained to look for the cause and root of sickness, he had diagnosed all the maladies afflicting "religion and Christianity" and concluded that they came from Italy and that, furthermore, the sickness could be traced more specifically to Rome and to the pope.[5] Moreover, in the second treatise he claimed that to remedy the problems the king should first go directly to the *capo,* or the pope, and make a fundamental change.[6]

A less biased observer, the Venetian ambassador to Rome, Michel Suriano, expressed more expansive but similar views some years later when he wrote a general essay on the impact on Italian affairs of the popes from Alexander VI (1492–1503) to his own day in 1571. According to his reading of history, Alexander VI had thrown Italy into disorder by bringing the king of France "over the mountains." Leo X, Clement VII, Julius II, and Julius III were all accused of building up their own wealth at the expense of Italy and peace. Only Paul III was seen as a good pope who maintained the peace of Italy and the dignity of the church, while the sharpest criticism was left for Paul IV, who "made the king of Spain spend many millions in gold and left a memorable example of trouble." It was impossible to think of a pope with worse judgment, in this writer's opinion.[7]

All this advice and historical interpretation was not lost on Philip and his ministers, who set about immediately to secure his political presence and power in Rome and Italy in the face of the papal and French challenge. Unlike Charles V, who had won the war against Clement VII but also lost reputation because of the sack of 1527, Philip had the advantages of a well-disciplined army and an ability to learn from the lessons of history. A good student of politics, if not of Latin, Philip II took the high road of restraint.

In this he was well served by the duke of Alba, who took charge of the military forces in the Kingdom of Naples. Far superior to the meager papal forces, Alba's huge army marched easily into the Papal State in the spring of 1556 and camped in the hill town of Grottaferrata, not more than twenty kilometers from Rome. Demonstrating great discipline and control of his troops as they amassed outside Rome, the duke sent couriers into the city urging the pope to negotiate a peaceful settlement.[8] Faced with sure defeat and certainly remembering the sack himself, the pope succumbed.

In a masterful piece of political theater, Alba played the role of obedient and faithful servant of the pope some months after the war was over. Visiting Rome in September 1557 the duke kissed the pope's feet and pledged the king's filial obedience, assuring Paul IV that he had not meant to menace the pope with his troops but aimed only to secure the king's realms.[9]

The extremely conciliatory tone (much too soft on the pope, according to an angry, but retired, Charles V) also marked the terms of the treaty.[10] The first article demanded only that the pope recognize the king as an "obedient son, and that he act toward him as an affectionate father, as he does for the other princes, and that he give to his majesty and to his subjects the same favors and gifts as to the other princes, kings, and nations."[11] The pope was also required to release any of the king's subjects imprisoned in Rome, allow other Spaniards whom he had expelled from the city to return, and restore the lands and offices of Roman supporters of the king, particularly those of Marcantonio Colonna. Most important, the pope was required never "to make war or offend the king and his states, nor to favor or help any prince or anyone else who wanted to," and to refrain from building new fortifications.[12]

In short, the treaty attempted to impose a Spanish alliance on the papacy, or at least to ensure the neutrality of the Papal State. From the Spanish perspective this was a fundamental relationship, which Philip and his successors worked hard to secure and maintain both for the sake of peace in Italy and because the papacy had many favors and gifts that the king depended upon. Rather than pursuing an innovative policy, Philip essentially took a conservative approach, preserving the financial privileges and political support his predecessors had procured from Rome. From the New World to Flanders, Naples, and Catalonia, Philip wanted and often needed papal support. The relationship was also one that the Catholic Kings were willing to pay for, and they ritually acted it out and reinforced it on an annual basis in Rome itself.

This ritualization of Spanish-papal cooperation was couched in traditional feudal language and embodied in the presentation of the annual feudal dues from Spain to the papacy for the fiefdom of Naples. The

MAP 2   ITALY, 1559 (WILLIAM L. NELSON)

Spanish victory in the war ensured that Philip would be recognized as the legitimate king of Naples, and also that he would pay only the 7,000 ducats negotiated by Charles V, along with the symbolic gift of the white Neapolitan horse, or *chinea*.

Indicative of the symbolic importance of the dues and the chinea was the fact that immediately after Paul's defeat, the duke of Alba attempted to present them to the pope as a sign of Spanish feudal and filial obedience.[13] Paul initially refused the formal presentation, considering it an insult. But he and his successors for the next 145 years did accept the chinea.

After fifty years of French challenge and repeated papal resistance, the Kingdom of Naples became after the Caraffa War one of the most secure dominions of the Spanish monarchy.

Moreover, from 1560 onward the presentation of the dues to the pope by the Spanish ambassador on the feast of Saint Peter grew into a major event, in which the procession sometimes overshadowed the feast of the saint itself. The chinea procession, which will be described in more detail below, thus served as one of the numerous annual political rituals that helped consolidate and demonstrate Spanish power in Rome. Far from mere ceremonials, these rituals were important parts of a public relations campaign that presented the Spaniards' interpretation of their role as loyal sons of the pope and Christendom to all those assembled in Rome. By its size and grandeur, moreover, the procession also displayed the power and wealth of the Spaniards and their allies in the city, a fact that would become most evident in the 1580s and 1590s.

The Spanish victory in the Caraffa War thus initiated a period of unparalleled influence in Rome. Moreover, the early death of Paul IV in 1559, and the defeat of the French in the larger Franco-Spanish wars that led to the Treaty of Cateau-Cambrésis that same year, left Spain virtually unchallenged in Italy. The Spanish Empire began a period of domination in Rome that would not be seriously challenged until the papacy of Urban VIII (1623–1644). For more than sixty years, then, as the French became consumed with internal religious wars and the Holy Roman Empire fell into line behind the more powerful, wealthier branch of the Habsburg dynasty, the Spanish monarchs were the de facto military protector of the Papal State and Rome's most powerful foreign financial patron.

POLITICAL POWER AND HISTORICAL MEMORY: THE SPANISH ARCHIVE IN ROME

A monument to the perceived importance of Rome in the Spanish Empire was the archive that Philip II ordered established in the city as soon as his ambassador, Don Juan de Figueroa, was established there. With characteristic bureaucratic efficiency, Philip wrote:

> Having seen and considered through the experience we have of the past the harm that ensued to our service and to the good of our affairs from

not having conserved in an archive the writings and briefs that past pontiffs who held the Holy See of Rome have conceded to our predecessors, as well as some of the investitures and agreements with which our royal authority and the good of our realms have been increased . . . we have resolved that a room in the church of Santiago of the Spaniards in Rome be used for this purpose, and for the conservation of such writings.[14]

Just as the king established fixed archives in Seville and Simancas embodying and authenticating his documentary and legal claims to the other centers of his empire, the New World, and the kingdoms of Castile and Aragon, respectively, he used his third archive in Rome as a tool for staking a claim to this religious and symbolic center of the Spanish Empire. With a permanent archive in Rome, the king could approach the papacy on its own terms, thereby proving that he understood and could use the power of documents to justify his historical claims as well as the papacy could. Whereas the papacy had long wielded archives as powerful arsenals of religious empire (frequently making recourse to documents that were centuries old, or at least reported to be, to back up temporal and spiritual claims), Philip II proved that he could do the same thing even in the heart of Rome.[15]

Philip's letter also reveals in broad but more concrete terms the primary benefits that the king saw in having good relations with the papacy: an increase in his authority and the betterment of his kingdoms through papal bulls and pronouncements. Since much of his own prestige and power was deeply interwoven with the interests and pervasive influence of the church throughout the Spanish Empire, papal cooperation and aid were essential to effective monarchical rule.[16] The critical factor in attaining cooperation, however, remained the pope himself; as soon as Paul IV died, Philip took action to ensure that a pro-Spanish pontiff was elected.

SPANISH PRECEDENCE, PAPAL ELECTIONS, AND ECCLESIASTICAL FINANCE

The conclave of 1559, like most of the papal elections for the remainder of the century, was marked by a strenuous attempt on the part of the Spanish monarch, working through his ambassador, the Spanish faction of cardinals, and "other Spaniards," to control the election.[17] Promises of gifts and pensions as well as personal letters to the conclave were central to the strategy, and Philip's machinations were so overt that some cardinals reportedly accused him of a "certain kind of simony."[18]

Indeed, one of the fundamental lessons Philip seems to have learned from both the successes and the mistakes of his father and his great-grandfather Ferdinand was that Spanish financial patronage was the most powerful political tool at his disposal in Rome. This point had also been emphasized by one of Iberia's most accomplished theologians, the Dominican Melchor Cano, whom the young monarch had turned to in 1556 for counsel during the war with Pope Paul IV.

In a generally balanced and realistic appraisal of the situation, Cano first noted the superior religious authority of the pope and the king's obligation to submit to him on spiritual matters. At the same time, he argued that the king had the right to defend his realms as a temporal ruler. More important, Cano pointed out that in economic matters the Spanish monarchy was the more powerful since the papacy depended upon Spain for its very bread and water.[19]

Cano's strong final claim, a certain level of patriotic rhetoric notwithstanding, was rooted in one of the fundamental, but unrecognized, realities of papal Rome in the late Renaissance and early baroque period: it was the Spanish Empire that was now providing many of the critical economic foundations for the development of the city. Rather than being the destructive and "barbaric" force described by early sixteenth-century Italian writers like Francesco Guicciardini, Spain had a far more positive influence in Rome between roughly 1540 and 1700.

During the reigns of Philip II, Philip III, and Philip IV, in particular, growing Spanish patronage and economic support on a variety of levels allowed the dramatic urban development of Catholic Reformation Rome. Churches and palaces, cardinals and courtiers, artists and musicians, hospitals and convents; these institutions and individuals, among many others, benefited from a large flow of Spanish revenue into the city, money that played a fundamental role in the transformation of Rome into what was arguably seventeenth-century Europe's most dramatic and impressive urban stage.

Whether this financial influence was a "certain form of simony" or simply the accepted form of patronage politics characteristic of sixteenth-century Europe is debatable. What is not is that it was extremely effective. In the case of the conclave of 1559, despite a formidable French faction it was clear from the beginning that the election was dependent upon Philip's approval. At one point the strongest supporters of the king, Cardinals Morone, Puteo, San Clemente, Perugia, Messina, Marsilia, and Cornago, all left the conclave to await the king's letter of instructions. A contemporary observer wrote, "It is certain . . . that it is not possible to elect anyone who does not fully satisfy the Catholic King."[20] The king went so far as to name his two main choices, Carpi and Pacheco, in a letter read to the conclave by the ambassador.

In the end, Philip's faction was not strong enough to push through either of his first choices, and a compromise candidate, Giovanni Angelo Medici, was elected. Although it was not initially obvious, Pius IV (1559–1565), who had left Rome in disgust at Paul IV's policies, would prove decidedly pro-Spanish in his inclinations. It is with his reign that some of the primary characteristics of the mutually beneficial exchange between Spain and Rome in the next six decades would emerge.

As it had been from the days of Ferdinand and Isabella, one of the strongest marks of the Roman-Spanish relationship was the common fight of the papacy and Spain against the Ottoman Empire, and their related financial interdependence.[21] Reports from Constantinople early in 1560 warned of the preparation of a large Turkish fleet,[22] and it thus became an urgent matter to do likewise in Italy. Of the three powers with large coastlines to protect — Venice, Spain, and the Papal State — the latter was clearly the weakest, with no fleet to speak of. It was no surprise, then, that the pope turned to Spain as the wealthiest of the Italian powers for help, and he was willing to grant papal favors in return.

Such was the case when the pope granted to Philip a renewal of the *subsidio,* a variable tax on ecclesiastical rents, ostensibly to aid in the fight against the barbary pirates, and a six-year renewal of the cruzada, the tax granted to many previous Spanish monarchs to subsidize the fight against the Moors in Spain; but these took on new meaning with the Ottoman threat.[23] In 1567 a third tax, the *excusado,* which took in 200,000 to 400,000 ducats annually, was granted to help pay for the war in Flanders.[24] By 1571 the subsidio was reported to be worth 200,000 ducats per year, and the cruzada was worth more than a million ducats during a three-year period.[25] These three taxes, known as the three *gracias,* became a staple of the king's military budget throughout the period, but they remained the pope's prerogative and his most powerful bargaining chip in negotiations with the monarch.

The pope, for his part, had an interest in the cruzada that went beyond military concerns, and he stipulated in his renewal of the tax that 20,000 ducats of it would be paid to the papacy every year to finish Saint Peter's.[26] This was one early example of the financial give-and-take between king and pope that characterized the future pattern of their negotiations. While Philip has often been depicted by pro-papal historians like Ludwig Pastor as trying to ravage the church of anything he could get, a close look at papal policy clearly shows that the king and pope often acted in collusion to gain access to the rich revenues of the Spanish church.

This was anything but unusual, given the great wealth that various Spanish dioceses, monasteries, and military orders had accumulated over the centuries, as well as the deep stake the monarchy had in the church, particularly through the *patronato real*.[27] According to a report of 1567 from the papal nuncio in Spain, for instance, total ecclesiastical rents in the kingdoms of Castile and León totaled 9 million ducats annually.[28] By 1630 the rents had increased to more than 12 million annually.[29] These sums were equal to the king's share of New World treasure over one of the best five-year periods of the late sixteenth century.[30] Subsequently, the constantly indebted Spanish monarchs had come to rely on being able to tax ecclesiastical revenues to help finance their expensive military ventures, taxes for which they needed papal approval and support.

The papacy, for its part, made a point of keeping itself well informed about Spanish church revenues;[31] and the fact that the money coming into Rome from France, Germany, and England had either completely vanished or was seriously declining in the late sixteenth century made papal income from the churches under the jurisdiction of the Spanish monarchs doubly important.

Part of this income came from the papal right to collect a share of Spanish ecclesiastical revenues during times of episcopal vacancy,[32] a sum that was reported to be 300,000 escudos in 1560 when Monsignor Francesco Aragona was sent to Spain as the papal collector.[33] Much of this money was already committed to other individuals, and the collector himself used a substantial quantity for his expenses. Nonetheless, registers for the period from 1589 to 1660 show that the pope's coffers regularly received 40,000 to 65,000 escudos per year from vacancies in the churches of Castile and Aragon, 15,000 from the churches of Naples, and 5,000 from the churches of Portugal.[34]

Together with this consistent source of Spanish revenue, the pope and his court also received other income from the Spanish church in the form of rich benefices controlled and granted by the king. This was already apparent in 1562 when Philip II gave the pope's nephews and Cardinal Borromeo a combined sum of 15,000 escudos from the revenues of the cathedral of Toledo.[35] Moreover, in that same year it was reported in Rome that "many cardinals and Italian prelates who were found at the court" in Spain were seeking money from the king.[36] Large-scale Spanish patronage of Roman ecclesiastical clients was thus a constant reality of life in the late sixteenth and early seventeenth centuries; and as the alliance between Rome and the king deepened, more and more Spanish income found its way to supportive members of the papal court. While some of the intricacies of the Spanish relationship with the cardinals will be examined in more detail in succeeding chapters, it is helpful to note for the broad political-economic picture that the Spanish monarch was granting between 30,000 and 75,000 ducats annually to the Spanish faction of cardinals between 1560 and 1625.

This role of benefactor and protector of the Roman court, and implicitly of Christendom, was one that Philip II sought to play from the beginning of his reign; but it was only in the context of the later sessions of the Council of Trent that it would be explicitly acknowledged by the pope.[37] Pius IV had been intent upon reconvening the council since early in 1560, but to do this he needed the consent of the three major powers: France, the Holy Roman Empire, and Spain. Of these Spain was the most supportive of his plans, and the pope looked upon Philip II as the ruler "in whom alone he had perfect confidence."[38]

While the interests of the Spanish church and those of the papacy were far from one, with disputes over ecclesiastical jurisdiction causing considerable acrimony,[39] the graver problems and challenges in Germany and France eventually forced the papacy to rely on Spain more and to grant concessions to the king.[40] Most important for the king's reputation, the pope decided in Spain's favor in the matter of precedence between French and Spanish representatives to the council.[41]

The dispute between the French and Spanish delegates, rather than being a simple matter of protocol in ecclesiastical functions, went to the heart of Philip's claims concerning his place in Christendom.[42] The French had held the traditional place of precedence in the papal court for centuries, and at Trent they initially retained the highest place of honor in processions and ecclesiastical functions. When the Spanish protested this

FIG. 8   TITIAN, *SPAIN COMING TO THE AID OF RELIGION,*
DORIA PAMPHILI GALLERY

arrangement, however, and threatened to leave the council if they were
not given precedence, Pius eventually ruled in their favor in 1563. According to the pope, the Spaniards deserved this place because they were "the
principal support of the Catholic religion." Philip's representatives subsequently "gave a solemn promise that their sovereign would defend the
authority of the pope with all his power."[43] With this exchange, Philip
attained, and possibly surpassed, what he had ultimately wanted from
his treaty with Paul IV: recognition as Christendom's most loyal son of
the papacy and a privileged position in Rome.[44]

At the same time, humanists provided the historical justification for
this exalted place. More specifically, the Italian writer Augustin di Cavallis, writing in June 1564, produced an elaborate synthesis of the historiography and political history that the Spaniards and their Italian supporters

had been developing in the previous decades. Drawing on everyone from Pliny to Annius of Viterbo, Cavallis compiled a list of Spanish histori-cal highlights, starting with antiquity and proceeding to his own day, to justify Spanish claims of precedence in Rome.[45]

Beginning with the cosmographers, Cavallis claimed that most of them, including Pliny, show "that Spain is the head of Europe." More-over, the author argues that Spain is a more ancient kingdom than France. For this, he cites a range of authors and texts including Beroso Caldeo, the history of the Spanish kings by Annius of Viterbo, the *Enchiridion delli tempi* by Alfonso Venero, the geography of Giovanni Fernandez d'Enciso, and the history of Anton Beuter.[46]

Drawing particularly on Beuter and Venero, Cavallis further claims that the first Christians among the gentiles appeared in Spain, and that the first churches were in Zaragoza and Santiago: the chapel of the Madonna in Zaragoza, he insisted, was founded in the first year after the Passion. Moreover, citing Favio Biondo and Paolo Orosio, Cavallis claims that after Saint James's disciples brought his body to Spain, they converted many natives, including Queen Lupa and her people. Many of the other early kings also converted, thus providing Spain with the first Christian monarchy.[47]

With record speed, Cavallis moved from antiquity to his own cen-tury in a matter of a few pages of text. In a section that focused on the "services and disservices" committed by the Spanish and the French for Christianity and the church, the author emphasized, in particular, the various leagues between Spain and the papacy from the time of Ferdi-nand to the present. In a loud affirmation of the priority that the Spanish monarchs placed on who took part in these holy leagues, the text con-cisely listed the history of the alliance. Ferdinand and Isabella intervened when Louis XII made war on Julius II and also attempted to help Leo X when the French broke a treaty and took Parma, Piacenza, and Milan. Charles V did the same for Clement VII, especially in the aid that he gave Clement in reinstating his family in Florence. The disastrous sack of 1527 was blamed on the French and on unruly soldiers who disobeyed the emperor's captain.

The Spanish kings also led in the fight against the Turks, as the vic-tory of Charles V over Barbarossa in Tunis had shown. Similarly, Charles gave help to Paul III in his many conflicts and aided Julius III in the war over Parma in which the French and the Farnese family had allied against the pope. And finally, Philip II had succeeded in making a general peace in Italy which "it pleased God to conserve."[48] In short, Cavallis could have called his treatise "The Manifest Destiny of the Pax Hispanica in Italy," for that is exactly what it was. Moreover, in the following decade the Spanish added yet another strong chapter to this text.

PIUS V AND LEPANTO

The election of Pope Pius V (1565–1572), a Dominican of humble birth, has often been described by contemporaries and earlier historians as free of the foreign influence and manipulation that had marked earlier conclaves.[49] Whether this was the result, as some claimed, of divine favor or of the election reforms of Pius IV that prohibited outside contact with the strictly cloistered cardinals, the fact was that this conclave lacked the brazen political maneuvering by the Spanish king that had characterized the previous election. Nonetheless, numerous other sources reveal that Philip considered the election extremely important and instructed his ambassador, Luís de Requeséns, to do all that was possible to steer the college in Spain's favor. When it was rumored in 1565 that Pius IV was ill, the king instructed Requeséns to "take great care to keep the College of Cardinals in our devotion" both generally and individually, and to "communicate with and visit especially those that are known as our servants and followers."[50] After the pope's death the king quickly wrote to Requeséns, again reminding him of the qualities to be sought in the new pope, namely someone who would "remove the errors and dissension that had arisen in religion" and "keep Christendom in peace, unity and conformity, and especially Italy, where there was always war . . . which has harmed us and harms us greatly."[51]

With regard to at least some of these particular qualities, Philip could not have hoped for a more suitable pope than Pius V. Coming from a humble past and relatively free of family ties and ambitions, Michele Ghislieri appealed to Philip's taste for low-born churchmen. At the same time, his work as an inquisitor and reputation as a strict reformer endeared him to the theologically conservative king. Thus, the perception that the Spanish party did not seem to dominate the conclave and explicitly determine the election actually favored the Catholic King, since he got what he had hoped for without giving the appearance of interference. There is also good reason to believe that the ambassador's earlier groundwork with the cardinals was seen by Philip as bearing good fruit in this election; and it was known in Rome that the king had given Requeséns 20,000 ducats shortly after the election.[52]

Despite the smooth conclave, Pius V was suspected of favoring the Spanish early in his reign, and it was reported that "other princes"—particularly the French—claimed that he was "inclined too much to the Spanish."[53] Certainly the quickness with which he granted another five-year extension of the subsidio, worth 400,000 gold ducats to the king, may have given this impression.[54] So, too, did the prayers of thanksgiving he ordered sung in the churches of Rome when news of Spanish military victories in Flanders reached the city, and the mass of the Holy Spirit he personally celebrated in Saint Peter's for the victory.[55] The pope also supported the king's plan to raise ten thousand troops in Italy for the Flanders campaign,[56] and the Spanish cavalry, some of whom had probably fought against papal troops in the Caraffa War in the not so distant past, were welcomed in Rome on their way to the war in Flanders in the spring of 1567.[57] Locally, a group of twelve Spanish Jews who were baptized in the church of Santiago were given 10,000 scudi by the pope to perform acts of charity.[58]

Clearly there were many examples of ways in which the pope did favor the Spanish king and his subjects in the realms of international politics and ecclesiastical affairs, as well as in the city of Rome itself. And there were many good motives for the pope to do so, since he believed from early on in his reign, as had Pius IV, that the stability of the Mediterranean region, including his own realms, depended heavily on Philip II.[59] This was most obvious in the case of the Turkish threat first to Malta and then to Italy itself.

An attack on Malta in 1565 had revealed the strength and proximity of Turkish power. But it also underlined the importance of Spanish naval power in the Mediterranean, since it was the fleet of Don García de Toledo, viceroy of Sicily, that ultimately forced the Turkish fleet to lift the siege of Malta and flee.[60] Pius V justifiably continued to be preoccupied with Turkish naval power and in 1566 pledged three thousand paid soldiers for Malta's defense under the command of Pompeo Colonna, a vassal of Philip's.[61] In the following year Pius asked the king to send Spanish troops to help defend the island, and in 1568, at Philip's prompting, the pope authorized a tax on the clergy of Naples which raised 30,000 scudi to build fortifications on Malta.[62]

With this defensive alliance growing throughout the early years of Pius V's pontificate, the pope was reluctant to hear any complaints against Philip from unhappy subjects. He subsequently sided with the king when representatives from the deputats of Catalonia in Rome protested the king's appointments of non-Catalan candidates to the bishoprics of Otranto and Piacenza. The representatives were eventually sent away and told that there was no place in the papal court for other representatives sent from the "laity of that kingdom."[63] Similarly, when a lawyer (avocato fiscale) was sent to Rome in 1567 by the senate of Milan to protest Spanish taxation policies and seek papal intervention, the pope turned him away, saying that he had no intention of interfering with this business of the king, whom he called "an obedient son of the Apostolic See." Upon the insistence of the Spanish ambassador and Cardinal Pacheco, the pope went so far as to excommunicate the president of the senate when he persisted in resisting the king's financial demands. The pope also acknowledged the king's right to use force to extract the revenues if necessary.[64]

In a variety of ways, then, the pope used the substantial tools of power at his disposal, including the right to impose ecclesiastical taxes, excommunicate, and arbitrate or intervene, particularly in Italian and ecclesiastical affairs, to help the king consolidate his own power. In Catalonia, Flanders, Milan, and Naples, the decisions of Pius V revealed explicitly or implicitly the support of the papacy toward an increasingly centralized Spanish monarchical authority. The symbiosis of spiritual and temporal authority that characterized the papal monarchy in this period, and led to such actions as excommunication for tax resistance, could be extended to the other monarchies as well when the pope cooperated.[65] At the same time, such actions often strengthened the position and image of the papacy. Thus papal absolutism and Spanish absolutism have to be seen as complementary and interdependent. Even in the delicate realm of ecclesiastical jurisdiction, where conflicts of interest between king and pope most often arose, compromises were sometimes reached that tended to benefit both monarchy and papacy.

The trial of the archbishop of Toledo, Bartolomé Carranza, illustrates this point. Carranza's trial has been the subject of much inquiry, and the basic facts of his condemnation by the Spanish Inquisition, imprisonment in Spain, and imprisonment in Rome are well known.[66] After Carranza's arrest in 1559, Pius IV had demanded that he be tried in Rome, arguing that it was an infringement on the rights of the papacy to do otherwise. With papal-Spanish relations still recovering from the war, however, Philip had kept Carranza in the hands of the Spanish Inquisition, whose authority he did not wish to see diminished, and it was not until 1566 that the king acquiesced to Pius V's demands and threats to excommunicate the Spanish inquisitors. Thus, in May 1567 the archbishop arrived in Rome with an entourage of servants, family, lawyers, inquisitors, and jailers and was promptly imprisoned in Castel Sant'Angelo.[67]

Philip's concession has been interpreted as a sign of the strength of Pius V and his strong defense of the rights of the papacy,[68] but it can also be interpreted as proof of Philip's growing influence in Rome and confidence that the pope would do nothing against his wishes in such an important matter. In fact, the pope acted as Philip's jailer for the next ten years, keeping Carranza in Castel Sant'Angelo and allowing the trial by the Roman Inquisition to drag on. In the meantime, Philip was allowed to make the secretary of the Spanish Inquisition provisional governor of the archdiocese of Toledo with the official support of a papal decree.[69] The king continued to control the bulk of the large revenues of the diocese, while the papal collector sent a percentage back to Rome since the archbishopric remained vacant.

A central fact that is sometimes lost in the details of the Carranza affair is that Philip's power over the Spanish church was substantially increased by the archbishop's imprisonment. By keeping the bishop's throne vacant for well over a decade, the king removed one of the few men in Spain who had tremendous financial resources, historical and moral prestige, and political power at his disposal. While Carranza himself had never been a threat, it was clearly to Philip's advantage to remove the traditional head of the Spanish church and assume his powers when the chance arose.

Thus, it was no surprise that Philip quickly wrote to Rome in 1568 when it was rumored that the archbishop was sick, urging the pope not to grant any premature concessions. To those in Rome it seemed that the king would be happy if the trial "never end[ed]."[70] Even though the Spanish ambassador visited the archbishop in prison a number of times with various conditions for his release, such as the renunciation of the revenues of the diocese and the acceptance of the king's nomination of his replacement, these demands were so extreme that they were sure to be refused.[71] Indeed they were, and the Carranza affair lingered on long after Pius V's death in 1572. When the archbishop finally died in Rome in 1576, having been released only when his death was imminent, Philip appointed the Inquisitor General Gaspar de Quiroga archbishop of Toledo, and thereby had one of his most loyal churchmen in Spain's most powerful episcopal see.

This strong demonstration of Philip's control over the church in Spain also points to the high level of subtle, if reluctant, cooperation the monarch now received from the papacy. While it was true that the king continued to rely heavily on the Spanish Inquisition for internal control of the church and people of his realms, by 1568 the papacy was also becoming much more supportive in this regard. Indeed, even when all the heated disputes over monarchical infringements of ecclesiastical privileges (particularly in Naples and Sicily) are taken into account,[72] the papacy still appears as an important instrument of ecclesiastical discipline that aided the king in keeping discontented clergy under control.

A prime example of this occurred when Philip pressured the pope to order all Spanish priests who held benefices in Spain out of Rome. Many of these clergy had been sent there by bishops or religious communities as procurators or ecclesiastical lawyers to undertake church business, and they sometimes lobbied the papacy and cardinals against the fiscal policies and taxes of the king. This was especially true when the king sought renewal or expansion of the general ecclesiastical taxes on their benefices, and Philip was well aware of their actions. Such was the case in January 1570 when the pope, under pressure from the king, issued an order that "all Spanish priests who are in this court who have benefices . . . must return to their residence."[73] Shortly thereafter, the pope granted a five-year renewal of the cruzada worth an estimated 334,000 ducats per year.[74]

All this papal cooperation did not come without expected Spanish reciprocation: the crucial factors that led Pius V to support and favor the king in matters ranging from the Carranza affair to monarchical taxes on ecclesiastical revenues were his overwhelming desire to form a league against the Turkish threat and his dependence on Spain as the backbone of such an alliance. The renewal of the cruzada is a case in point. When Pius gave preliminary approval to this grant in August 1570, he required that the king use part of the money to make the following contributions to the proposed alliance: four hundred ships of various sizes, ten thousand infantry, five thousand cavalry, and grain for the fleet.[75] Although this did not turn out to be the exact configuration of the Spanish contribution to the league, Philip did provide the majority of ships, men, and food for the alliance, which was formally announced less than six months after the cruzada was renewed.[76]

The formal announcement of the alliance occurred on May 23, 1571, when a solemn mass, attended by the pope, various cardinals, and the ambassadors of the Catholic princes, was said in Saint Peter's. At the end of the mass Monsignor Aragona preached a "very beautiful, spiritual, and Christian sermon" in which he proclaimed the formation of a military league between the pope, the Republic of Venice, and the king of Spain. A Te Deum was then sung, and the pope ended the ceremonies with a benediction. There followed a gathering marked by "much happiness."[77] The following week the pope ordered three processions, all of which he personally led on foot, to Saint Peter's, Saint Mark's, and Santiago of the Spaniards to pray for a victory over the Turks.[78] As an added sign of pleasure with the Spaniards, he gave the chaplains of the church 800 scudi "because they ran the church well."[79]

So began the military alliance between the papacy and Spanish monarchy that would continue in one fashion or another for the next fifty years. More than any other single event or agreement, the Holy League of 1571 solidified the close relationship between Spain and the papacy and demonstrated to both the people of Rome and the international community the central position of Spain in the new world order of the late sixteenth-century Mediterranean world. Philip II, for his part, proved himself a master at the political game fashioned by his great-grandparents and his father.

This was doubly true after the famous victory at Lepanto in October 1571. According to the first dispatch that the Spanish ambassador, Don Juan de Zúñiga, sent to the king after the victory, the pope had celebrated a Te Deum in Saint Peter's immediately upon receiving the news and later talked to the ambassadors, where he let it be known that "his happiness is great and that he knows that the *república cristiana* would not have been able to enjoy this [victory] but through the intervention of the king."[80] The celebration parades in Rome passed under various triumphal arches decorated with the names of the pope, Philip II, and Venice. Engraved marble plaques praising the Spanish king were hung in the church of Santa Maria in Aracoeli on the Capitoline Hill. Pius urged the Spanish ambassador to have the commander of the fleet, Don Juan of Austria, come to Rome so that he could be given the same elaborate

FIG. 9   GIORGIO VASARI, *THE BATTLE OF LEPANTO*, SALA REGIA, VATICAN
(MONUMENTI MUSEI E GALLERIE PONTIFICIE, CITTÀ DEL VATICANO)

triumphal entry that had been granted Marcantonio Colonna upon his
return from the battle.[81]

Long after the death of Pius V in May 1572, memories of Lepanto
would continue to shape the political imagination of Rome. The new
pope, Gregory XIII, commissioned a series of paintings by Giorgio Vasari
for the Vatican palace to commemorate the victory. In what remains one
of the largest physical monuments to Lepanto and the transformed relationship between king and pope that now prevailed, the large series of

canvases include allegorical human representations of the papacy and the Spanish monarchy with arms lovingly draped over each other's shoulders beholding the naval battle.

SPANISH HEGEMONY IN ROME IN THE AGE OF GREGORY XIII

By 1572, when Ugo Boncompagni—Gregory XIII—was elected to succeed Pius V in the chair of Saint Peter, Spanish power, reputation, and influence in Rome had reached unprecedented levels, and the king's role in the conclave was decisive. Although Alessandro Farnese had a strong following for his own papal ambitions, Philip made it be known through his special envoy, Cardinal Granvelle, that he opposed the plan. Farnese, who received substantial revenues from Spanish benefices, quickly backed down.[82] Boncompagni, on the other hand, who was a known quantity in Spain, where he had twice served on papal diplomatic missions, was on the Spanish list of possibilities and was quickly elected.[83]

The reign of Gregory XIII thus began with the clear support and intervention of the Catholic King. During Gregory's thirteen-year pontificate, moreover, the dominant position of Philip II in Spain's relationship with Rome and the pope would continue and even be strengthened, a fact that first became evident in military affairs. The Battle of Lepanto had effectively underlined not only the naval supremacy of the Spanish fleet—it comprised more than 50 percent of all ships and men of the combined fleet—but also pointed out the relatively small military capacity of the papal forces: the pope was able to provide only 12 ships, 3,000 soldiers, and 270 cavalry for the expedition.[84] While not inconsequential, the papal forces were certainly not comparable to the Spanish and Venetian fleets.

This was a basic military reality that was never far in the background when other papal-Spanish matters were negotiated. If Philip had sought to neutralize and generally reduce the papacy to a weak and subservient military ally after the war with Paul IV, he had succeeded masterfully by 1572. Gregory XIII, for his part, was well aware of this dependency, especially after Venice reached a separate treaty with Sultan Selim shortly after Lepanto, which led to the formal dissolution of the league. In 1574, for instance, the pope instructed his special envoy to beseech Philip in these words to renew the league: "Our Lord God, having preserved

FIG. 10   TITIAN, *ALLEGORY OF LEPANTO AND PHILIP II* (PRADO MUSEUM)

Your Majesty with such power together with Christian piety, almost, one
could say, as the only sustenance of our holy church and of the Catholic
faith; His Holiness has desired to communicate to you his holy thoughts
regarding all the help that Your Majesty owes to God for the many graces
and gifts that he has given you."[85] After this preface the pope asked Philip
to maintain a large fleet in Italy under the command of Don Juan, with an
amount of ships, money, and men equal to that of the previous alliance.

The king responded to such pleas with characteristic requests for more financial concessions from the Spanish church, supported and approved by the papacy. In a letter to Rome that revealed Philip's view of the world and his place in it — and which also provides a valuable estimation of Spanish military expenses — the king wrote,

> Only I as an obedient son have always come to the aid of and offered myself to defend the Holy Apostolic See, bearing the burden, costs, and expenses that are required for this, sustaining an army on the borders of Africa formed against the Moors and Turks; and this costs great sums of gold ducats with no income coming from these areas. And on the frontiers of Spain, and on the islands of the Mediterranean, and the frontiers of Naples and Sicily to resist and defend against all of the invasions of the Turks costs 3 million gold escudos every year, and in the war with the Turks and Moors in Granada 2 million and in Flanders 25 million; the fleet of ships that we bring to the sea against the Turks and heretics cost more than 2 million annually, including the war and defense of Malta.[86]

With this litany of self-praise, as well as self-pity, Philip II requested that the pope grant him the *tres gracias* — subsidio, cruzada, excusado — perpetually.[87] Gregory, while reluctant to grant a favor that would have taken away future bargaining power, did nonetheless quickly grant the *decima* (the 10 percent grant on ecclesiastical income that went to the king) and continued to renew all the gracias throughout his pontificate.[88] Philip responded with a letter in his own hand saying, "I am very sure of how much Your Holiness loves me, and I value this more than anything else in this life, to see signs and proof of this love."[89]

This exchange underlines the strength of the Spanish monarchy by 1574, the increasing dependency of the papacy on the Spanish military for its own defense, and the warm rhetoric that characterized much, if not all, papal-monarchical correspondence in this period.[90] Philip could justifiably claim his role as defender of the faith, having defeated the Moors in Granada in 1569, the Protestants in their ongoing rebellions in Flanders, and the Turks at Malta and Lepanto in 1565 and 1571, respectively. These were basic facts of international affairs that the pope could not deny.

This is not to say that Gregory always supported the Spanish monarch's imperial designs: he opposed the annexation of Portugal and encouraged more compromise in Flanders than Philip would entertain.[91] Nonetheless, he was unable because of his own relative military weakness and dependency on Spanish forces to act in any way that would cause a serious breach of relations.[92]

In fact, the pope could not even keep his own vassals from supporting Spain in military campaigns he opposed. Although Gregory had forbidden his subjects to join Spanish forces in Portugal upon penalty of excommunication and loss of property, the Roman nobleman Martio Colonna took three hundred of his men with him for the campaign, claiming that they were his personal guards. So, too, did Roman allies of the king; Pompeo Colonna was named a general of five thousand men for a potential Portuguese war.[93] After Philip successfully took control of Portugal, the pope bowed to reality, sending his congratulations and receiving the king's ambassador. No papal vassals were prosecuted for their involvement in the campaign.

In the case of Flanders, Gregory supported Philip's request that 10,000 troops be raised in Italy for that campaign; and in 1578 a Roman nobleman, Camillo Capitucco, was named general of 4,500 Italian troops.[94] This appointment, as well as the Portuguese appointments, reveals how the Spanish king built up his military strength and presence within the papal states by giving commissions to Roman noblemen. Although these Romans technically operated as vassals of both king and pope, it was clear that because of Philip's financial power he was often able to exert the stronger influence.

These are but a few examples of Romans who became Spanish military vassals. In the following chapter more details on the large number of Roman nobles who joined one of the Spanish military orders will be examined as part of an analysis of the Spanish faction in the city. It is helpful to note here, however, that during the reigns of Philip II and Philip III a few Romans typically joined these orders each year, so that by the early seventeenth century a sizable number of Spanish military vassals resided in Rome and were considered an important, visible part of the Spanish faction.

This is precisely the type of situation Philip had vehemently protested in the 1560s when the shoe was on the other foot and there was a military order in Spain attached directly to the pope: the order of Saint Lazarus. Writing to Pius V, Philip had complained that for the pope to have a military order in his realms constituted a usurpation of his rights: "Since the Roman pontiffs oftentimes have pretensions, ends, and human wars that they conduct as temporal princes, it is not just that they have and take

arms from our house and our realms for such things."[95] For the politically
astute in Rome, it must have been obvious that by cultivating a group
of loyal military knights in the Papal State, the Catholic King was successfully accomplishing in Rome the same thing he accused the pope of
doing in Spain. Yet during the pontificate of Gregory XIII he met with
little official resistance.

Indeed, many Roman and Neapolitan servants of the pope had close
ties to Philip II, so that in the defense of the city of Rome itself double
vassals of king and pope served in high places. The pope's natural son,
Giacomo Boncompagni, also known as the duke of Sora, was named
a general of the Papal State and the commander (*castellano*) of Castel
Sant'Angelo, with two hundred soldiers and sixty cavalry from his duchy
serving under him. At the same time, he was also indebted to the king
for a benefice of 7,000 escudos which he held from a church in Spain,[96]
and there was little question but that he was counted among the allies
of the Spaniards. When the new Spanish ambassador, the count of Olivares, entered the city in 1582, the duke gave him such an extraordinary
salute (*salva estraordinaria*) with the guns of Castel Sant'Angelo that the
French complained bitterly that other ambassadors were given no such
treatment. This was because "the duke of Sora is not a servant of France
as he is of Spain,"[97] according to one Roman observer.

Martio Colonna, who also served as an officer in the papal guard, was
another double vassal who commanded fifty soldiers. When the pope
offered him fifty cavalry as well, he responded that the fifty "men of arms
that he has from the Catholic King" were enough.[98] Combined, the duke
of Sora's men and Colonna's soldiers made up roughly one-third of a
papal force reported in 1583 to number five hundred Swiss guards, four
hundred soldiers, and sixty more soldiers with arquebuses.[99] This was
not an insignificant number and points to the deep Spanish sympathies
of the many troops closest to the pope himself.

This submission to Spain in military matters did not come without
benefits for the Papal State. Most apparent was the protection the papacy
received from possible internal and external enemies. In 1580 the league
against the Turks had been renewed, and in 1583 the Spanish fleet was
used to rid the papal coasts of Turkish pirate ships.[100] At the same time,
banditry in the papal states had reached alarming proportions, and there
were a number of disgruntled vassals of the pope who were known to
be harboring bandits and causing general unrest. Pope Gregory's policy

of claiming long-overdue feudal dues and confiscating land when the money was not forthcoming contributed to this chronic problem. Banditry also afflicted most of the other Italian territories in the late sixteenth century, including those of Spain.[101] Making it clear that he would tolerate no rebellion in the Papal State, Philip sent 1,500 soldiers from Naples to the Roman port of Civitavecchia in 1583 in case the pope should need them.[102] The ambassador also reportedly told Cardinal Colonna that the king was ready to move "all the force that he has in Italy against those who want to disturb the pope and bother the Papal State."[103]

Although Spanish troops and royal threats against banditry were frequently as futile in the Papal State as they were in their own realms (the Spaniards were actually suspected of supporting the bandits a few years later, when they showed themselves discontented with Sixtus V), they still acted as a strong deterrent against outright rebellion. In fact, the Papal State in the period between Paul IV's war against the Spaniards and Urban VIII's War of Castro in 1642 (when Spanish military support was absent) was largely free of the destabilizing and costly civil unrest that had often drained it of financial and human resources in the previous centuries. Thus, in the period of the strongest Spanish presence in Rome and the Papal State, the pope's domestic authority can also be said to have grown. In short, the Spanish military may have bolstered papal absolutism, even if the latter government was for all practical purposes a military dependency of the former.

The greatest benefit of Spanish military assistance, and possibly of greatest importance for the long-term development and domestic stability of Rome and the Papal State in this period, was the financial advantage the papacy gained from not having to support a large military force. While the Spanish king spent himself into repeated bankruptcy trying to defend and expand his empire—recall the king's earlier letter to Gregory XIII citing 32 million gold escudos in military expenses—the papacy after the pontificate of Paul IV spent a comparatively small percentage of its budget on military forces until the War of Castro.[104] Papal expenses for the Lepanto expedition, for instance, were 140,000 scudi, or roughly 15 percent of the papal income, and from 1560 to 1620 the total military budget rarely exceeded 20 percent of the total annual budget, which grew in this period from approximately 1 to 2 million scudi. This was in comparison to the 50 or 60 percent of the papal budget for military expenses that was common in the fourteenth and fifteenth centuries, and the enormous costs of Paul IV's war with Spain, which was two or three times the annual papal income from 1555 to 1557.[105]

Clearly, the Papal State benefited financially from Spanish military protection, primarily at the expense of the ecclesiastical states in the realms of the Spanish king, which were repeatedly taxed, with papal consent, to support the military budget. At the same time, Rome and the papal court of Gregory XIII continued to benefit more directly from the Spanish money that flowed into the city in a variety of forms for cardinals, courtiers, Spanish agents, and the papal family.

From the perspective of public relations the most important Spanish financial contribution to Rome was the feudal dues paid to the pope from the Kingdom of Naples. By the late 1570s the related problems of banditry and papal vassals reluctant to pay feudal dues had given the Spaniards the opportunity to emphasize, by contrast, their own obedience and fidelity to the pope. The presentation of the 7,000 gold ducats and the white horse for the papal stable on the feast of Saint Peter subsequently rose in importance and stature. In 1578, for example, a Roman report noted that after the pope celebrated mass on the feast day he waited for "the chinea that had to come accompanied by the Catholic ambassador and Señor Castellano in the coach of Señor Vicenzo Vitello, by Señor Honorato Chrietano, and by all the nobility of Rome with the Spanish nation."[106] When the large procession of people arrived, Gregory welcomed them, "commending the Catholic King for the obedience rendered." It was noted that "the chinea was very beautiful" that year.[107]

For all its symbolic importance to both king and pope, the money involved was small compared to the other Spanish revenues that came into Rome. The income or papal share of the "spoils" from Spanish vacancies, most noticeably, brought into the papal coffers a reported 50,000 scudi in 1577.[108] This appears to have been the average payment made to Rome by the office of the "collector" during the 1570s and 1580s, a period for which there are no detailed papal registers. We know more specifically from the papal economic registers starting in 1589 that the Spanish contributions from the vacancies were equal to or greater than this in the following decades. In 1589, for example, we find entries that put contributions from the Spanish realms at the following levels: "Dalla Colletoria di Spagna—50,000"; "Dalla Colletoria di Portugallo—4,000"; "Da Cleri del Regno di Napoli—15,090"; "Da Su Maesta Cattolica per il Censo del Regno di Napoli, 8,251."[109] This 77,000 scudi, which included the chinea, constituted roughly 5 percent of the recorded papal income of 1,546,279 scudi and was the sixth-largest item on the papal register, following taxes from other parts of the papal states.

Besides this direct income from realms of the Catholic King, the papal court more generally benefited from the growing patronage of Philip II throughout the pontificate of Gregory XIII. Among the larger pensions granted were those from the revenues of Toledo in 1577: Cardinals San Sisto and Madruccio received 4,000 ducats each, Vastavallano 3,000, Aragona and Orsini 2,500 each, and Maffeo, Mont'Albano, Colonna, Delfino, Comillino, Gambara, and Napoli 1,000 each.[110] Early in 1578 Cardinal Alessandrino was given a monastery in Sicily with a 4,000-ducat pension,[111] and one of the auditors of the Rota was given 14,000 ducats from the bishopric of Lérida in 1579.[112]

Large-scale Spanish gifts also contributed substantially to the papal treasury without being recorded in the registers. In 1578, after the pope had awarded Pedro Deza his cardinal's hat, the king sent the same Roman envoy who had delivered the hat back to the pope with a gift of 7,000 ducats, together with a necklace worth 700 ducats and a jewel worth some thousands.[113] A year later the papal envoy, Giovanni Batta, after delivering a cardinal's hat to Quiroga, the archbishop of Toledo, was given 2,000 ducats for himself, a 500-ducat pension from a church in Sicily, and a reported 50,000 ducats' worth of jewels for the pope.[114] Combined with the many pensions and other smaller gifts and commissions from Spain, these larger gifts made it clear that the Catholic King's treasure chest was, indeed, a critical part of the courtly society and economy of Rome in the late sixteenth and early seventeenth centuries.

PHILIP II AND TRAJAN: POLITICAL POWER AND THE RHETORIC OF TRIUMPH

As Spanish political domination in Rome increased, so too did the rhetorical production that claimed a place of precedence for Spain in both contemporary and ancient Rome. Ambrosio Morales, a contemporary and friend of Ocampo's as well as a professor of rhetoric at the University of Alcalá, took up the task of finishing Ocampo's *Crónica* upon his death.[115] Even more than Ocampo, Morales was a servant of the king, eventually becoming a courtier in the royal household. In addition to finishing the *Crónica,* he was given the task of writing a life of San Diego of Alcalá, something that meant a great deal to Philip II personally, as we shall see later.[116] Morales's addition to Ocampo's work began with the Roman period and continued through the reign of Fernando I of Castile, who was credited with unifying Castile, León, Galicia, and Asturias in 1037.

Since the Roman period was Morales's first concern and the topic of no fewer than the first ten books of his *Crónica,* it was the Romans above all others who were presented as the primary point of contrast and comparison to the Spaniards. Initially, the Romans were depicted with admiration as the most astute in war and most politically sophisticated people of the ancient world. Morales followed Livy closely as he described in some detail the functioning of the Senate, the tribunes, the consuls, and the mysteries of the Roman religion.[117] In the midst of such greatness, the author initially made no attempt to compare any autonomous Spanish rulers or accomplishments but, like Ocampo, sought only to claim a part of the Roman glory for Spain. To this end he claimed that aside from the Italians, the "first allies the Romans had were the Spaniards, which was no small glory for our nation."[118] Moreover, he contended that the Senate and people of Rome were no less concerned with the affairs of Spain than with those of Italy.[119]

To prove this point, Morales argued that the Spaniards were quick to aid the Romans in their war with the Carthaginians and that the Romans sent one of their best leaders, Scipio Africanus, to subdue and govern the peninsula. Scipio, in fact, became not just a Roman military leader in the *Crónica* but was said to have been taken as king by the Spaniards. According to Morales, the Spaniards of that time were not very sophisticated in their politics, but they knew a strong king when they saw one and immediately began to call Scipio king.[120] The Spaniards were presented as naturally well-disposed to and desirous of a strong monarch; and it is obvious that Morales was referring not to a regional or provincial leader but to a king of all the Spaniards. Scipio was credited with conquering the whole of Spain, and, most important, of doing so with the assistance of Spaniards.[121]

The depiction of the Spaniards as a nation was one of the dominant characteristics of Morales's history of the Roman period, and even in his description of the most notable early instance of regional separatism, the revolt of the people of Numancia against Roman rule, the *Numantinos* are described as "our Numantinos" and as valiant Spaniards (*Españoles*).[122] It was one of the telling ironies of the *Crónica* that the author was able, in his recounting of the rebellion and subsequent destruction of the separatists, to praise the "great strength and valor of our Numantinos" at the same time that he acknowledges the role of other Spaniards in their defeat: "The Spaniards could not be conquered unless other Spaniards helped to conquer them."[123]

It was at this point in the history that the Romans were criticized and contrasted to the Spaniards, whose virtues the Numantinos were said to embody. Morales here turned to the ancient Spanish historian Paulo Orosio, a contemporary of Saint Augustine's, who chastised the Romans for claiming the great virtues of "faith, justice, and strength" when, in fact, it was the Numantinos who had now taken on these qualities.[124] The Romans, in the meantime, had already begun to be corrupted. They lost their empire because of a lack of precisely those virtues the ancient Spaniards had.

The claiming of Roman glory, virtue, even the founding of Rome, for Spain by Ocampo and Morales provides much insight into the attitude of the Spanish ruling class toward Rome throughout the Golden Age. From this historical perspective, Spain was the true heir to what was best about the Roman Empire; and it was this view, in part, that allowed Spaniards to think of Italy and Rome "as an extension of their own country."[125] At the same time, the Spanish monarchs were fashioned as the true descendants of the ancient Roman emperors and were described with the appropriated language and imagery of classical empire.[126]

Consistent with the literary moves of Annius of Viterbo, Ocampo, Valdes, and others, Morales and his generation of Spanish humanists thus deepened the literary conquest of Rome. To accompany the contemporary political reality, these writers created a version of history that subjugated Rome to Spanish designs. In the words of Tzvetan Todorov (describing the world of Machiavelli and Ferdinand), their "discourse was not determined by the object it described . . . rather, it was constructed solely in view of the objective it sought to attain."[127] In this case, the objective was to present Spain as a central part of the Roman past and the historical heir of the Roman Empire, as well as the legitimate contemporary protector and reformer of the city.

Moreover, by the middle years of the reign of Philip II, these views were also being presented and produced in Rome itself by Spanish humanists. The most direct descendent of the historical tradition of Ocampo

and Morales was the Dominican Alfonso Chacón. He had built a reputation as a theologian while in Spain, where he was the prior of the convent
of San Tommaso in Seville.[128] He was called to Rome by Pius V in 1567,
initially lived in the palace of the Spanish cardinal Pacheco, and served as
a confessor for the Vatican in the *penitenziere* for some time.[129]

Chacón was the most important Spanish humanist of classical and
Christian antiquity working in Rome in the sixteenth century, and he
had begun his studies in Spain under Ambrosio Morales.[130] In Rome he
was able to indulge this passion more fully. He eventually produced more
than twenty works, including *De antiquitatibus Romani, Historica descriptio urbis Romae,* and *Historia utriusque belli datici a Traiano Caesare gesti quae
in columna eiusdem Romae visuntur, collecta.*[131] In the course of his study,
Chacón collected a large library, including numerous manuscripts of classical texts that he intended to give as a gift to Philip II when he died. The
fame of the library, however, was such that Clement VIII claimed it for
the Vatican upon Chacón's death in 1599.[132]

Among his classical works, the most important was the *Historia utriusque belli,* the first detailed study of one of ancient Rome's best-preserved
and most dramatic monuments, Trajan's Column. This book added yet
another subtle contribution to the rhetoric of Spanish triumph in Rome.
Like his teachers, Chacón wrote, in part, to underline Spain's role in
Rome's greatness both past and present. The famous relief sculptures that
wind their way up Trajan's Column in a corkscrew pattern tell the story
of the Spanish emperor's victory over the Germanic tribe of the Dacians.
And like the ancient Roman history of Ocampo and Morales, the analysis
of the story told by the sculptures is given a distinctly Spanish twist.

Initially, Chacón set the stage for his work by making a clear connection between the contemporary Spanish monarch and the ancient
Roman emperors. In the dedication to Philip II, Chacón declared that
it was particularly appropriate that his work should be dedicated to the
king. Indeed, he claimed that it was right to call Philip the successor of
Trajan because both were Spanish, both were kings of Spain, and both
ruled a large portion of the world.[133] Moreover, Chacón noted that he was
sending a copy of the book to the king for his new library in the Escorial,
confident that Philip knew, like the ancient Romans, that a wise ruler
conquered and defended his realms with books as well as arms.[134]

In the text itself, Chacón made a point of writing Spaniards into the story of Trajan's victory over the Dacians wherever possible. He claimed, for instance, that the victorious military forces were made up of Italians and Spaniards and that it was a Spanish soldier, Leucas Hispanicas, who led a company of one thousand Italians. According to Chacón, the shoes and dress of many of the soldiers on the column revealed them to be Spanish, as did their beards and hairstyle. A similar point was made about priests.[135] More generally, Chacón emphasized that the Spanish soldiers were the natural choice to be friends of a Spanish emperor.[136]

While it would be wrong to overstate the degree to which Chacón tried to make a Spanish fiction of Trajan's Column—he was too good a humanist to stretch the facts too much—the dedication and repeated references to Spaniards in the text give the work a distinctly Spanish flavor. This appears to have been clear, for example, to a later Italian translator of the text, Giovanni Pietro Bellori, who created a new version that was dedicated to Louis XIV of France in 1686. Gone, of course, was the original dedication to the Spanish king, and gone, too, were any references to anything Spanish in the text. No Spanish clothing, soldiers, or reference to Trajan's place of origin were left in Bellori's version.[137] The text, in short, was ethnically cleansed; even the author had been given an Italianized name, Ciaccone.

But in 1576, when it was first published, Chacón's work was another addition to the Spanish version of Roman history. Combined with the writing of his teacher Morales, his text claimed still another piece of Roman history for Spain at a time when "Trajan's successor," Philip II, was claiming an unprecedented level of influence in the sixteenth-century city. Not surprisingly, this was an influence that not everyone in Rome celebrated, and the pope who succeeded Gregory XIII in 1585, Sixtus V, was determined to reassert papal power and autonomy.

RESISTANCE AND REACTION UNDER SIXTUS V

When Cardinal Montalto, the former Franciscan friar Felice Peretti, was elected to succeed Gregory XIII, he brought with him characteristics common to his two predecessors that made him *papabile* (eligible for election) for the Spanish. Of low birth, he, like Pius V, had been an inquisitor with a reputation for ecclesiastical strictness and, like Gregory XIII, had served on diplomatic missions to Spain and was known there. While not the first choice of the Spanish faction in the conclave, he was known as a supporter of the Catholic King and was among those who were acceptable to the monarch.[138]

His pontificate therefore began with no surprises or changes in the close relationship between Spain and Rome that had developed over the past twenty-five years. On the contrary, in the early months an exchange of favors and aid between king and pope deepened the alliance generally, and strengthened Philip's hand internationally. In Rome the presentation of the chinea and dues from Naples went on with its usual pomp, and a few months later the king ordered one of his vassals, the duke of Mantua, to give the pope another fine horse as well as two horses and a carriage for his nephew, Cardinal Montalto, and four horses and a coach for his sister.[139] The "spoils" from Spanish church vacancies also continued to make their way to Rome uninterrupted.

The pope, for his part, pledged a million scudi for a Spanish-led war against England, which he urged Philip to undertake.[140] When representatives of the king pressed for papal support in Flanders, moreover, Sixtus committed himself to either provide or pay for four thousand infantry and six hundred cavalry for the latest campaign.[141] At the same time, the pope renewed the subsidio for five years and the excusado and cruzada for six. By this time these ecclesiastical taxes alone raised more than 2 million ducats annually for Philip.[142] On a smaller scale, the pope sent many prisoners held in Rome to serve on the Spanish galleys in Naples.[143] In return for these concessions and grants, the Papal State continued to receive the usual Spanish naval protection—the cruzada was in part justified by the costs of the Spanish fleet in Italy—and the more general military support of the king.[144]

In addition to direct financial contributions and military aid, the pope, beginning in the 1580s, became increasingly dependent upon the realms of the Spanish monarch for another necessity of internal stability: grain to supplement the decreasing production and increasing numbers of bad harvests in the Papal State.[145] The population of Rome, in particular, had been growing rapidly over the previous two decades and suffered greatly under food shortages; in 1582 Gregory XIII had imported more than 4,000 rubbi of grain from Sicily to help feed the city.[146] Late in 1585 Sixtus V asked the king for increased imports of roughly 7,000 rubbi, and in 1586 Spanish realms sent almost 3,000 rubbi.[147] In fact, over the fifty-year period from 1582 to 1631 the Papal State depended on grain imports from Spanish territories (Sicily, Naples, Sardinia), and Spain itself, as the following representative figures reveal:[148]

TABLE I: GRAIN IMPORTS TO ROME

Year	Total Imports by Rubbio	Imports from Spanish Realms
1582	21,045	4,029
1585	38,956	6,906
1586	12,346	2,846
1590	21,072	11,139
1592	42,041	33,898
1593	27,668	7,614
1596	20,782	19,112
1599	4,510	4,510
1600	43,856	24,400
1601	24,336	19,450
1605	18,517	10,440
1612	4,793	4,793
1615	6,582	6,582
1616	886	886
1617	55,949	8,849
1618	19,382	9,279
1620	7,915	7,915
1621	20,579	1,133
1622	30,676	17,706
1623	3,581	3,581
1624	8,462	3,332
1627	6,247	1,460
1630	38,265	10,678
1631	2,209	2,209

This dependence on grain from Spanish realms gave the monarch yet another powerful bargaining chip with which to try to shape Roman policy, and it was especially clear in the late 1580s and early 1590s that Philip would not hesitate to use the weapon of food to pressure popes and conclaves. It appears to have been no accident, for example, that shortly after Philip granted the pope his needed grain concessions in 1586, Sixtus V awarded him the long sought-after right of presentation to all the bishoprics of Sicily for himself and his son.[149]

With this ongoing exchange of favors, and with their interests more tightly interwoven than ever, the papacy and the Spanish monarchy continued to present a united front throughout Europe and in Rome itself. In 1586, when news reached Rome that the city of Cologne had been retaken by Spanish and German forces, for instance, Sixtus V ordered major prayers of thanksgiving and "the following morning the pope proceeded from Monte Cavallo with twenty cardinals to the church of Santiago, where there was a mass *pro gratiarum actione,* and from there he went to the church of [Santa Maria] dell'Anima, where the Te Deum was sung."[150]

In France, too, the king and pope were initially united in their support of Henry III, the duke of Guise, and the Holy League. Sixtus V excommunicated the Protestant Henry of Navarre in 1585, and granted Henry III more than 2 million livres in church taxes to aid him in the fight against the Huguenots. Philip II, however, sought even more overt papal intervention, especially after Guise was killed and Henry III assassinated in 1589.

By this time, however, growing Spanish power throughout Europe and territorial pretensions in France were feared and resented by Spain's enemies and allies alike, and the pope was no exception. As early as 1586 Philip had deeply angered Sixtus by claiming the right of bestowing ecclesiastical titles, a traditional prerogative of the pope, and Sixtus threatened him with excommunication.[151] In addition, continuing struggles over ecclesiastical jurisdiction strained relations, and the king and pope grew to dislike each other personally as well. Philip was particularly angered by the pope's refusal to pay him the million scudi pledged to the English campaign after the disaster with the armada in 1588 and by his perceived reluctance to contribute to the Holy League.

While Sixtus could not help but initially support the Holy League and the Catholic King, he had grown weary of Spanish power and presumption in French affairs, especially as they were manifested in Rome in the person of the Spanish ambassador. The count of Olivares was relentless in demands that the pope move with all his force against Navarre and the Protestants in France and went so far as to issue formal protests against his receiving the French king's emissary. The fact that the pope could even discuss reconciliation with the lapsed monarch outraged the Spaniards, who expected complete support from the papacy for their own agenda in France.[152] Reports from Rome, on the other hand, bitterly accused the Spaniards of seeking to reduce the papacy to a Spanish vassal and complained that "neither the Neros, nor the Diocletians" had tried to usurp pontifical authority as much as the Spaniards now tried to.[153] The angry exchanges and accusations included military posturing from Spanish troops in Naples, the withholding of badly needed Sicilian grain during a serious bread shortage in Rome, and even rumors that renewed banditry in the Papal State was sponsored by Spain. Sixtus responded with threats of excommunication, and for the first time since the days of Paul IV a breach of relations was a serious possibility.[154]

By July 1590, however, the pope had been worn down by Spanish military threats and economic coercion as well as by the deteriorating situation in France. He agreed to have a treaty drawn up for a formal military alliance with Spain, pledging both money and men to aid the Holy League.[155] Despite his disgust with Spanish intimidation in Rome and fear of Spanish domination of Europe, Sixtus was faced with the Papal State's deep-rooted dependency on Spain and the lack of alternatives or stronger allies. As much as he hoped that Catholic France would become strong enough to offset Spanish power, this was still only a distant possibility. Sixtus was also forced to acknowledge the allegiance Philip enjoyed among the cardinals and nobility of Rome. The result was that even this most powerful and wealthy pope was forced to acquiesce to Spanish pressure, revealing the extent to which the politics of Rome had become hispanized.

ROME AS A SPANISH AVIGNON?

The strengths, innovations, and many successes of Sixtus V in governing the Papal State and building up the city of Rome have often overshadowed the other basic fact of his pontificate, his dependence on Spain. But if there had been any doubt about the depth of Spanish power and influence in the eternal city, it was eliminated during the quick succession of conclaves that followed his death in 1590. The Catholic King, determined to prevent a repeat of the last years of Sixtus's pontificate, dropped all pretense of detachment from the election. Spanish troops and galleys from Naples moved toward Rome,[156] while strong members of the Spanish faction of cardinals like Cardinal Sforza hung the Spanish coat of arms on the doors of their palaces.[157] Combined with popular hatred of Sixtus V, whose statue on the Capitoline was quickly smashed by a mob after his death, these strong displays of Spanish power and dislike of Sixtus—it was reported that the pope's death consoled all Spain; some towns even held celebrations [158]—overwhelmed any possible attempt to elect a member of the opposition faction, led by Sixtus V's nephew Cardinal Montalto. When Giovanni Batista Castagna, who took the name of Urban VII, was elected, it came as no surprise to anyone that he "was unequivocally attached to the Spanish interests." [159]

The sudden death of this pope only twelve days after his election forced another conclave. With Rome unsettled and the French situation at a critical stage, Philip made his boldest move yet in a papal election by simply providing a list of seven cardinals who would be acceptable to him. No others would even be considered, according to his chief representatives in the city.[160] At the same time, the king let it be known to the conclave that the grain ships destined for Rome would be kept in Sicily until they had concluded a satisfactory election.[161] When Cardinal Sfondrato, an old member of the Spanish faction who appeared on the list, was subsequently elected in December 1590, he quickly indicated in his choice of a name, Gregory XIV, that like Gregory XIII he would firmly support Spanish policies. The king was pleased and a short time later sent a list of pensions worth 30,000 scudi to be distributed among the Spanish faction of cardinals in Rome.[162]

Perhaps more than any of his predecessors, Gregory XIV opened the papal coffers and the papal court to Spanish interests with an abandon that astonished and angered many other parties in Rome. This did not occur, however, without early tensions caused by continuing Spanish coercion, exercised primarily through the grain supply. The food shortages in Rome had grown even worse over the year, and bread riots broke out early in 1591. Popular, as well as official, opinion held the Spaniards responsible: a Roman report from late 1590 noted that six Spaniards walking past the Pantheon were chased by a Roman mob who blamed them for the famine and claimed that they would be the first to suffer, followed by the Jews and the merchants.[163] Promises of Sicilian grain had been made shortly after Gregory's election through the papal nuncio in Madrid, but the pope was also being pressured to pay the Spaniards the 500,000 scudi that they alleged Sixtus V owed them from the failed English campaign.[164] The grain shipments were seemingly being used to squeeze this payment from the pope, and he responded with a threat not to renew the three gracias.[165] When the grain finally arrived in Rome a few weeks later, however, he promptly renewed the gracias and also formally committed six thousand infantry, five hundred cavalry, and five hundred pikemen to the French League.[166] Within a few months, he had gone further to pledge an additional 200,000 scudi to the league and was quickly spending the treasure Sixtus V had accumulated in Castel Sant'Angelo in the way Philip had always wanted.

Besides this compliance in international affairs, the new pope was also predisposed toward Spanish appointments in Rome. The naming of Pompeo Arigoni, one of the king's key lawyers, as an auditor of the Rota, the most important ecclesiastical court in Rome, was a clear example of the pope's favor.[167] So, too, was appointing the Spanish banking company of Herrera and Costa papal bankers, or holders of the office of the *depositaria generale*.[168] Together with the first, pro-Spanish cardinals created by the pope, these actions led to the growing perception that the Spaniards were dominating the entire papal court, which caused much consternation among other factions. The Venetian ambassador, for instance, complained that the pope's appointments were "all devoted to the Spaniards, who want to dominate all this court and to create in their style the popes, cardinals, auditors of the Rota, and every other official of the Apostolic See."[169]

This stark assessment of affairs was, of course, an accurate description of Spanish designs. Philip was constantly maneuvering, through his many vassals and agents, to place Spaniards in positions of power in the papal court. By 1591 and the pontificate of Gregory XIV, moreover, the old king, together with his agents and his ambassador the count of Olivares, had become masters at the complicated game of Roman politics. As one Roman observer put it, "The solicitude and art that these Spaniards use to procure" the various things they desire at court, "is an incredible thing."[170]

Spanish political power reached its zenith in Rome and throughout the Italian peninsula in the early years of this decade, and no pope capitulated to it more than Gregory XIV. Had he lived beyond the ten months and ten days of his pontificate, the fears that Rome would become a "Spanish Avignon" might not have been far from the mark. A contemporary observer summed up the situation well when he wrote, "These Spaniards boast of having obtained in the pontificate of Gregory XIV as much as is possible to have conceded from the Apostolic See for their king, who now has no other need but of popes who are confidants and friends of his majesty."[171] Thus, it was no overstatement when Leopold von Ranke wrote, "The loss of this pontiff was the heaviest affliction that could possibly have befallen the party of Spain."[172]

The Spaniards, for all their acumen in electing a series of overtly pro-Spanish popes, were obviously having a bad string of luck with papal health. This continued to be the case with the successor to Gregory XIV, Innocent IX, who lived only two months after his election on October 29. During his short reign he pledged continued support to the Holy League but displayed disgust at the depletion of the papal treasury that had occurred during his predecessors' time under pressure from the Spaniards. It was reported that the pope was especially pained by the fact that "the aim of the Spaniards has been to consume and destroy the Apostolic treasury first with one strategy and then with another";[173] and he took back 150,000 of 200,000 scudi that Olivares and Sessa had procured from Gregory XIV for the league shortly before he died.[174]

In what was probably his only other notable sign of defiance toward Spanish coercion, Innocent IX threatened the Spanish authorities in Naples with excommunication for allegedly withholding a shipment of wine for the papal tables.[175] This last act, while possibly one of the more timely excommunications since the Neapolitan wine was best consumed young, nonetheless revealed yet another area of dependency and the desperate, exaggerated measures the papacy was driven to by its own weakness. Relying on the Spanish king for bread, wine, domestic and international military support, and direct financial support, the Papal State was close to becoming, if it was not already, a Spanish client state. Although a shrewd and able pope could still wield considerable power in the realms of ecclesiastical and international affairs, it was the challenge of the next pope, Clement VIII, to use this power to recapture a greater measure of political and domestic independence from the Spanish monarchy.

CONTINUITY AND CHANGE
UNDER CLEMENT VIII

The election of Ippolito Aldobrandini, Clement VIII (1592–1605), as the successor of Innocent IX did not signal an immediate change in the status quo in Rome. A Florentine by birth, he had enjoyed the support of Cardinal Farnese and Sixtus V and had served on a diplomatic mission to Spain. Although a compromise candidate, he was approved by Philip II and demonstrated in the first months of his pontificate that he would support the king's French policy by sending 50,000 scudi to the Holy League.[176] Before 1592 was over the pope had also pledged 15,000 scudi per month to the French cause under pressure from the Spanish ambassador, who sought enough papal funding for three thousand troops and five hundred cavalry.[177]

At the same time warm royal letters from Madrid assured the pope of continued general support and specific help in eradicating banditry from the Papal State.[178] The largest shipments of grain from Naples and Sicily yet sent to Rome also arrived in the first year of Clement VIII's reign: more than 33,000 rubbi of a total 39,000 imported.[179] The duke of Sessa informed his king that the pope was "content and very grateful for the favor that Your Majesty has done for him," and that these imports "caused the price of bread to go down in this city."[180]

Other forms of direct financial exchange also continued between the courts of Rome and Madrid; for example, the pope granted Philip 200,000 ducats from vacant benefices of the Order of Santiago early in 1593.[181] In that same year he also gave the king the right to new annual financial concessions from the clergy of Catalonia, who were now required to pay the king two fifths of the decima.[182]

Meanwhile, in Rome various cardinals received substantial pensions from Spanish realms, including 5,000 ducats to Cardinal Terranova (or Terranuova) from a monastery in Sicily,[183] 2,000 to Cardinal Farnese, 6,000 to Cardinal Deza,[184] 3,000 to Cardinal Sfondrato,[185] and 1,000 each to the cardinal nephews of the pope.[186]

The number of pensions from church lands in Spanish realms that went to Rome during Philip II's long reign began to breed resentment in Spain, ultimately producing a revealing exchange late in 1593. The Council of State, the king's primary advisory body for political affairs,[187] declared that no foreigners should be allowed to hold benefices in the kingdoms of Castile and Aragon.[188] This affected Italian churchmen more than any other group, Romans in particular. When the Spaniards published the official proclamation in Rome, the pope summoned the ambassador to make known his deep displeasure with the innovation: he reportedly claimed that if the new order, which would affect an estimated 30,000 ducats per year of Roman income, were acted upon he would "revoke the many concessions and useful engorgements that Spain has from this See from the excusado, subsidio, triennale, decima, cruzada, and similar things that bring in more than 3 million [ducats] in gold annually." The pope would then "have his and the Spaniards theirs," if that was how they wanted it.[189]

Here was the clearest acknowledgement to date of the reciprocal economic arrangement—albeit an unwritten one—that marked Spanish-papal relations throughout this period. While the pope's estimate that only 30,000 ducats came into Rome from Spanish benefices was low, ignoring the many pensions from Sicily and Naples that also benefited Romans, it expressed the common perception in Rome that the Spaniards were getting the better end of the bargain. Even given the unmentioned financial benefits that came to the Papal State in the form of revenues from Spanish vacancies and military support, it was true that the amount gained by the royal treasury in Spain from ecclesiastical concessions was proportionately far greater. The estimated 3 million gold ducats of annual ecclesiastical revenue for the king was a critical part of the royal finances that became even more important in the following decades as the flow of New World treasure decreased. In reality, this revenue constituted the unnoticed safety net for the royal treasury, a fact that became most apparent after it went bankrupt in 1596.

This being the case, Philip was not about to stop paying Roman pensions that by all accounts brought him a good return. In a shrewd move that placated the unhappy Spaniards at home while demanding an even greater display of allegiance from the cardinals in Rome, the king let the council's prohibition stand but granted cardinals receiving pensions from Castile and Aragon the naturaleza from these realms.

The rights of naturaleza, or naturalization, for the kingdom of Castile was a common favor used by the king to gain allegiance: he granted naturalezas on a large scale to Portuguese churchmen after 1580, as well as to important clerics from Aragon in order to allow them to benefit from the far richer benefices of Castile. The powerful and loyal auditor of the Rota, Francisco Peña, for example, who was from the Kingdom of Aragon, was given the naturaleza of Castile in 1592, along with a pension from the bishopric of Ciudad Rodrigo. Peña acknowledged the gift in the following letter to the king: "The duke of Sessa has told me about the favor that Your Majesty has been pleased to grant me of a pension and naturaleza so as to be able to have more in the kingdom of Castile, and although no temporal prize can increase the obligations and desire that are within me to serve Your Majesty as your faithful vassal and creature, this gesture that Your Majesty has made through his greatness and goodness is appreciated more than I know how to say."[190]

For Italians, too, this royal tool was used to maintain a strong allegiance among cardinals and the Roman nobility, and the council's prohibition had little effect. While a more detailed look at how naturaleza, pensions, and other Spanish concessions were used to build up the Spanish faction in Rome will come in the next chapter, it is important to note here that Spanish pensions continued to flow into Rome in the months and years following the contentious decree. In 1593 Cardinal Farnese received 10,000 ducats from the bishopric of Zaragoza and Cardinal Sfondrato 3,000.[191] In 1594 the pope's nephews were given an additional 2,000 ducats in pension and the auditor of the Camera received 2,000 from the bishopric of Placencia; it was noted that he was "brought the naturaleza of Spain in order to be able to obtain those benefices."[192] In 1595, moreover, 20,000 ducats from the vacant archbishopric of Toledo were distributed in Rome upon the death of Cardinal Quiroga, with the largest amounts given to the following clerics: 3,000 to Cardinals Aldobrandino and San Jorge; 1,500 to Cardinals Toledo and Santi Quatri; and 1,000 to Cardinals Pallavicino, Pinto, and Aquaviva.[193]

Spanish patronage and pensions therefore continued unabated in the early years of Clement VIII's reign, as did the broader military alliance that included a renewed league against the Turks as well as cooperation with the French League. Just as the Turkish threat had led all the popes from Pius IV to Sixtus V to rely on Spanish help, so too did it lead Clement VIII to write Philip II in 1592 to call for a new league against the old nemesis.[194]

On the Mediterranean front a joint Spanish-Italian fleet was formed, with Spain and the Papal State providing the bulk of ships and men. It was reported that the fleet consisted of forty-seven galleys, eight supply ships, five thousand Spanish and six thousand Italian infantry—but only the vessels from the Papal State and Spain would have the honor of sailing with their standards at full mast, "everyone having been given his place."[195]

At the same time, the pope urgently called for joint action against the Turkish threat to Hungary and Austria. As early as 1592 he had asked the king to send money and men to Emperor Rudolph II, and after the sultan formally declared war in 1593 this support became all the more vital.

Philip responded reluctantly to these overtures, but he did send 300,000 ducats in 1593–1594.[196] Moreover, when the See of Toledo fell vacant, and tensions arose between pope and king over the use of the "spoils," it was eventually agreed that a third of the money would be sent to the Holy Roman emperor.[197]

Briefly summarized, papal-Spanish cooperation in the international arena remained strong until 1595, when the pope, after long negotiations, finally resolved to absolve Henry of Navarre, now Henry IV, following his conversion to Catholicism. Having successfully persuaded (or intimidated) a number of popes against considering such a move, Philip now lost out in the face of growing French Catholic support for their king, Henry's repeated and increasingly humble requests for papal absolution, and Clement's belief that the king was sincere and that his absolution could "prevent the apostasy of France."[198]

Surprisingly, the absolution of Navarre did not bring the threats that had characterized Philip's response seven years previously, when Sixtus V first considered the possibility of doing so. Nor did it bring any serious breach of relations between Spain and the papacy. While Philip was obviously against the move, he was faced with a financial crisis at home, increasingly bad health, and the need to secure a solid position with the pope for his son and successor. The pope, for his part, had no desire to alienate the Catholic King and made the important gesture of appointing two cardinals at Philip's personal request early in 1596: Don Francisco de Avila and Don Hernando Niño de Guevara. The king responded with an ingratiating letter, noting that the pope had performed "a very particular favor and benefit for me, and for that I kiss the very holy feet and hands of Your Holiness."[199] Clearly times had changed from the days of Sixtus V.

This exchange underlines the new tone that marked the last years of Philip's life; and generally the years between 1595 and 1598 have to be seen as the most important period of transition in Spanish-papal relations since the time of Paul IV. Two fundamental changes, the imminent re-entry of France onto the Roman stage and the imminent exit of Philip II from the earthly one, lay at the heart of this transformation. The old Spanish king had arguably been the single most powerful force in Rome over the previous forty years without ever having set foot in the city. Yet his quickly approaching death signaled an inevitable, if temporary, diminution in the prestige, influence, and power of the Spanish monarchy.[200]

It is both a strength and weakness of absolute monarchy that much of its power and prestige depends upon the longevity of the king. In the case of Philip II and his relationship with Rome, his long rule had allowed him to build up a vast network of dependents, which, in part, maintained a personal quality.[201] Moreover, the virtual absence of his most powerful competitor for Roman clients, the king of France, had greatly increased his influence.

After the absolution of Henry IV, however, all this began to change, for the French began competing more actively with Spain for clients in Rome. Already in 1595, for instance, it was reported that Don Michele Peretti, a minor Roman nobleman, had been sought out by a Frenchman for service to the French king. He declined, asserting, "I am Spanish and not French."[202] More important, early in 1596 Henry IV had agreed to allow the papacy a larger role in the appointment of bishops, and it was noted that French benefices would now be coming into Rome more regularly, something that gave the pope "great consolation."[203] Spain, in short, was no longer the only player in town.

French support also served to strengthen the hand of the papacy in wider Italian affairs, and to free Rome from almost sole dependence on Spain. The annexation of the vacant fiefdom of Ferrara by Clement VIII in 1598, an event that more than any other marked the new papal strength, was accomplished largely through the support of Henry IV. Turning on his old allies, the house of Este, the French king claimed that he was ready to lead an army across the Alps himself, if necessary, to defend the pope. Although the Spanish initially supported Cesare d'Este, the pretender to the duchy, an increasingly sick Philip II was loath to become involved in a conflict with the pope that could be used as an excuse for the French to gain a serious foothold in Italy.[204]

When Clement VIII subsequently rode into Ferrara on May 8, 1598, to take peaceful possession of the duchy for the Papal State, he enjoyed a prestige and authority that the papacy had not experienced in many years.[205] Moreover, only six days later he was advised that the treaty between Spain and France that he had helped mediate had been signed on May 2.[206] Besides restoring the terms and boundaries determined at the Peace of Cateau-Cambrésis in 1559, the Peace of Vervins enhanced Rome's international position and emphasized the pope's favored traditional role as peacemaker and arbitrator between the Christian princes.

Combined with one last momentous event in 1598, the death of Philip II in September, these earlier victories served to solidify Clement's position internationally and meant that at least for a brief time he could negotiate with Spain from a position of strength. They did not mean, however, that there would be an immediate realignment in Rome or that the pope would seek to radically change the relationship with the Spanish monarchy that had developed over the previous forty years. On the contrary, this relationship had benefited Rome a great deal, and the first years of Philip III's reign were no exception.

The primary early example of Spain's continued position as economic benefactor of Rome, and an event that served to emphasize the new king's position as faithful servant of the pope, was the reinvestiture of the fiefdoms of Naples and Sicily. Clement and a congregation of cardinals had decreed in the summer of 1599 that each new king of Spain would have to render formal homage and fidelity to the pope for these kingdoms upon assuming the throne and to be reinvested by the pope with the rights of the *feudo*. Not surprisingly, a payment was also included in the act of investiture, and the duke of Sessa skillfully negotiated the sum of 100,000 scudi as the new king's initial feudal dues.[207] With both sides agreeing amicably to these terms, Sessa took advantage of the event to stage a large procession from the Piazza Navona to Monte Cavallo, where the congregation of cardinals and pope received him in October. According to Roman reports, Sessa was accompanied by "a hundred coaches and all the princes, barons, and nobility of Rome" when he arrived to render formal homage and fidelity in the name of Philip III. Only the French protested.[208]

This procession was followed by another in May 1600, when the viceroy of Naples, the count of Lemos, entered Rome to render formal homage from the kingdom to the pope. According to contemporary reports, the count made his way to the papal audience "with one of the most beautiful cavalcades that this city has seen in many years, because in it were counted more than 860 horses, all cloaked, and among them 40 [carrying] bishops and other prelates."[209]

The processions, more than any other event, publicly reaffirmed and re-presented the close relationship between pope and king to the city of Rome and made it clear to everyone present that the Spaniards still dominated the city. Although Philip III came to power owing millions of ducats to his bankers, his many possessions still produced great wealth;

and in the case of Naples and Sicily it was a wealth that benefited Rome in a variety of ways. The viceroys of these kingdoms, of course, sometimes complained that their economies were already hard-pressed, but this kept neither pope nor king from using the territories for their own designs.

This was also the case with church lands in the Iberian kingdoms. More specifically, after the bankruptcy of 1596 Philip II had pressured the pope to allow him and his son to take the income from the major offices of the three military orders of Alcántara, Calatrava, and Santiago to pay the large royal debt. By 1602 Philip III could write to the pope with the news that he had paid off the large sum of 6 million gold ducats with the help of this concession.[210]

Although there was no direct benefit to the papacy from this favor, such was not the case when Clement allowed the bishopric of Zaragoza to be secularized and subsumed into the royal patronato in 1600. This gave the king the right to appoint the canons of the church, as well as direct control over its income. To expedite the paperwork for this process, 25,000 ducats were sent to Rome.[211]

In addition to this kind of direct payment to the papal coffers, Spanish money continued to flow to Rome in the form of pensions. By 1600 Philip III had begun to benefit from peace with France, the arrival of a large treasure fleet from the New World, and the ecclesiastical concessions. Those who would date the decline of Spanish power in Rome from 1598 overlook this resiliency and, more specifically, the skill of the duke of Sessa in cultivating a strong Spanish faction of cardinals, a practice he had learned under the tutelage of Olivares and Philip II.[212] While the French were now more actively seeking to lure cardinals and Roman nobles into their faction, the Spanish party remained strong throughout the reign of Clement VIII.

This did not occur without resistance on the part of the pope, however. It is an oft-noted fact of Clement VIII's reign that he successfully sought to increase the number of neutral cardinals in order to prevent the Spaniards from dominating the college and the conclaves as they had throughout Philip II's reign.[213] Moreover, he had considered prohibiting new cardinals from receiving pensions from Spain, a move that increased tensions between himself and the duke of Sessa.[214] In this matter the duke and the Spanish faction of cardinals won out: it was agreed that the prelates could continue to receive Spanish benefices. Even after the celebrated creation of eighteen new cardinals in 1604, the Spaniards still counted as the largest faction, with twenty-eight cardinals in their party.[215]

Thus, when Clement died in March 1605, the position of the Spaniards in Rome remained strong. The political-economic relationship between Rome and Madrid retained many of the essential characteristics that had developed over a fifty-year span: the alliance against the Turks continued, as did a joint naval fleet for protection of the Italian coast; papal financial concessions contributed substantially to royal finances; and Spanish money and aid in the form of the feudal dues from Naples spoils, pensions, and grain bolstered the economy of the Papal State and gained the Spaniards deep influence in the Roman court.

On the other hand, the reentry of the French onto the Roman scene, the death of Philip II, the increased political stature of the papacy, and the departure of the duke of Sessa from Rome in 1603 combined to weaken Spanish supremacy and signified that a new stage in the politics of Spanish Rome had begun. The Catholic King and his ambassadors would no longer dictate commands with the same confidence that had characterized the days of Philip II and the count of Olivares, and Spaniards no longer walked the streets of the city as representatives of the unchallenged foreign power in Rome. Still, the Spanish party remained strong throughout the reign of Clement VIII and celebrated the virtues of a Rome they continued to dominate.

THE RHETORIC OF PRAISE

By the first decade of the seventeenth century, with the Spanish monarchy enjoying unprecedented influence in Rome and the Spanish community in the city at its peak, a final theme emerged in the Spanish myth of Rome to match the moment: the rhetoric of praise. Gone were the days of criticism. As the preeminent foreign power in the city, Spaniards felt increasingly positive about Rome, a fact reflected in Spanish writing celebrating the *spiritual city,* the mother of the church, the most holy center of Christendom.

One of the most detailed—and florid—examples of this heroic version of Rome was the treatise by Jerónimo Gracián entitled *Trattato del giubileo dell'anno santo* (Treatise on the Jubilee of the Holy Year; 1599), written and printed in Rome.[216] Gracián, a Carmelite who was born in

Granada in 1540 and had been an early spiritual director to Saint Teresa of Avila, spent roughly a decade in Rome at the end of the sixteenth century.[217] As a theologian in the household of the wealthy and powerful Spanish cardinal Pedro Deza, Gracián was instructed to write the treatise to demonstrate why Rome would be the best location for the Jubilee of 1600. Cardinal Deza was then in charge of the group responsible for organizing the Jubilee, the Congregatione dello Spirituale del Giubileo, and the treatise was primarily meant as a laudatory preface to the events he planned for the holy year, rather than an inquiry about other possible sites for it.

Rome, Gracián wrote, was more appropriate than any other location for the Jubilee because it was the "universal fatherland" (*patria universale*) of all Christians and their common spiritual capital as members of the church. Thus, it did not matter whether a person "was born in Spain or France, or in any other land, according to the flesh," because "in the spirit" everybody was a Roman.[218] Quoting the early pope Anacletus (79–91), Gracián called Rome the head and heart of the church and claimed that all business pertaining to the good of Christianity was conducted there.

In what developed into a lengthy litany of Roman virtues, as well as a demonstration of his own patristic and classical training, Gracián sought to evoke the central place of the city in world civilization. He therefore drew on the supposed Greek definition of the word *Rome* as "strength" and the Hebrew definition of it as "sublimity." Not satisfied with these brief descriptions, he went further to claim that in Hebrew, *Rome* also signifies "strong," "robust," "sublime," and "consecrated," among other things.[219]

All these adjectives were fitting and self-evident, the author claimed, when one considered the many martyrs the city had produced. Most important, Rome served as the residence of the vicar of Christ. This was the central contemporary and historical reason why Rome was the head and lord of the world, not to mention its priestly city and queen.

Gracián compiled a formidable list of earlier authors to substantiate his claims, accumulating titles and quotations by everyone from Virgil to Saint John Chrysostom. Rome, he claimed, possessed two resplendent eyes, the bodies of Saint Peter and Saint Paul. Far from being simple reminders of the past or even powerful relics for present use, they ensured that Rome would enjoy a glorious future, since it was here that the two apostles would rise from their graves at the Last Judgment. As Gracián rhetorically asked, referring to Peter and Paul, "What roses will Rome send to Christ at that hour?" Thus, the city was holy, august, and the most favored and loved city of God. Indeed, Gracián claimed as a climax, "With truth one can say she is a new, and beloved, Jerusalem." [220]

At first sight, this treatise may seem an overzealous, isolated work by a priest out to impress his patron, the cardinal—and even the pope himself. And unfortunately, it is impossible to know how many copies were printed or distributed among Italians or Spanish pilgrims. What is known, however, is that by the late sixteenth and early seventeenth centuries such ornate and romantic praise was not limited to Spanish theologians. A literary example from Spain's most famous Golden Age writer, Miguel de Cervantes, serves to illustrate the point.

Published posthumously in 1619, *The Trials of Persiles and Sigismunda* was Cervantes's last work, and its subject was the long pilgrimage to Rome of the eponymous heroes. [221] The body of the text focused on the problems the two encountered on their way to the city; Rome was presented as the reward at the end of an arduous struggle. The pilgrimage and trials functioned as a metaphor for every human's journey through life, while Rome became the metaphor for the desired end, or heaven itself. As Persiles explicitly states at an early stage of their travels, "For although Rome is heaven on earth, it isn't located in the heavens, and there'll be no trials or danger to prevent us from finally reaching it." [222]

With that said, Rome fades into the background of the story until the final pages, when the group of pilgrims finally arrive at the city. As the weary travelers catch a glimpse of their destination from a high hill, they are overwhelmed with emotion and "[kneel] down as though before something sacred and [begin] to worship it." Then one of them recites the following poem:

> Oh great, oh strong, oh sacred soul of Rome!
> This lowly pilgrim bows before your might.
> Devout and humble now I kneel to you
> And view, astonished, all your beauty grand.
>
> With tender reverence and unshod feet
> I've come to gaze on you and worship you.
> My mind, though made to hope for the divine,
> Is stunned to see that you transcend your fame.

> The soil of this fair land that I survey,
> So tilled and mixed with all your martyr's blood,
> Is everywhere esteemed a relic dear.
>
> There is no part of you that does not serve
> to show example of His holiness;
> For God's own City was your model fair.[223]

Here, then, is the culmination of the journey—as well as of the praise of Rome—for the Spaniards, the pilgrims, and Cervantes. Surpassing even Gracián, which seems impossible, Cervantes here describes Rome not just as the New Jerusalem but as the City of God on earth. Possibly an allusion to Augustine's city, or perhaps a more poetic way of calling forth Gracián's New Jerusalem imagery, Cervantes gives us in the pilgrim's poem the idealized, heroic Rome of the Catholic and Spanish restoration.

With no hint of criticism of the city or calls for reform there, Cervantes takes us far from the world of Alfonso de Valdés. Instead, we are presented with a version of Rome that was made possible by sixty years of strong Spanish influence and ties to the city. To praise Rome at this point, after all, was to praise a place that Spain had had a large hand in creating. It was, in fact, to praise oneself.

PHILIP III, PAUL V, AND THE
NEW BALANCE OF POWER

Soaring rhetoric notwithstanding, the vulnerability of the Spanish position and the revived threat of French power were also apparent in the early years of the seventeenth century. This was first revealed in the conclave that elected Leo XI in 1605. The relatively inexperienced duke of Escalona was a poor replacement as Spanish ambassador for the duke of Sessa and exercised little influence among the cardinals, even though he had called in an intimidating company of soldiers from Naples, ostensibly for protection.[224] At the same time, the French cardinals and ambassador had already built up a sizable coalition, and Henry IV was playing Philip II's old game of giving his faction a list of cardinals whom he explicitly excluded. Although neither the French nor the Spanish succeeded in getting one of their first choices elected, the eventual election of Cardinal Alessandro de' Medici, who had been excluded by the Spanish, was a clear victory for the French, despite the fact that he died less than a month after the election.[225]

The Spanish agents in Rome, and especially Cardinal Avila, who had been embarrassed by the last conclave, were angered and frightened by the new level of French machinations in Rome and especially by reports that "the king of France in imitation of the Spanish has reserved 30,000 scudi of pensions from the church of his kingdom to distribute among cardinals."[226] While unable to elect one of their own favorites at the next conclave, the Spanish faction did have the votes to exclude all the French choices and eventually settled on the election of Cardinal Borghese, who held a 2,000-ducat pension from Spain.[227]

Camillo Borghese, who took the name of Paul V (1605–1621), had spent time in Spain on a diplomatic mission and was described by the Roman reports as being very affectionate toward the Spanish crown.[228] Moreover, in 1601 the Council of State in Spain had judged him the most eminent of the young cardinals.[229] He was also on particularly good terms with the Spaniards resident in Rome and had purchased the palace — thereafter and still known as the Palazzo Borghese — of Cardinal Deza near the Piazza di San Lorenzo in Lucina. It was unlikely, then, that even though the French were making a strong attempt to exercise influence in Rome the new pope would upset the strong ties between Rome and Madrid.

Rather, the exchange between the two courts continued much as before, with the pope renewing the subsidio, excusado, and cruzada in June 1605,[230] and Philip III sending many pensions to Rome, including 4,000 ducats for the pope's nephew, that same year.[231] The Spanish viceroy in Sicily also shipped more than 10,000 rubbi of grain to Rome, for the Papal State had suffered yet another bad harvest and shortage in 1605.[232] The Sicilian grain was used to good advantage by the Spanish ambassador in Rome, and when the pope ordered his nephew Cardinal Borghese to attend to the needs of the poor in the summer of 1606, the ambassador rode with him for two days throughout the city, helping to distribute bread.[233] Acknowledging this help, the pope wrote the king a warm letter of thanks.[234]

As important as this reciprocal domestic aid between Paul V and Philip III was as an early sign of continued close relations, the primary events that cemented the alliance and ensured a continuation of Spanish supremacy throughout this pontificate occurred in the realm of broader Italian affairs. More specifically, tensions between Paul V and the Republic of Venice in 1606, escalating into a full-scale break in relations in 1607, served to reveal the continuing dependency of the papacy on Spanish military assistance and the unreliability of France as an ally of Rome.

Paul V's dispute with the Senate of Venice began with a conflict over the arrest and trial in the civil courts of Venice of two priests; it was compounded by age-old distrust owing to a variety of perceived infringements upon ecclesiastical jurisdiction by Venice as well as on the sovereignty of Venice by Rome. With the Jesuits voicing strong support for papal supremacy even in the temporal sphere and the Venetian Servite, Paolo Sarpi, promoting the opposite view, there was little chance of reconciliation. Matters came to a head in April 1606 when Paul V demanded the release of the two clerics and the repeal of recent laws that had forbidden both the building of new churches without secular permission and the alienation of property to clerics. When the demands were refused, he excommunicated the doge, Senate, and government of Venice and placed the entire republic under interdict.[235]

Talk of open war between the two powers began, and the true loyalties of France and Spain, as well as the dependency of Rome on the latter, were brought into full relief. Although Henry IV had initially attempted to play the role of mediator, the Venetians held fast to their positions, and the discussions in Rome became increasingly bellicose. In the meantime, Philip III wrote to the pope pledging his assistance to the Holy See. Repeated interventions by both the Spanish and the French ambassadors, including the duke of Lerma's nephew Francisco de Castro, failed, and preparations for war began.[236]

In Rome reports estimated that a full-scale conflict would involve fifty thousand infantry and four thousand cavalry at a cost of 600,000 scudi per month.[237] It was obvious that the Papal State could not hope to finance a war of this magnitude, and it fell to the Spaniards to provide the bulk of the forces for the expected conflict. More specifically, Philip III ordered his governor in Milan, the count of Fuentes, to raise an army of twenty-six thousand infantry and four thousand cavalry to defend the papal interests.[238] Early in 1607, moreover, Alfonso de Avalos, a Spanish colonel serving in Milan, was called to Rome by Paul V and charged with organizing the papal forces, reportedly twenty-two thousand infantry and two thousand cavalry.[239] Shortly thereafter, Alessandro Monti, a captain fighting for the Catholic King in Flanders, was called to Rome and named Maestro di Campo Generale of the papal forces.[240]

The clear necessity for Spanish military aid emphasized the king's role as protector of the papacy to a greater degree than any other single event during the pontificate of Paul V. Moreover, the threat of large-scale Spanish military intervention in Venice forced Henry IV to show his true sympathies. When he subsequently ordered twenty-four thousand troops and four thousand cavalry raised to aid the Republic, it further accentuated the fact that the Spanish monarchy was the sole power Rome could depend upon.[241] The Venetian affair, in short, became for Philip III, albeit on a smaller scale, what the Battle of Lepanto had been for Philip II: the major international event that showed him to be the most loyal son of the papacy and protector of the Papal State.

Even though an actual war was averted and a formal reconciliation between the papacy and Venice reached in April 1607, the year of tension had undermined the advances the French had made in Rome in the previous decade and reaffirmed Spanish preeminence in the city. This was already apparent in the large procession held shortly after the peace had been announced, in which the new Spanish ambassador and a contingent of two hundred Spanish gentlemen carrying torches, accompanied by various Roman confraternities, made their way to Saint Peter's, where they were welcomed by the pope.[242]

Over the next fifteen years, the position of Spain as the most loyal servant of the pope would be ritually acted out with growing pomp and pageantry in the chinea procession. Such was the case in 1608, when the procession included "around five hundred horses," with many nobles and prelates, including the pope's brother;[243] and in 1609, when the new ambassador, Francisco de Castro, led "around six hundred horses."[244] Year after year the procession served as one of Spain's best public relations opportunities and demonstrated to all assembled that the relationship between king and pope remained strong.

Throughout the pontificate of Paul V, in fact, the military alliance originally formed against the Venetians continued in one form or another, although it was not explicitly directed against the Republic of Venice. In 1617 Spain and the papacy agreed to join their fleets to defend the Italian coasts, for instance, and a few years earlier the pope had agreed to use the papal share of vacancy revenues collected in Naples, 20,000 ducats, to build papal galleys for the Spanish fleet.[245] After the 1617 agreement the pope wrote Philip III a letter thanking him for the peace of Italy and "assuring Your Majesty of the paternal affection and care we bear toward you, and of the desire we have for your every happiness."[246]

In that same year the pope gave the king a more tangible sign of his affection in the form of a renewal of the three gracias for five years; and generally the pope continued to cooperate with royal requests to secure more revenues from the church in Spain.[247] In 1618, most noticeably, Paul granted the king the right to raise 18 million ducats from the *estado eclesiástico* (ecclesiastical state) in the form of increased taxes in order to help the monarch pay off his debts.[248] While this last act was performed under pressure from Madrid and reportedly left the pope "displeased" because it upset the Spanish clergy and compelled them to go before the secular courts to contest the ruling, it was another example of the give-and-take between monarch and pope that may have alienated the ruled but aided the rulers. The pope, briefly stated, could not afford a bankrupt Spanish monarchy, for the economies of the two powers overlapped in crucial spheres, such as the military; he was subsequently willing to grant ecclesiastical concessions at the cost of the church in Spanish realms.

At the same time, the papal court was itself the continued beneficiary of the by now traditional Spanish revenues to Rome: from the papal collectors came roughly 70,000 scudi annually during the pontificate of Paul V;[249] from the many pensions for the cardinals came as much as 60,000 ducats per year;[250] and from the office of the coadjutor in Rome, which reserved the right to distribute many lesser Spanish benefices, came at least 20,000 ducats, which the pope often granted to members of the papal household.[251] These substantial quantities were only the most obvious Spanish revenues that benefited Rome—the numerous other ways in which the large Spanish presence in Rome bolstered the local economy will be examined in the next chapter.

The close relations between Rome and Madrid, solidified by this substantial economic exchange and military cooperation, also led to a strengthening of the Spanish faction of cardinals in Rome and generally put the Spaniards in a good position to influence the next election. Possibly the most important among these cardinals was the pope's nephew Cardinal Borghese, who held at least 10,000 ducats in pensions from Spain. Upon the death of Philip III in 1621 Borghese wrote the following letter to Philip IV, expressing the loyalty many prelates and Roman nobles felt toward the Spanish crown: "The memory of the favor we have received from Your Majesty's father, the king, who now enjoys heaven, will live perpetually in me and in my house, and so a singular and devout regard will always be inviolably held by us, which we owe to his royal crown."[252]

These sentiments, echoed by the correspondence of more than twenty cardinals and dozens of Roman nobles, were another indication that Philip III had successfully repeated his father's policies and retained the basic characteristics of the Spanish-papal alliance throughout his reign. Two months earlier, after the death of Paul V, the conclave that elected Gregory XV had provided yet another sign that Spanish influence still remained strong and, at least temporarily, was still the decisive factor in papal elections.

When Alessandro Ludovisi, the archbishop of Bologna, was elected to succeed Paul V in February 1621, he was one of the four cardinals on the Spanish list of acceptable candidates and held pensions from Spain.[253] The Spanish cardinals in Rome, Borgia and Zappata, had combined with the powerful Cardinal Borghese to secure the election, and ensured, even after the death of Philip III, that all the customary signs and exchanges of the alliance remained in place.

In July, for instance, the new pope received the chinea from the Spanish ambassador, the duke of Albuquerque, who was accompanied by a procession described as both "noble and numerous," which included the pope's nephew Nicolò Ludovisi.[254] In both 1621 and 1622 Sicilian grain was again shipped to Rome to alleviate shortages, although there had also been bad harvests on the island. In fact, in 1622 the Spanish ambassador had sought the pope's permission to imprison clerics in Sicily who were charged with hoarding grain.[255]

The pope, on his side, had little time in his short pontificate to give the Spaniards the kind of financial assistance many of his predecessors had provided, beyond the traditional concessions. He did, however, give them a precious commodity for which they had lobbied the papacy with great vigor ever since the time of Philip II, namely, four new Spanish saints. The subject of saint-making will be taken up in greater detail in Chapter 4 within the broader area of the piety of Spanish Rome. Still, it is important to note here that the canonizations that took place in March 1622 were one of the most important signs of papal favor the Spaniards had ever received in Rome. They revealed as much as any financial or political concession the enormous degree of influence and goodwill that the Catholic King enjoyed in the eternal city. Saint Isidore the plowman, Saint Ignatius of Loyola, Saint Teresa of Avila, and Saint Francis Xavier all joined the Roman calendar on March 16, 1622; and the festivities that preceded the actual canonizations included the formal rendering of obedience to the pope by the representative of the new Spanish monarch, Philip IV.

This was Don Manuel Zúñiga y Fonseca, who offered obedience in the name of "the most powerful king of Spain, Philip IV, who, singularly blessed by God among all the princes of the earth, possesses great dominions in its four parts, Europe, Asia, Africa, and America" and whose many prosperous subjects constantly "asked God for an increase of the church and the prosperity and long rule of the most high pontiff."[256] The pope's spokesman, in the meantime, praised the kings of Spain, who had freed their kingdom of heretics and had spread the knowledge of the virtues and glory of Christianity and the name of the Roman pontiff to the ends of the earth—so much so that one could say that where the flag of the king of Spain was planted, so too was the trophy of the cross.[257]

The speeches, in short, were the rhetorical equivalent of Vasari's painting of the Battle of Lepanto that showed the allegorical figures of papacy and monarchy sharing a friendly embrace. The pontificate of Gregory XV, coming at the end of more than sixty years of increasing Spanish power, can be seen as the late summer of Spanish dominance in Rome, the last full season in which the warmth of papal favor shone on the Spanish monarchy and its subjects.

Most unfortunate for the Spaniards, however, was the double loss of both this amiable pontiff and of their king, Philip III, in the space of two years. The next pope, Urban VIII (1623–1644), would be decidedly pro-French. Over his twenty-year reign he undermined much of the power that the Spaniards had built up in Rome. Combined with the young and inexperienced king, the internal financial and military problems of the Spanish Empire, and growing French power, the efforts of Urban VIII and the Barberini cardinals to substantially weaken Spanish influence and presence in Rome signaled the end of the era of Spanish preponderance.

Still, the Spanish Empire had sunk deep roots in the city in the form of Spanish patronage, the Spanish faction of cardinals, and the colony of transplanted Spaniards. Even the long reign of Urban VIII could not entirely dislodge Spain from its position of affluence and influence. Spain would subsequently enjoy surprising control until the end of the century. The Spanish faction of cardinals and the colony of Spaniards had always constituted the most visible manifestation of Spanish power in Rome, and during the reigns of Philip II and Philip III Spaniards became the most influential foreign group in the city. It is to this local presence, the people of Spanish Rome, that this study now turns.

CHAPTER 4

THE PEOPLE OF SPANISH ROME

THE domination of Rome, the center of the Old World, by the Spanish Empire from the time of Ferdinand and Isabella through the reign of Philip III paralleled and ran simultaneously with the conquest and consolidation of Spanish power in the New World. Indeed, the two theaters of Spanish imperialism shared many features: large-scale literary production, military operations, and economic exchange. In both the New World and Rome, moreover, Spanish imperialism also relied on another practice that has most often been associated only with the New World, namely, colonization. In Rome, too, the Catholic Kings encouraged, directly or indirectly, the growth of a large Spanish community made up of both Iberians and Italians who helped carry out their agenda. At the same time, many Spaniards moved to Rome for the opportunities the city offered. In the first half of the sixteenth century, Spanish immigration to Rome was not well organized, and even occasionally disrupted, and the community subsequently remained small, as we have seen. During the reign of Philip II, however, the Spanish community and its adherents grew until they constituted a large percentage of the Roman population and were the dominant foreign faction. The main players have already been introduced in the persons of cardinals, ambassadors, soldiers, artists, and priests. But there were many others, besides, representing every segment of society. These were the living face of Spanish Rome.

SPANISH PLAYERS ON THE ROMAN STAGE

O n Easter morning 1596 a skirmish occurred between a Spanish galleon and four smaller galleys, which seemed to come from the four
corners of the earth. For more than two hours the adversaries exchanged
fire, but the Spanish galleon prevailed like a "very strong rock," according
to one observer.[1] In the distance a Spanish castle adorned with images
of saints, the Virgin, and a lion clutching a cross towered over the scene.
So, too, did a church dedicated to Spain's patron, Santiago, that had been
richly decorated with gold and rose-damask banners for the Easter celebration.

Protected by the galleon, a dawn procession celebrating the Resurrection was leaving the church, led by a choir of twenty-four members
who preceded a priest carrying the consecrated Host. A group of high-
ranking Spaniards, including the Spanish ambassador, the archdeacon
of Calatrava, and a canon of the cathedral of Toledo, also accompanied
the Host, which was covered by a richly embroidered baldachin. A large
crowd surrounded the heart of the procession, and another seven choirs
of twenty-four musicians each sang songs of praise from various points
along the path.

From the church the worshipers proceeded to an elaborate theatrical
construction decorated with angels and harps, verses of Scripture celebrating the Resurrection, and a life-sized statue of the resurrected Christ.
Fireworks were set off from various windows and arches of the Resurrection monument when the sacrament arrived, and afterward the procession returned to the church of Santiago for morning prayers, this time
accompanied by five hundred torch-carrying members of the Confraternity of the Most Holy Resurrection, which had organized the festivities.

Quite a spectacle, even for sixteenth-century Spain, but this battle and
this procession did not occur on the rocky coasts of Galicia, the smooth
beaches of Andalusia, or the shores of the kingdom of Aragon. Rather,
the mock naval battle and the procession took place in the Piazza Navona,
in the heart of Rome. In fact, every Easter since its founding in 1579,
the Spanish Confraternity of the Most Holy Resurrection in Rome had
hosted an elaborate dawn procession for the city; but this particular year's
festivities had been outstanding, according to the Italian courtier Girolamo Accolti, and therefore merited a written memorial in honor of the
"majesty and greatness of the most noble nation of Spain" in the city

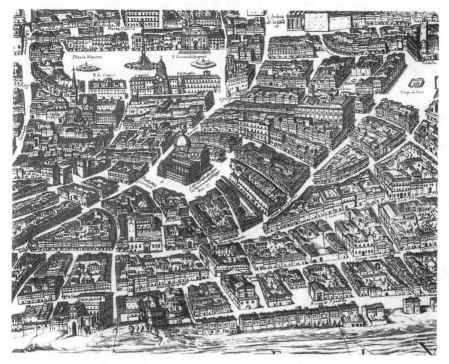

FIG. II   TEMPESTA-ROSSI PLAN OF ROME, 1693, DETAIL SHOWING
PIAZZA NAVONA WITH THE CHURCH OF SANTIAGO

of Rome. An independent account gave a more general but supporting version of the extravagant festivities.[2]

The day after this triumphal celebration of Spanish military and religious power, however, the scene in the Piazza Navona was quite different: dozens of poor Spaniards lined up outside the church of Santiago to receive free bread, beg for alms, and seek medical care in the adjacent Spanish hospital. While the confraternity's more glamorous task was the Easter ritual, their daily duties included distribution of alms, visiting and aiding the many Spaniards in Roman prisons, and generally trying to care for the multitudes of poor Spaniards in the city. The line of impoverished Spaniards was the daily reality in Rome and provided a stark contrast to the image of Spanish strength projected by the procession.[3]

These accounts of the Resurrection procession and the Spanish beggars underline both the strong presence and the wide social span of the Spaniards in Rome in the late sixteenth century. They also conveniently bring together many of the major Spanish players and institutions assembled on the Roman stage: the ambassador, high churchmen, the national church of Santiago, the Confraternity of the Most Holy Resurrection, and the poor. Together, they made up the Spanish "nation" in Rome, which by the 1590s had reached its peak as the most powerful foreign community in the city. The Resurrection procession was a visible annual reminder of this social reality for visitors and residents alike.

Like the annual procession that accompanied the presentation of the chinea and feudal dues for the fiefdom of Naples, this was a political ritual that emphasized the role of the Spaniards as loyal servants of the church and thus provided a point of continuity with the politics of Spanish Rome. At the same time, it was high religious theater, coming at the crux of the Christian calendar, which functioned as a living "text" on the Roman stage depicting the Spanish interpretation of Spain's role in the Christian republic. It was, to use anthropological terms, the Spanish version of a master myth that shaped the ongoing history of victorious Christendom according to Spanish design.

The myth presented here might best be seen as a form of triumphal procession that celebrated simultaneously the victory of the cross and the victory of the Spaniards over heresy. The Spanish galleon (actually a model that was hung on ropes between the columns of the arch at the north end of the piazza) fires salvos at the opposing ships (also models, pushed around on carts throughout the piazza) in order to protect the Easter procession, to protect Christ himself. The victorious heroes, represented by the ambassador, churchmen, and members of the confraternity, march through the arches of the piazza and around the castle with the spoils of the victory, namely the body of Christ, covered by the baldachin.

We can see here many of the features of triumphal processions that marked sixteenth-century Roman history from the entry of Charles V to the victory at Lepanto and beyond. One recent description of the triumphal ceremonies, for example, sums up these features in the following terms: "Reduced to essentials, the public celebration of a real or imagined triumph called for processions and ritual passageways through gates or arches, conquering heroes and the display of the spoils of conquest, and a more or less elaborate 'program' and 'production team' to organize the spectacle."[4]

Adopting these terms, we can see the importance of the broader Spanish community and faction in Rome and the role they played as supporters of the Spanish Empire and its agenda in Rome. In short, the officers of the confraternity were the "production team" that organized the festival and also provided the stars and supporting cast. Regardless of their parts—central actors like the ambassador and major prelates, peripheral players like the musicians and confraternity members, or poor servants who built the ephemera and decorated the piazza—these Spaniards all acted together in the name of their king. They were the early modern spin doctors, giving the Spanish version of important events to the city and, through it, the world. In this sense, their role in the production of the Resurrection procession can be seen as a microcosm of the larger role they played in the politics of Spanish Rome.

SPANISH NATION-BUILDING IN ROME

At the same time, the confraternity and its procession reveal another central aspect of the Spanish imperial project in Rome that was both a cause and an effect of growing Spanish power in the city: Spanish nation-building on a local level. Although a substantial Iberian presence in Italy and Rome went back at least to the time of the Borgia popes, it was only in the second half of the sixteenth century, during the height of the "Spanish preponderance" in Italy, that the previously disparate Iberian "nations," including the Castilians, Catalans, and Portuguese, were effectively consolidated in Rome by the Spanish monarch, his ministers, and the confraternity as the much stronger and effective Spanish "nation."[5]

Not to be confused with the ideologies of nineteenth-century and twentieth-century nationalism or nation states, Spanish nation-building in Rome was more about "practices of collective representation, of national self-constitution, of imagining a people that emerged in Early Modern Europe before ideology."[6] This kind of Spanish nation-building and Spanish empire-building went hand in hand on the streets of Rome as the merging of the monarchy's disparate subjects into the Spanish "nation" contributed to the rise of Spanish power in Rome.

More specifically, two major aspects of Spanish nation-building— achieving a union in name for all Iberians and institutionalizing a union of charity by means of the confraternity—coincided with the rise of Spanish influence in Roman society and the strength of Spaniards in the Roman patronage system. The Roman context thus served as a microcosm of both Spanish imperial practices of political domination and of the related process of the hispanization of the smaller Iberian "nations" occurring in Iberia in the second half of the sixteenth century.[7] In Rome, the Spanish monarchs, ambassadors, cardinals and other leading figures generally succeeded in achieving the union in name that they were also advocating at home. Reference to, and identification with, other Iberian "nations" took a second seat to, or were immersed in, the larger Spanish "nation."[8] Moreover, as the disparate nations consolidated their forces into the larger Spanish nation, their reputation and influence grew, attracting many other Roman clients by means of economic and social incentives. Thus, the unified "nation" served as the nucleus of a broader Spanish faction that dominated the patronage-based politics of Rome for at least half of a century and won for the Spanish monarchs unprecedented influence in, and benefits from, the papal court. With this strong local base of political strength, the Spanish monarchs shaped papal elections, gained ecclesiastical taxes from the church throughout their empire, and kept the papacy aligned with both their domestic and their foreign political agenda.

The Spaniards in Rome therefore played a critical part in both foreign and internal Iberian affairs, and many Spanish ambassadors who had resided in Rome returned home to serve on the king's Council of State. At the same time, through the confraternity, the Spanish "nation" gained institutional definition and structure, and for both the resident Iberians and other Romans it became a highly visible patron through its rituals, its charitable work, and its endowment. Thousands of Spaniards who joined the confraternity and subsequently returned to Spain took with them memories of this model of pan-Iberian cooperation.

The Easter ceremony is a good example of these parallel practices of political domination and nation-building. A triumphal procession to mark the highlight of the Christian calendar, the ceremony forcefully demonstrated the power and wealth of the Spaniards in the city. To use the words that Edward Muir chose to describe the Easter ritual in Venice in the same period, the "drama affirmed that even the greatest mysteries, such as the resurrection, had to be illustrated in a worldly way, and that individuals, especially politically powerful ones, sought to share the sacred power of the host."[9] Unlike in Venice, where the Doge and the senators were at the center of the procession sharing this power, in Rome it was the Spaniards and their allies who tasted the first fruits of the triumph of the cross in a display of music, fireworks, and theatrical pageantry that rivaled any liturgical celebration at Saint Peter's.

At the same time, the procession was the central Spanish annual event, bringing together a wide range of Iberians from every geographical region and social class, which ritually built and promoted the impression of a unified nation for participants and observers alike. Thus, in 1596 the wealthy Portuguese merchant Jerónimo Fonseca, one of the two highest ranking officers of the confraternity, was in charge of coordinating much of the procession, especially the fireworks, while his fellow prior Pedro Deza, a canon from the cathedral of Toledo and nephew of Cardinal Deza, coordinated the choirs and music. Francisco Peña, an auditor of the Rota from Zaragoza, was also present at the center of the procession. Clearly, in the foreign setting of Rome there were benefits associated with belonging to the larger Spanish "nation" for these expatriot Iberians from Portugal, Castile, and Aragon which ranged from social prestige to economic, spiritual, and social advantages. Italians who benefited from the patronage of the Spanish crown, such as Pietro de' Medici, also demonstrated their allegiance through their participation.[10]

Besides giving the Iberians the ritual experience of unity, the confraternity also gave the terms *Spanish* and *nation* clearer definition. The Roman courtier Girolamo Accolti used *Spanish nation* to describe a community composed of disparate Iberian groups, also referred to as nations: Galicians, Castilians, Catalans, Andalusians, and, after 1580, Portuguese. In the fifteenth century, three of these groups, the Castilians, Portuguese, and Catalans, had established their own churches, of Santiago, San Antonio, and Santa Maria de Montserrat, respectively, and often functioned as separate groups in Rome. In the early years of Philip II's reign, moreover, the interests of the Catalans and Portuguese were at odds with the designs of the Catholic King, and they retained their own representatives and pursued their own agendas in Rome. By 1570, in the case of Catalonia, and 1580, in the case of Portugal, however, these separate representatives or ambassadors had been suppressed upon the insistence of Philip II. Pope Pius V sent a Catalan representative home in 1570, explaining that since their king already had an ambassador in the papal court there was no need for another "sent by the laity of that kingdom."[11] At the same time, the churches of Santa Maria de Montserrat and San Antonio were in decline. They seldom show up in the local records, received few special favors or grants from pope or king, and were generally overwhelmed and overshadowed by the Spanish ambassador, by the traditional Castilian church, Santiago (which now functioned as the church of the broader Spanish nation), and by the Confraternity of the Most Holy Resurrection, which always was known as the confraternity of the Spanish nation.

The confraternity took it upon itself to define what constituted a Spaniard. One of the first articles of the organization's 1580 charter stated:

> This confraternity being properly of the Spanish nation, it is necessary that he who would be admitted to it should be Spanish and not of another nation; he is understood to have the said quality of being Spanish if he is from the crown of Castile or the crown of Aragon, or from the kingdom of Portugal and the islands of Majorca, Minorca, and Sardinia, or both the islands and mainland of the Indies with no distinction of age or sex or rank.[12]

The confraternity subsequently served to define and unite the various groups of Iberians in Rome in a way they had not previously been identified, and it constituted a striking example of how traditional corporate groups built a national identity that is most often associated with a modern corporate structure, namely, the nation state. More specifically, from 1579 on, members of the expanded Spanish nation would be brought together in a corporate group which had common stated goals, duties, and services to perform, as well as property to manage. These were the basic marks that differentiated this form of political alliance from a simple personal, or dyadic, alliance.[13]

These were also the basic marks of the Spanish confraternity. In addition to putting on the Resurrection procession, the confraternity took care of the many needs of the poorer Spaniards in the city through the management of an endowment that passed from generation to generation. Men and women, laity and clergy, poor and rich could join.

It should not be surprising that this evolution of the local Spanish nation, and of the identity attached to belonging to the larger Spanish state, occurred in Rome. Long the sacred center of Christendom and a major pilgrimage destination, Rome had been shaping and defining a common Christian identity for the disparate peoples of Europe throughout the Middle Ages, as Benedict Anderson has eloquently pointed out.[14] At the same time, however, it was in Rome that the numerous local identities of Europe were commonly grouped under the five major "nations": France, England, Spain, Italy, and Germany. Similarly, the papacy named the monarchs of France, Germany, Spain, and England protectors of the major churches of Rome. Thus, long before the emergence of the modern nation states, the naming of the five major western European nations had taken root in Rome.

In the evolution to a corporate form of organization, however, the Spanish confraternity gave institutional definition and structure to an expanded version of the Spanish nation that included all subjects of the Spanish crown in Iberia, the Indies, Sardinia, and Majorca. This must be seen as nothing less than a masterful act of impromptu early modern nation-building on the edges of empire by Philip II and his ambassadors. Although it remained true in Rome, as in the rest of the Spanish Empire, that "there was no legal concept of a 'Spanish' nationality during the early modern period,"[15] the confraternity allowed the monarch to unify his subjects institutionally, in a union of charity. Not surprisingly for a most conservative regime, this task was not accomplished with radical new political institutions, constitutions, or laws. Rather, the forging of a broader Spanish identity relied upon the traditional crucible of medieval corporate organization, the confraternity.[16]

Moreover, it would be simplistic to assume that the confraternity arose initially or primarily from this political motive. Instead, a genuine social need for an ongoing institution to serve the needs of poor, weak, and unwell Iberians in Rome served as a catalyst for a new, highly political organization. Nonetheless, in seizing the chance to use the benevolent confraternity as a way of strengthening and unifying his subjects in Rome, the king and his ambassadors revealed a shrewd political opportunism; and it was precisely this ability to manipulate medieval social structures and traditions both in Rome and at home that contributed to the strength and success of the Spanish monarch's programs.

The king and his ambassador were always the first members of the confraternity listed in the organization's registers, and it was under Don Juan de Zúñiga in 1579 that the confraternity was formed to serve as an ongoing guardian of both the material and the spiritual interests of the Spaniards in Rome. A statement of its historical origins and purpose drawn up in 1603 serves well to summarize the organization's raison d'être:

> Don Juan de Zúñiga, considering . . . the needs that are continuously presented to persons of the Spanish nation in this court, both by the distance from their own lands and by the frequency with which Spaniards

gather here; and considering that many of those who reside here have a particular obligation to give alms and to do other works of charity, arranged with the counsel and consent of important people of the same nation to institute with Apostolic consent the "hermandad y Cofradía" of the most Holy Resurrection in the church of the glorious apostle Santiago.[17]

With the confraternity thus serving visibly to represent the collective identity of the Spanish empire in the city through ritual activity and charitable work, thousands of men and women from various professions and classes joined, served as officers, and participated in the work of the organization. Indeed, when the group first began to keep its membership roster, in 1603, more than two hundred new members a year were being added, and between 1603 and 1625 more than three thousand Spaniards joined.[18] A letter from Philip III in 1607 to his ambassador in Rome described the confraternity as representing the "entire body of the Spanish nation."[19]

Thus, during the period between 1580 and 1640, the terms *Spanish nation* and *Spaniard* served to identify anyone from Iberia, the islands of Sardinia and Majorca, and the Indies. A king, his ambassador, the confraternity, and the name itself were the primary political bonds that united them in this early representation of the "Spanish nation." While this understanding of nation is not to be confused with that of the modern nation state or of modern Spain, with all of their juridical and constitutional trappings, it clearly played an important role in forging a new, expanded version of the Spanish nation that represents an important transition between the medieval and modern understanding of Spain. Moreover, it suggests that there was a more complex and developed sense of the "Spanish nation" during the reigns of Philip II and Philip III than has often been suggested.[20]

With a complex agenda in Rome, a united Spanish "nation" was more impressive and effective than a group of smaller, divided groups, and Philip II cultivated this image by naming the Spanish nation in virtually all his correspondence with the papacy and his subjects in Rome.

Trying to cultivate unity of purpose and loyalty through evocations of ancient and mythic España was by no means a novel idea in early modern Iberia. As John Elliott has pointed out, although the Spanish monarchy from the time of Ferdinand and Isabella ruled over many different kingdoms and political entities, monarchs often "sought to revive shadowy memories of a Roman or Visigothic Hispania in order to suggest a wider potential focus of loyalty in the form of a historically revived 'Spain.'"[21] And though this could be difficult in Iberia, where local allegiances and loyalty tended to be primary, "in certain contexts" where "the advantages of political union could be considered, at least by influential groups in society, as outweighing the drawbacks," it was possible for a strong loyalty to the wider community of "Spain" to exist.[22] Rome provided such a context, where the monarchs and their primary subjects generally succeeded in achieving the "Union in Name" that was often so elusive in Iberia itself.[23]

In Rome, at least, regional "national" identities, although they did not disappear, took second place to the larger Spanish nation. Some individuals continued to assert their local identity through the bequests they left to churches and charities in their homeland and by choosing to be buried in their national churches in Rome. Still, most Iberians from nations other than Castile joined the confraternity, enjoyed the prestige and benefits of the larger Spanish nation, and showed little sign of resistance to this designation. We might go so far as to say that the Castilian humanist dream of a unified Iberia under the name of the classical Hispania was created and existed more fully in Rome in this period than it ever did in Iberia itself, along with a distinctly Spanish identity. Since *Spanish nation* was the repeated usage in the primary documents, and the dominant perception in Rome itself, I shall continue to use it here, albeit not without attention to the other local identities that members sometimes used.

In order to understand how the Spanish community reached the point of influence demonstrated by the Easter procession of 1596 and to grasp its size, strength, and influence beyond pageantry and processions, it is essential to step back to 1558 and look again at the role of Philip II in Rome. Just as the furthering of his reputation and authority had led Philip to establish an archive in the city to preserve the many papal bulls and briefs that granted him various privileges, so too did it lead him to cultivate and encourage a strong Spanish community there. This was something neither Ferdinand and Isabella nor Charles V had ever achieved, and it constituted Philip's biggest contribution to the creation of Spanish Rome.

With communications slow—it usually took twenty-eight days for a letter to go from Madrid to Rome—Philip understood better than any of his predecessors that he needed to create a strong presence of his vassals and subjects on the ground in order to effect his many Roman projects.[24] More specifically, a sizable part of the community which will be examined below served as a powerful lobbying group that pressured the papacy to support Spanish military adventures, grant ecclesiastical taxes, approve spiritual dispensations and favors, and put its moral authority, financial resources, and military forces at the disposal of the wide variety of Spanish domestic and international policies charted in the previous chapter.

While the king was a critical force, other motives, such as ecclesiastical business, the traditional lure of Rome as a source of both material and spiritual treasures, and pilgrimage, also contributed to the rise of a strong community. The Spanish historian and first biographer of Philip II, Luís Cabrera de Córdoba, for example, gave voice to the broader Spanish fascination with Rome when he wrote in 1600 that "the court of Rome is . . . the common fatherland [patria] of all Catholics, in which all have a part and can enter, and can aspire to that which they wish: virtue, nobility, wealth, and favor. . . . [Rome] is full of splendor, business, judgments on the actions of princes, discourses about the state [estado], and science."[25] Inspired by any or all of these attractions, thousands of Spaniards traveled to Rome during the late sixteenth and early seventeenth centuries, and many made it their residence.

Just how numerous were the Spaniards in this period? In the spring of 1582, the count of Olivares, father of the more famous count duke, arrived in Rome to take up his office as Philip II's ambassador to Pope Gregory XIII. His arrival in town was a major event, and a Roman observer described the count's household, income, and general welcome by the Roman nobility and papal court in some detail. Included in this report was a description of the procession that accompanied the new ambassador to the papal palace for his first visit, which noted that he was "followed by two hundred coaches" of the Spanish nation. This was a large procession even by the standards of Rome, but it was apparently not surprising to the author, a diplomatic spy for the duke of Urbino, since, as he noted, "the Spanish nation here numbers thirty thousand."[26]

This casual report is the only reference I can find to the population of the Spanish community in Rome during this period. If accurate, it would mean that the Spaniards constituted roughly 25 percent of an estimated population of 115,000.[27] Since we have no detailed census records from the period or other documents such as tax registers that would allow us

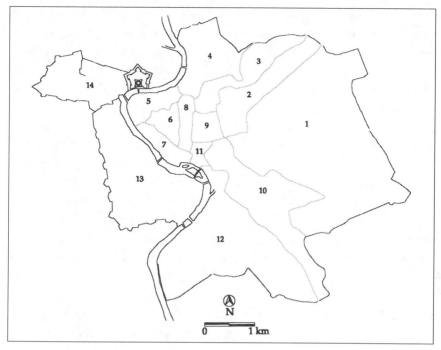

MAP 3   THE NEIGHBORHOODS (RIONI) OF ROME (SHAWNA LEIGH)
(1) Monti; (2) Trevi; (3) Colonna; (4) Campo Marzio; (5) Ponte; (6) Parione;
(7) Regola; (8) Sant'Eustachio; (9) Pigna; (10) Campitelli; (11) Sant'Angelo; (12) Ripa;
(13) Trastevere; (14) Borgo (or Castelli)

to verify or discount this estimate, it is impossible to know with certainty
the true number. Nonetheless, as with much of the social documentation of the period, it gives us a valuable, if impressionistic, perception of
the large Spanish presence in Rome. At the same time there are a variety
of other records—confraternity and baptismal registers, dowry records,
diplomatic correspondence, and notarial records—that allow us to re-
construct in clearer detail a large part of the social picture.

THE SPANISH FACTION AND THE ROMAN
PATRONAGE SYSTEM

To understand how the Spanish nation, as well as the broader Spanish faction, functioned and exercised power in Roman society, it is
helpful to approach them as part of a large patronage network loosely
unified by a variety of powerful individuals and institutions that advanced

and protected their widely varying interests.[28] Cardinals, ambassadors, courtiers, artists, artisans, lawyers, priests, merchants, widows, peasant women and men: everyone in the city at some time relied on a patron for income, work, legal representation, housing, spiritual intervention, dowries, a bride, a husband, charity, or a burial. Degrees of dependence varied, of course, and many people, including Spaniards, served Italian patrons, such as the pope or a noble family, thereby removing themselves from the direct orbit of the Spanish crown and community. Through this same patronage system, however, the central Spanish patrons of the city claimed many direct vassals and servants for the Catholic King.[29]

The Roman court of the late sixteenth and early seventeenth centuries was dominated by the politics of patronage, factions, and competing patron networks, but the complex details of how this system functioned (or didn't) have rarely been discussed in other important works on the papal court.[30] No study of early modern Rome, for example, attempts to show how patronage relationships shaped, and were shaped by, the development of papal absolutism and the politics of the Papal State in the same way that Sharon Kettering has analyzed the role of patron-broker-client relations for French absolutism and state-building in the seventeenth century.[31] An analysis of how the Spanish nation and its adherents developed and functioned as a part of the broader patronage network of the papal court thus promises to shed light on some of the larger questions surrounding papal absolutism and the politics of patronage for Roman society in general and the Papal State in particular.

Providing theoretical insight and models for this task are recent historical works on early modern court factions such as Kettering's study, which in turn has drawn on more than thirty years of anthropological work on the related issues of client-patron relations, factions, corporations, and the relationships among these various forms of social and political alliance.[32] Anthropologists, and historians after them, rightly caution against simplistic or overly general interpretations of clientage systems, since each local situation has its own nuances and variations. Still, much of their work can serve to illuminate the broad outlines of the complicated web of Spanish relationships in Rome. More specifically, a study of the various levels of Spanish patronage, which ranged from simple personal relationships, or dyadic alliances between two people, to loose associations of large numbers of both Spaniards and Romans (referred to as the Spanish faction), to large, complex corporate organizations like the confraternity, promises to reveal how the Spaniards exercised political power in Rome, how this power evolved over time, and what the broader impact of their faction and colony was on the papal court and city at large.

Initially, the primary patron-client relationship was the dyadic exchange that has already been examined in some detail, between the pope and the king. This relationship was fundamental to all others in the patronage network, and these two forces were clearly at the top of the pyramid of patron-client relations.

Rather than being a simple dyadic relationship, however, characterized by a basic exchange of services between two people,[33] this relationship also had a more formal, contractual nature embodied in the treaties, alliances, and financial exchanges between the institutions of the papacy and the Spanish monarchy.[34] Moreover, the fact that the papacy was a hybrid institution serving as both spiritual head of the Roman Catholic Church and temporal ruler of the Papal State further complicated matters since it meant that on the spiritual level the pope was the patron and the king the client but on the temporal level the king was an equal and, in fact, often a far more powerful patron.

From the perspective of the rhetorical exchange between the papacy and monarchy, we have already seen that the general tone of the correspondence reflected a warm personal relationship between father and son: Philip II, for example, frequently signed his letters to the pope "Your very humble and devout son," and the popes, such as Gregory XIII, who wrote to the king in Castilian, similarly called the monarch "Our much loved son."[35]

Thus, at least on the rhetorical level, it was the religious role of the pope that set the terms of the discourse, and this placed the pope in the superior position of the patron dispensing spiritual and financial favors to the client monarch. This also allowed him to take on the scolding tone of the angry father when the monarch infringed on church privilege, also a frequent part of the exchange.

On the other hand, the fact that the Spanish monarch had, again in the words of Gregory XIII, "always been at the defense of Christendom and of the Holy Apostolic See opposing with his military forces of sea and land the inhuman beast of the Turk . . . and the heretics of these times" was the dominant factor that led the papacy to grant its favors.[36] The exchange as it actually played out in the practical realms of political and economic support might then be characterized not as a vertical but as a horizontal relationship between two princes, each of whom possessed powerful and essential favors the other needed.

The reciprocal exchange of favors, moreover, was often couched in the language used for the traditional giving of gifts between personal friends, which points to the strong residual element of the medieval gift economy in the papal-Spanish relationship. In this system favors and gifts built ties and strengthened alliances; and everything from ecclesiastical financial concessions to cardinals' hats, books, jewels, relics, and the ancient marble bust of Antonia Pia that Pius IV bought for Philip II at a cost of 770 gold scudi in 1559 was part of a gift economy between the two powers.[37]

Gift giving and the exchange of services at the top level of the patron-client pyramid in Rome affected other levels of the social structure as well, and although the pope was clearly the most visible and directly powerful patron in the city, the Spanish monarch, too, gained great influence through the power of patronage. This was most apparent in the emergence of what was known as the Spanish faction in Rome.

The Spanish faction, which included but was not limited to the Spanish nation, also comprised the many Italians living in Rome who were allied with the Spanish monarchy in one fashion or another. The term *faction,* it is helpful to note, was "used traditionally to denote groups engaged in political rivalry prior to the appearance of modern political parties in the West," groups that were generally not driven by ideology but by competition for material resources.[38]

This definition, translated to the Roman scene, well describes the Spanish faction, which was composed of a fluid, constantly changing group of cardinals, soldiers, lawyers, noblemen, courtiers, couriers, artists, and working-class Spaniards and Italians who were all involved in some direct or indirect exchange of goods and services with the Catholic King, although seldom on a contractual basis. Political exchange in this context encompassed a wide range of activities, from the king directly giving out a Spanish pension to secure a cardinal's vote, to a wealthy Spaniard encouraging his servants to take part in processions to celebrate Spanish military victories, to a Roman nobleman's presence in the chinea procession either because of, or with the hope of gaining, a Spanish military pension for himself or his son.

Another way of describing or visualizing these various clients in the broader faction is as vertically arranged dyadic chains of patrons and clients that pyramided upon one another to form the broad base of support for the patron, or patrons, at the top of the pyramid.[39] In this system a cardinal, for example, was both client and patron, as were most nobles, and it was not uncommon to be a client of more than one wealthy patron. What this meant in Rome was that the patron-client pyramid, the peak of which was, in part, shared by pope and monarch, also had an interlocking base. The most basic version of this pyramid can consequently be viewed as follows:

POPE

SPANISH MONARCH

ROMAN NOBILITY — CARDINALS

SPANISH FACTION — OTHER FOREIGN FACTIONS — ROMAN PEOPLE

The Ambassadors

With the general framework of social and political relations defined in this way, it is easier to understand the importance of local intermediaries in building a faction and maintaining loyalties. This was especially true in the case of the Spanish monarchs, since neither Philip II nor Philip III ever set foot in Rome and therefore relied upon their most immediate representatives, the ambassadors, to gain and influence clients for them. In this system, the "personalistic leadership" of the king and his most direct intermediaries were crucial factors, for there were no formal contracts binding either client or patron to any specific exchange, and no formal organization, at least on this broader factional level.[40] The cultivation of loyalty was therefore the constant work of the ambassadors, and the wealth and power of the Spanish monarchy made them some of Rome's most influential men, since in Rome there was usually "a greater concern with power and spoils than with ideology or policy." A patron's status as a foreigner and the policies of his king mattered less than his ability to confer favors.

As leaders of the Spanish faction, the ambassadors thus occupied a place on the patron-client pyramid that might be conceived of as being in parentheses just below the king's.[41] The fact that they were the arbiters of monarchical favor meant that with the right personal capabilities these men could rise to equal the wealthiest Roman noblemen and ecclesiastics in revenues and influence. In the words of a modern historian of Rome during the reign of Urban VIII (when Spanish power was on the decline), they constituted one of the primary "nodes of power" in the city.[42]

This ambassadorial power, and the full potential of the faction, became most apparent in the 1580s and 1590s; but by the early years of Philip II's reign, the king and his representative were already well aware of the ambassador's tasks and goals in cultivating a group of followers. Writing to his new ambassador, Don Juan de Figueroa, in 1558, Philip gave him the following instructions: "Toward the Roman courtiers who are Spanish, and all the Spanish nation, and all our other subjects and vassals, you shall favor them always in all that would be just, gathering them to yourself and treating them well, and not allowing them to be mistreated by anyone, because this will give you much reputation and authority in that court."[43]

With the Spanish faction — or, in the king's words, "the Roman courtiers who are Spanish, and all the Spanish nation, and all our other subjects and vassals" — serving as his base for reputation and authority in Rome, Figueroa came to Rome from Milan, where he had been commander of the Spanish fortress, with the immediate tasks of projecting an image of military strength and of building up the faction.[44] This double role was routine for the ambassadors, especially in the first decades of Philip II's reign but also throughout the period between 1558 and 1626. The fourteen men who served the Catholic Kings as ambassadors during this period are listed in table 2.

Between 1558 and 1563, however, preoccupation with the immediate business of papal elections and the relatively short tenures of Figueroa and Vargas meant that the task of cultivating the broader faction proceeded slowly. It subsequently fell to Requeséns and Zúñiga to lay the foundations for their young king's influence by securing a client base in Rome.

In 1566, for example, Requeséns wrote urging the king to extend his favor to a Spanish member of the papal court, Don Diego de Vargas Manríquez. In a letter of recommendation that typified the genre and became more and more common as the years passed, the ambassador wrote that this courtier (*camerero secreto*) of the pope's was "very honored, handsome, virtuous, and very learned," and that he was one of those given the task of preaching in the papal chapel, having earned a doctorate in theology in Rome.[45] Requeséns shrewdly noted that a Spaniard so close to the pope could be very useful to the king.

TABLE 2. SPANISH AMBASSADORS
TO ROME, 1558–1626

Juan de Figueroa, 1558
Francisco de Vargas, 1559–1563
Luís de Requeséns, 1563–1568
Juan de Zúñiga, 1568–1574
Marquis de Alcañices, 1574–1581
Abad Briceño, 1581
Count of Olivares, 1582–1592
Duke of Sessa, 1592–1603
Duke of Escalona, 1603–1606
Marquis de Aitona, 1606–1609
Duke de Taurisano, 1609–1616
Cardinal Borgia, interim, 1616–1618
Duke of Albuquerque, 1618–1623
Duke of Pastrana, 1623

On a more local and public level, Requeséns took on one of the most traditional patron roles when he attended the baptisms of Jewish converts; he even became a godfather of one in a baptismal ceremony in the Dominican church of the Minerva in 1566.[46] The Spanish ambassador was present at the baptism of numerous Jews in this period, and in at least one case, the baptism of twelve "Hebreos" in the church of Santiago in 1567, it appears clear that these were members of the Spanish-Jewish community in Rome.[47]

Other, more extravagant public displays also pointed to the growing presence of the ambassador and of the Spanish faction in Rome during the tenures of Requeséns and Zúñiga. In 1566 and 1567, in addition to the annual presentation of the chinea, the Spaniards held solemn celebrations in the church of Santiago when the birth of the king's daughter was announced. The ceremony included processions in the Piazza Navona followed by fireworks, and the large expenses of the festivities were reportedly paid by the Kingdom of Naples.[48] Similarly, when military victories in Flanders were announced a few months later, Te Deums were sung in Santiago with accompanying festivities in the piazza.[49]

The coming of a new Spanish ambassador to Rome developed into a major occasion for the Spanish adherents to present themselves to the city during this period. When Don Juan de Zúñiga, the comendador of

Castile, arrived in the city late in 1568, for example, he was "met by all the nation, and the court, and without dismounting went to the [papal] palace to kiss the pope's feet. Present were twenty-five cardinals, and when he crossed the bridge [of Castel Sant'Angelo], and when he returned, he was much saluted from the castle."[50]

Zúñiga did a good job of picking up where Requeséns had left off and quickly established himself as a prominent presence on the Roman social scene as well as a master of ceremonies for the Spanish faction. He was at the head of a procession that welcomed the prince of Parma to the city in July 1569; it also included the pope's cavalry and numerous cardinals.[51] A few weeks later, moreover, he was present at the mass and festivities celebrating the feast of Santiago, which was naturally held in the church of Santiago and also included "all the other knights of that order." Afterward the ambassador hosted a "beautiful banquet" in the palace he had rented in the Piazza Navona.[52]

As noted earlier, Zúñiga was also responsible for one of the most important developments in the consolidation of the Spanish presence in Rome, the founding of the Spanish Confraternity of the Most Holy Resurrection in 1579. Responding to both the needs of the growing Iberian population for charitable assistance and the political opportunity to bring the disparate Iberians together in an organization that had monarchical authority and ambassadorial supervision, Zúñiga functioned as a nation-builder on a local level. Ambassadors have not traditionally been noted for this role, it is consistent with the role of broker between monarch and subjects found in other absolutist settings, such as France, and it needs to be seen as one of the most important functions of the Spanish ambassador in Rome.[53]

The wealth and social influence of the ambassadors thus continued to grow throughout the early decades of Philip II's reign but reached a high point when the count of Olivares arrived in 1582. It was reported that he had 40,000 ducats to spend annually, of which 34,000 came from his estates and 6,000 from the king.[54] It was also noted that he brought thirty-four servants and immediately acquired fifteen more to help him set up his palazzo off the Piazza Navona, rented from the Sforza family for 1,300 scudi per year. During the decade he spent in Rome, Olivares's household grew to number well over a hundred dependents, typical for a man of his rank.

A decade later the next ambassador, the duke of Sessa, brought with

him an income from one of the richest estates in Spain, worth an estimated 100,000 ducats a year.[55] Yet even this was not enough, and when he
finally returned to Spain, he was deeply in debt, having spent his entire
income on an extensive household and a network of Roman and Spanish
clients.

Roman Knights of Iberian Military Orders

Large incomes and extensive households constituted power. Moreover, wealth and a strong social presence were increasingly necessary for
both cultivating and leading the growing Spanish faction, which included
more and more Roman noblemen, many of whom owed the Spanish
monarchs loyalty as members of the Iberian military orders. The feast of
Santiago and its accompanying festivities, for example, was another annual Spanish celebration in Rome that was led by the ambassador and that
served the important function of bringing together part of this important subgroup of the Spanish faction, the knights of Santiago who lived
in Rome. Members were commissioned by the king, received a pension
for their service, and represented a key Spanish military presence in the
city. Both Requeséns and Zúñiga were comendadors of the Order of Santiago in Castile,[56] the highest-ranking knights of the order after the king
himself, and it was the ambassador who actually initiated new knights
into the order. This was the case early in 1571 when the oldest son of the
Roman Angelo Cesis took the habit in the church of Santiago [57] and again
in 1575 when Count Fabio Landriano was brought into the order.[58]

The initiation ceremonies for these men and numerous others were
central examples of how a Roman became a client of the Catholic King,
and thanks to surviving notarial records we have descriptions of the ritual
that give us details of the language and gestures involved in creating a vassal for Philip II. The induction of Stephano Mutino, a "gentilhombre Romano," in 1579 is representative of the initiation rite. Gathered together
with the other knights of the order in the church of Santiago, who were
dressed in their white habits sporting the cross of Santiago, the prospec-
tive knight was led by the ambassador to the high altar. Then the ambassador took the scroll, or royal "carta y provisión del Rey Phelipe," which
he first kissed, and placed it on top of the head of Mutino, instructing him
to serve the perpetual administrator of the order, the king, with reverence and obedience.[59] The novice was then presented with a sword by the

ambassador and two other Roman knights, Jacob Rusticuccio and Juan Baptista Madaleni, and asked, "Do you want to be a knight?" three times. After Mutino answered yes, the ambassador took the sword, touched the young man's head with it, and then presented him to the other knights. He was then assigned to serve on the Spanish galleys for six months, and after that to spend a year of training in one of the order's monasteries in Spain before returning to Rome.[60]

The number of knights in the four major Iberian military orders, both Iberians and Italians, who lived in Rome continued to grow throughout Philip II's rule. They included young initiates like Mutino as well as established and powerful figures like Gregory XIII's son Giacomo Boncompagno, the duke of Sora, who was also the governor of the Borgo and military commander of the Castel Sant'Angelo during the pontificate of his father. Philip sent Boncompagno the habit of Calatrava in 1576 with a reported 12,000-ducat pension,[61] and a habit of Alcántara in 1579 worth 14,000 ducats, 4,000 of which were reserved for Boncompagno's son Geronimo,[62] who was also granted the naturaleza of Castile so that he could receive up to 8,000 ducats in pensions from that kingdom.[63] Not surprisingly, the duke, while most immediately a servant of the pope's, was also one of the king's most valuable and visible vassals in Rome. He was present with the Spanish ambassador and the cardinals of the Spanish faction at numerous public celebrations and processions, such as the presentation of the chinea, the reception of new ambassadors, the solemnity of Santiago, the Easter procession, and various banquets thrown by the Spanish ambassador and the cardinals.[64]

Initiating young men into the various military orders also helped to build ties with other members of the Roman court, as was the case in 1583 when Marcantonio Bianchetti, the brother of the pope's maestro da camara Ludovico Bianchetti, was given the habit of Calatrava in the church of Santiago.[65] Similarly, requests from cardinals for habits for their family or household members were common, particularly in the later years of Philip II's reign. Cardinal Farnese, for instance, wrote to Philip personally asking that the "cross of Calatrava" be granted to Bertoldo Orsino, the second son of the count of Pitigliano, "to signal his service to Your Majesty."[66]

By the 1590s, in fact, more and more Romans were seeking and receiving the habit. A 1595 letter from the most effective ambassador of the entire period, the duke of Sessa, illuminates how the growing patronage web connected a wide variety of Roman clients to the Spanish monarch. Entitled "Report of That Which the Cardinals and Other People Who Have Served Your Majesty in Rome Seek," the letter listed the following requests:

- Cardinal Sarnano requested the habit of Santiago for Justiniano Bartuli.
- Cardinal Farnese requested a habit of Santiago for Baltazar Palazo, a "principal knight of this city."
- Cardinal Montalto requested a habit of Santiago for Scipione Dentici, who is described as a great *músico de tecla* (keyboard player).
- Cardinal Aldobrandino requested a habit of Santiago for Oracio Coloreto.
- Cardinal San Jorge requested a habit of Santiago for Sigismundo Quartari.
- Cardinal Ascoli requested a habit of Santiago for Geronimo Bernerio.
- Cardinal Altemps requested a habit of Santiago for his grandson, the duke of Galesi.
- The pope asked for a habit of Christ for Juan Antonio Romano, a courtier in the papal household.
- A ranking member of the Curia, Paolo Copercio, requested a habit of Christ for his gentleman, Dominico Cachio.
- Alexandro Boloneti, a knight of Santiago, requested a habit for his son.
- Cardinal Marcantonio Colonna requested a habit of Santiago for a member of his household, the knight Fontana Bolones.
- The duke of Mantua requested a habit for a knight in his household.
- Count Geronimo Giliolo requested a habit of Calatrava for himself; he is supported by Cardinal Gesualdo.
- Monsignor Tarugio requested the habit of Christ for his nephew.[67]

The duke of Sessa encouraged the king to honor all these requests, using a succinct justification that can be considered a basic Spanish axiom of patron-client relations in Rome: "Besides giving satisfaction to the cardinals it seems that with this [action] servants and friends are gained for Your Majesty in somebody else's states."[68] The duke could also be more specific in his support when necessary, as he was in the case of Monsignor Tarugio. The ambassador backed his request because "the said monsignor is the secretary of the congregation of bishops and regulars where every day much business [concerning] your majesty's states is conducted; and because he is the one who talks to His Holiness about this, he can provide much knowledge or benefit. Up until now he has attended very well to all that has related to the service of Your Majesty."[69]

The king was clearly interested in knowing this kind of detail even late in his reign, and it was a reflection of the careful attention he paid to his interests in Rome that he would sometimes ask the ambassador for more information about someone who sought the relatively small favor of a habit for a military order. Such was the case when Philip wrote to Sessa, again in 1595, for further particulars concerning Juan Andrea Rucci and Horacio Coloreto, who had written to Madrid seeking habits. The duke responded that Rucci was the first son of Julio Rucci, the son of Cardinal Montepulciano, and a knight of Santiago. The father had an estimated income of 6,000 scudi from land in Tuscany and a house in Rome, and now wanted to marry his son Juan to a daughter of Fabio Matei, a Roman nobleman.[70] This was the kind of information that mattered, since it located the young man in the broader patron-client network and showed the long family history of service to the Spanish crown.

This was also true when the ambassador requested a habit in 1593 for Don Benito de Córdoba, the "son of Don Iñigo, who served Your Majesty for many years in Rome,"[71] and when he intervened in favor of "a Roman noble named Baltasar Paluchi Albertini . . . who is of the nobility of this city, and whose two uncles have had the same habit."[72]
By 1600 a family tradition of service to the king through one of the military orders had become common in Rome and extended from the pope's family to the cardinals' households to the other nobility of the city. Gaspar de Cavalieri, a "gentilhombre Romano," was typical of this group, being described by Sessa as the brother of Mucio Cavalieri, a knight of Calatrava from a noble Roman family who had served the king for twenty-three years. The family, moreover, had old and warm ties of service to the Spanish crown and to Cardinal Borghese (soon to be Pope Paul V), to whom they were attached by marriage. They desired the habit for Gaspar to ensure "that those of his family continue always in the service of Your Majesty which he was born into, as were his ancestors."[73]

The Cardinals

The request concerning Gaspar de Cavalieri, as well as the long list of requests sent by Sessa to the king in 1595, underlines the important role that a number of cardinals also played in the Spanish faction. Indeed, we have already seen the importance of the cardinals to the political, economic, and social life of Spanish Rome, and a more precise picture of their evolving role in Spanish-Roman affairs as both clients and patrons in the Spanish faction can now be drawn.

The cultivation of a Spanish faction in the College of Cardinals was perhaps the ambassadors' most important role and one which the king made sure they understood. Writing to Requeséns in 1565, for example, Philip II emphasized the importance of the ambassador's presence in the city during such tumultuous times and advised him "to take great care to keep in our devotion the College of Cardinals universally and particularly, . . . and to communicate with and visit especially those who are known as our friends and servants."[74]

In the patron-client pyramid the cardinals occupied a position on the second tier directly below pope and king, and as princes of the church they had substantial power in their own right. This power, as well as their wealth and social status, varied widely, of course; one recent study distinguishes at least four classes among the larger group: (1) nobility, (2) patriciate, (3) new families, and (4) humble families.[75]

Among these classes, cardinals from the noble families like the Colonnas, Farneses, and Medicis were the most influential, with large incomes and extended households that could include as many as two hundred direct members; the Spanish king especially desired to secure their loyalty. In addition to this group, and also ranking among the more powerful cardinals, were the Spanish prelates who had resided in Rome for long periods and were loyal supporters of the king. Between 1561 and 1625, Cardinals Pacheco, Deza, Mendoza, and Borgia, especially, occupied a place in the Spanish faction just below that of the ambassador and frequently worked closely with him. (Cardinals Pacheco and Borgia, in fact, acted as ambassadors for short interim periods.) Even the most humble cardinal held a vote in the conclave, however, and many of these men were the object of Spanish lobbying and recipients of favors and also became loyal supporters of the king.

The number of cardinals in Rome who were known to be part of the Spanish faction of the college usually ranged between twenty and thirty-five at this time, with a relatively high turnover rate; a detailed analysis of Spanish relations with each cardinal necessarily exceeds the boundaries of this work. Moreover, it would be misleading to assume that because a cardinal voted with the Spanish party in a conclave or received a small pension from Spain that he was a reliable member of the broader Spanish faction in Rome.[76] Divided, and sometimes conflicting, loyalties were a fact of life in the politics of early modern Rome, as Ambassador Zúñiga complained to the king in a letter of 1569 which warned that not all the cardinals who "claim to be servants of Your Majesty" could be trusted because "they have given their pledge to many."[77]

Nonetheless, a number of cardinals stand out in the surviving records for their role as strong members of the Spanish faction, and their correspondence with the king, combined with the ambassador's supporting correspondence, reveals the complex patron-client exchange that existed between the Catholic King and a sizable group of cardinals.

Chief among these in the 1560s and 1570s were the cardinals named by the ambassador as leaders of the Spanish faction, namely Pacheco and Medici, who maintained primary residences in Rome, and Granvelle, who stayed in Rome for scattered periods of time as a special emissary of the king for critical negotiations.[78]

Of the three, Pacheco was the most effective patron and advocate of Spanish interests over the long term, probably because he enjoyed extensive revenues from Spain that bound him tightly to the Catholic King. Born to a noble family in Ciudad Rodrigo, Francesco Pacheco held a substantial pension from his early position as a canon of the cathedral of Toledo. In 1568 Philip II had nominated him to the wealthy archbishopric of Burgos, whose income was reported to be 40,000 ducats.[79] Pacheco also had been given an additional 6,000 ducats in pension from the diocese of Porta Nueva in 1571.[80] While maintaining strong ties to Castile, this cardinal also knew the Roman system extremely well, having been brought to Rome by his uncle Cardinal Pedro Pacheco, whose red hat he all but inherited in 1561. Besides holding the title of the cardinal of Santa Croce in Gerusaleme, he was also the protector of the kingdoms of Spain for the eighteen years that he resided there (1561–1579).

His wealth meant that in addition to pressuring the papacy and fellow cardinals to move in ways that benefited the Spanish Empire, Pacheco could act as a patron in his own right. We frequently find him in the notarial record as the executor of wills, for instance, for members of his household and other predominantly Spanish residents in Rome. Such was the case with Lope Rodríguez Gallo, a cleric from Burgos who, besides having 1,000 gold ducats, included among his possessions "in the house of the most illustrious and most reverend Cardinal Pacheco, my patron, the furnishings and belongings of my room."[81] Alonso de Villalobos, a priest from Toledo and a knight of the order of Saint Peter and Saint Paul, also named the cardinal as the executor of his much more humble estate in 1567,[82] as did Pedro Xuaxel from Seville in 1571, who served in the cardinal's palace as a courtier.[83]

Like Pacheco, Cardinals Granvelle and Medici also had large incomes from Spanish benefices and served as important intermediaries for the king in Rome.[84] Granvelle was noted by Roman observers for the great feasts he held for cardinals and prelates.[85] In 1569 he remarked in a letter to Philip II that he had recently distributed information received from the king to his servants in Rome, and that it had given "infinite content-ment" to all of the "vassals and creatures of Your Majesty here."[86] This, of course, was precisely the role he was supposed to be playing in addition to lobbying the pope on more particular matters, and he made a point of letting his royal patron know that he was doing it well.

Cardinal Giovanni de' Medici,[87] the son of Cosimo, was indebted to the king for favors granted not only to himself but also to other family members, such as his brother Pietro, to whom the king had given a mili-tary commission worth 500 ducats per month in times of peace and 1,000 in times of war. This favor and numerous others led the cardinal to write the king a letter of thanks that expressed the sense of obligation com-mon to major Spanish vassals in Rome: "Many are the favors that by now oblige my house entirely owing to Your Majesty."[88]

In addition to these leaders of the faction, there were other cardi-nals in the 1560s and 1570s who were loyal vassals of the king. In 1569, for example, Cardinal Marcantonio Colonna[89] wrote to Philip II thanking him for the royal favor that had been shown to his family—he had just been granted a 3,000-ducat pension from the diocese of Siguenza[90]—and assuring the king that he would work hard to secure the renewal of the cruzada.[91] Both Colonna and Cardinal Sforza sat on the congrega-tion that handled the cruzada, and Sforza, too, wrote to the king in 1569 assuring him that he "worked in your service in the negotiation of the cruzada" and that "the desire to serve Your Majesty grows always greater in me."[92]

Cardinals Aragona, Chiesa, Gesualdo, and Alciato were also recom-mended by Zúñiga as "good vassals," and by the early 1570s Aquaviva, Giustiniano, and Alessandrino were being included in the expanding group of trustworthy servants of the Catholic King.[93] Not surprisingly, all these prelates received generous pensions from churches controlled by Philip II, including 1,500 ducats to Aragona and Alessandrino from the bishopric of Catania, and 1,000 ducats to Giustiniano in 1574 from an unspecified church.[94]

Generally speaking, during the 1570s and 1580s there was a noticeable increase in pensions granted by the king, an increase that not surprisingly coincided with the growing strength of the Spanish faction of cardinals. Cardinal Farnese was reportedly receiving 20,000 ducats in pensions from Toledo by 1571;[95] Cardinals San Sisto, Madruzzo, and Vastanillano received 4,000, 4,000, and 3,000, respectively, from Toledo by 1576;[96] and Alessandrino received 4,000 from a monastery in Sicily in 1578.[97] When the count of Olivares arrived in Rome in 1582, moreover, he brought 20,000 ducats to be distributed among cardinals.[98]

These are but a few of the larger pensions, but there were literally dozens of others ranging in size from a few hundred ducats to a few thousand that came into Rome from Spain during the 1570s and 1580s. Indeed, when reading the record of the weekly meetings of cardinals as reported by the Avvisi, one gets the impression that by this time one of the key pieces of business of the consistory was the dispensing of ecclesiastical pensions controlled by the Catholic King. And the money clearly had its desired effect of building up the number of loyal servants and of cardinals considered leaders of the Spanish faction in the college.

Whereas only Medici and Pacheco were considered leaders in 1569, for example, Philip II was able to count a considerably larger group of cardinals as heads of the Spanish party by 1586, when he instructed his ambassador to recognize the following men as deserving of that rank: Farnese, Medici, Gesualdo, Colonna, Madruzzo, Aragona, Montalto, Alessandrino, and Deza. The king went further, offering a brief, but revealing, rationale for this choice: Farnese, Medici, Gesualdo, and Colonna because they were "protectors of my states"; Madruzzo because he was "a prince of the empire"; Aragona because his ancestry made him practically a member of the royal household;[99] Montalto because he was related to the pope; and Deza because he was Spanish.[100]

Many of the members of this inner group sat on powerful congregations such as the one in charge of the Inquisition,[101] and beyond official church business they also appeared together in a variety of other social contexts that served to bolster the prestige of the Spanish faction in Rome and to underline their loyalty to it. When Marcantonio Colonna, the hero of Lepanto, viceroy of Sicily, and long-time servant of Philip II, came to town in 1584 on his way to Spain, for example, he was welcomed by Cardinals Medici, Deza, Alessandrino, and Colonna, who had gathered in the ambassador's palace together with the governor of Rome, the duke of Sora, and many other Spanish prelates.[102]

Of this group of cardinals, Pedro Deza, who had been made cardinal of Seville upon the urging of Philip II in 1578 and resided in Rome for most of the next twenty-two years, became one of the most significant Spanish patrons in the city. Together with the two ambassadors, Olivares and the duke of Sessa, who lived in Rome for roughly the same period, Deza became a center of the Roman social, ecclesiastical, and political scene, demonstrating how influential the Spanish presence had become.

In addition to receiving pensions connected to earlier offices he had held in Spain, Deza was given the diocese of Zaragoza, with a 45,000-ducat pension, in 1586.[103] Numerous smaller benefices followed, and the wealth of the cardinal of Seville was great enough that he was able to build a large palace behind the Piazza di San Lorenzo in Lucina, in the *rione* (neighborhood) of Campo Marzio.[104] By the time he died in 1600, he had an annual income of 100,000 ducats, which made him, together with Cardinal Farnese, one of the wealthiest cardinals in Rome.

Deza had an extensive household to match his income, and his will reveals that at his death he left 20,000 scudi in gold in his palace, owned a library of more than seven hundred volumes, and possessed twenty-two paintings, four canopied beds with gilded columns, numerous coaches, a stable of horses, and other domestic goods that took forty pages to list.[105] During his time in Rome, he had attached various Spanish theologians and writers to his household and contributed more broadly to Roman courtly society by holding frequent banquets and sponsoring many comedies.

Together with his powerful position as head of numerous congregations and of the Spanish faction in the College of Cardinals, Deza's social prominence, his wealth, and his longevity made him one of the most influential members of Roman society.[106]

With men like Deza in the forefront, and with international and local Spanish power rising throughout the 1570s and 1580s, the size and influence of the Spanish faction of cardinals reached new heights by 1590. A letter from Olivares to the king concerning the conclave in that year described the situation well: "I believe that Your Majesty's faction has never entered into a conclave with such great reputation, since many are the subjects that depend upon Your Majesty, with Montalto also having declared that he wishes to depend on your will, and without opposition from France, nor from any [ally] of theirs."[107]

Indeed, during his more than three decades in power, Philip II and his primary intermediaries in Rome had succeeded brilliantly in winning over or creating a large number of cardinals, including many of the most powerful. Thus, by 1590, a contemporary report counted at least twenty-three cardinals as strong followers of the king,[108] and it was no surprise that the subsequent conclaves quickly elected a Spanish favorite. Cardinal Sforza went so far as to hang the king's coat of arms on the door of his palace after the conclave of 1590 to demonstrate that he was, in the words of one observer, the best conclavist and the most ardent creature of the king.[109]

The fact that cardinals continued to be well rewarded for their loyalty certainly played a large role in Philip's success, and in 1591, 30,000 ducats' worth of pensions were again distributed among them, including 8,000 to Terranova.[110] In that same year 2,000 ducats from Seville went to Cardinal Rusticucci,[111] and 4,000 to Cardinal Farnese.[112] The pattern of the 1590 conclave was subsequently repeated in 1592, when the Spanish faction's twenty-four votes again dominated the election.[113]

These "Spanish" cardinals frequently appeared together at functions like the feast of Corpus Domini and Spanish masses of thanksgiving in the church of Santiago to further publicize their allegiance to the Spanish crown. Ironically, it was precisely at this point of highly visible success that some of the weaknesses inherent in factional politics began to surface, and the Spanish faction of cardinals began to be challenged and undermined by two powerful opponents: death and the French.

Because the strength of the factions depended heavily upon the patron-client bond, the longevity of both Philip II and many of the cardinals of his era was crucial to the strength of the Spanish faction. For many of these men, the old king had been their or their family's patron for ten, twenty, even thirty years, something that could not be said of any pope of the period. This led to a deepening sense of loyalty as well as dependence on the part of both patron and clients.

Beginning in the early 1590s, however, death began to claim many of the players of the older generation, and its potential impact upon Spanish interests did not go unnoticed. In a letter to the king in 1594, for example, the duke of Sessa pointed out, "From the vacant See of Sixtus V [1590] until now the following cardinals and servants of Your Majesty have died: Gastano, Albano, San Jorge, Caraffa, Cremona, the two Gonzagas, Santi Quatro [Coronati], la Rovere, Mendoza, Canano, Sans, Espiñola, and Alano, and so Your Majesty has lost fourteen sure votes."[114] Only ten, according to the duke, could now be counted upon as "vassals of your majesty": Sfrondrato, Farnese, Pallavicino, Pinto, Aquaviva, Santi Quatro Coronati, Sasso, Toledo, Aldobrandino, and Gaetano.[115]

With characteristic tenacity, Philip continued to attend to this group, giving most of them part of the 20,000 ducats in pension that he granted in the following year from the diocese of Toledo.[116] At the same time, the king continued to lobby the papacy to create new cardinals, including Giovanni Doria, who had studied at Salamanca and Alcalá, and Don Francisco de Avila, the archdeacon of Toledo, who was given the red hat in 1596.[117] The king himself, however, died in 1598, and the enormous influence and power he exercised in Rome were not automatically transferred to his son. When Philip III named the auditor of the Rota, Francesco Peña, and Andrés de Córdoba as his candidates for the cardinal's hat in 1600, he was refused.[118]

Also in 1600, one of the most outspoken cardinals of the Spanish faction, Cardinal Madruzzo, died, which prompted the duke of Sessa to write a letter to the king warning him of the increasingly grim situation for the Spanish party. According to the ambassador, "very few cardinals remain[ed]" in the Spanish faction.[119] Correspondence to the Council of State earlier that same year counted only five men who remained strongly devoted to the Catholic King—Avila, Zappata, Doria, Madruzzo, and Dietrichstein—and went further to warn that the French king had begun to spend 60,000 scudi annually in Rome to build a French faction in the college.[120]

Attrition and competition, then, seriously undermined the strength of the Catholic King's faction in the College of Cardinals in the first years of the seventeenth century, forcing the king to spend more and the ambassador and Spanish cardinals to work harder to rebuild their earlier position. In 1604 Clement VIII created eighteen new cardinals, and Olivares and Sessa, who were now back in Madrid, sent advice to the new ambassador, the less capable marquis of Aytona, on how to win the cardinals over to the Spanish king.[121]

Although few in Madrid or Rome were happy with the performance of the new ambassador in a variety of other respects, he nonetheless did a fairly good job in this regard with the help of the king's generous pen-

sions; by 1608 he was able to send to Philip III a growing list of cardinals who were at least inclined toward Spain. More specifically, Aytona's
list counted twenty-three cardinals who held pensions totaling roughly
60,000 ducats from churches in the Spanish Empire. These included Cardinal Farnese, with 16,000, 10,000 of which came from the archbishopric
of Monreale in Sicily; the pope's nephew Cardinal Borghese, who held
7,000 in pensions; and Cardinal Montalto, who had 3,000.[122] These men
and others, such as Colonna, Sforza, and Madruzzo, were described as
generally attached and obligated "as vassals" of the king, and also were
praised for their role in gaining other servants for him. Cardinal Borghese, in particular, was lauded as being "one with the Spaniards"; and it
was noted that as long as his uncle the pope lived, he would gain many
creatures for the Catholic King.

Other cardinals, however, who held lesser pensions, were described
as being held "en poca opinión" and of "poco servicio," although their
vote in the conclave was secure. Cardinal Gallo was representative of
these less dependable princes of the church since he also held pensions
from France, and the ambassador warned that "he is not a trustworthy
man."[123]

Thus, by 1608, the Spanish faction of cardinals was again wielding
considerable influence, but it fell short of the level of strength it had enjoyed in the 1580s and early 1590s, and a number of the cardinals counted
as members were weak in their support. With the French faction now
also numbering between twenty and twenty-five supporters, moreover,
Spain's was not the only game in town; and the French king's party served
as formidable opposition, actively recruiting cardinals and poised to capi-
talize on Spanish weaknesses. And although the French were not strong
enough to shape the conclave that followed Paul V's death in January
1621, they had become so by 1623, when Gregory XV died.

A young and inexperienced Philip IV had been on the throne only
two years at this point, and the French were quick to take advantage of the
weak loyalties in the college to the new monarch. The fact that a French
candidate, Maffeo Barberini, was elected by fifty of the fifty-five voting
cardinals revealed more than any other event that the hegemony enjoyed
by the Spanish faction for more than sixty years had been broken.

But it did not mean that the Spanish presence in Rome had disappeared, for the Spanish faction also included the many knights of the religious orders and the broader Spanish nation. The prince of Sulmona, for

example, was given the cross of Calatrava early in 1624, and a few months later the ambassador gave the habit of Santiago to another Roman nobleman, Baldassare Cafarelli. A contemporary observer noted that by this time the order of Santiago was recognized as being "favored by much of the Roman nobility."[124]

THE SPANISH NATION: THE CLERICS

In addition to these Roman servants of the king, the broader Spanish nation had become firmly entrenched in the city during the reigns of Philip II and Philip III. Not surprisingly in a city that served as the institutional and symbolic center of Christendom, churchmen were the most visible and prominent subsection of the nation after the ambassadors and cardinals, while lawyers, merchants, notaries, and working-class Iberians provided the remaining base of support for Spanish interests in the city.[125] There was a wide social range among the clerics themselves, of course, but for purposes of analysis we can discern at least four major groups: clergy who served in the Curia or papal household; members of Iberian religious orders or dioceses who came to Rome on official business for the king, their orders, or both; members of religious houses in Rome or members of cardinals' households; and clerics of lower rank who came to Rome to seek a benefice or some other advancement from the papacy.

Representative of Spanish clerics who served in the Curia or papal household was Constantino de Castillo, a canon of the Cathedral of Cuenca, who held the powerful position of *referendario y scriptor Apostólico* in the Segnatura di Giustizia from at least 1551 to 1566, when he died in Rome.[126] The referendarios ruled on matters both civil and ecclesiastical, and the Segnatura di Giustizia has been called "the supreme tribunal of the Roman curia" in this period.[127]

Although this position and the long duration of his stay in Rome imply a loyalty to the papacy and a deep faith, as his will puts it, in the "Santa Madre Iglesia Romana," Castillo also remained attached to the Spanish community and church in Rome. In fact, he began the tradition of setting up endowments for the dowries of poor Spanish women, donating three houses in Rome to the church of Santiago and directing that their rents should be used for the dowries.[128] He also gave the funds to build the chapel of the Assumption within the church of Santiago, where he was subsequently buried.[129]

Castillo was thus a man of substantial wealth and connections with an extensive household in Rome,[130] and he serves as a good example of how Spaniards increasingly tried to ensure through property and wealth that after their deaths their church and their fellow Iberians would flourish in Rome. Castillo stipulated, for instance, that all the women who received dowries from his endowment had to stay in Rome.[131]

Another Spaniard who held the same position as Castillo some years later was Don Pedro de Foix Montoya, a cleric from Seville who died in Rome in 1623.[132] He, too, expressed a deep loyalty to the papacy and also gave a considerable part of his estate to the Spanish nation and church in the city. He established an endowment of 2,333 scudi of silver, for example, which yielded 77 scudi per year for the salary of a chaplain in the church of Santiago. Similarly, he established a larger charitable endowment with the rest of his property. The interest of this *patronato,* as he called it, was to be divided into three parts, with the first going to Spaniards in debtors' prison, the second for the dowry of a poor Spanish girl, and the third for masses to be said for his soul.[133]

In addition to the two referendarios, Foix Montoya and Castillo, there appeared in the papal court in the 1580s and 1590s two of the most prominent Spanish churchmen of the entire period, Francisco Toledo and Francisco de la Peña. Toledo, a native of Cordova who became a Jesuit in 1558, was a gifted philosopher, theologian, writer, and preacher who was sent to Rome to teach in the Collegio Romano in 1560.[134] Like most Jesuits in Rome, he initially appears to have been involved primarily in the local work of his order rather than in the affairs of the papal court or Spanish politics. Teaching and writing were his main duties in the 1560s and 1570s. He published an introduction to Aristotle's *Dialectic* (1561), and commentaries on Aristotle's *Logic* (1572), *Physics* (1573), *De anima* (1574), and *De generatione et corruptione* (1575).[135]

By the early 1580s, however, Toledo's intellectual and rhetorical reputation had grown to the point where he was one of the main preachers in the pope's chapel. He preached an Advent cycle in 1585, for example, that caused one observer to remark, "Blessed are those who have been in Rome to listen to the word of the Lord" when Toledo preached his spiritual doctrine at the papal palace.[136] From this point on he was a regular preacher at Saint Peter's and was appointed a member of the board of episcopal examiners in 1592.[137] More notably, in that same year Toledo was made cardinal by his close friend Pope Clement VIII, becoming the first Jesuit to wear the red hat and to break the prohibition in the original Jesuit charter against its members holding such high ecclesiastical honors. He moved into the papal palace in 1593,[138] and was appointed a leading role as theologian in the special congregation that recommended the absolution of Henry IV of France.[139]

The case of Toledo, like that of most Spanish Jesuits who lived in Rome, represents a more clouded example of allegiance and support for Spanish policies. On the one hand, he was strongly supported by Philip II, received a pension from Spain, and did much to bolster the reputation of the Spaniards as theologians and leaders of the Roman church generally. Still, Toledo was also closely tied to the papacy and particularly to Clement. Allegiance to both powers was not unusual, particularly in a period when relations were close or at least relatively smooth. When a point of serious difference arose between king and pope, however, such as the absolution of Henry IV, it tested the loyalties of Spanish churchmen like Toledo and Peña and revealed different levels of affinity.

Toledo, for example, was instrumental in organizing the theological justification for Henry IV's reconciliation with Rome, a role that earned him a solemn funeral memorial in Paris when he died in 1596.[140] Peña, on the contrary, fought vigorously against the absolution, throwing all of his considerable power as jurist and member of the Rota behind his monarch's staunch opposition to the move.

Peña, who held the powerful position of auditor of the Rota from 1588 to 1612, was an accomplished canon lawyer from Zaragoza who also held the offices of archdeacon of that church and general counsel to the Inquisition.[141] He was granted the naturaleza from Castile in 1592, along with a pension from the church of Ciudad Rodrigo, and expressed his thanks to the king for these favors in a letter that also emphasized his desire to serve the monarch "as a faithful vassal and creature of yours."[142] This he did for his two decades in Rome, often under the direct instructions of the ambassador. He was so upset when he failed in the negotiations over Henry IV that he asked the king for permission to return to Spain.[143]

He was refused this request, not surprisingly, because as a powerful and wealthy member of the Curia who was deeply tied to the king, Peña came close to the Spanish cardinals in both his institutional power and his ability to act as a local patron and supporter of the Spanish nation. Living in his household, for example, were Cardinal Don Felipe Filonardo and Paolo Emilio Filonardo, an officer of the Roman Inquisition. So, too, were the doctor Lucas Anton Visilai and a Padre Lemos.[144] When Peña died, all these "good companions" were bequeathed books and relics from the auditor. Numerous other Romans and Spaniards, including the Confraternity of the Most Holy Resurrection, also benefited from his considerable estate, the bulk of which was invested in fifteen shares, or "places" (*luoghi*) in the Roman *monti* (bond issues, or administrative state loans). Most of his property in Spain, on the other hand, went to his nephew and namesake in Zaragoza, his universal heir (residuary legatee).[145]

While not as powerful as Peña or Toledo, a number of other Spaniards, like the friar Tomas Manríquez, master of the sacred palace, were also closely tied to the papal court in this period.[146] The duties of the master of the papal palace included sitting on the influential congregation for the examination of bishops, which oversaw episcopal appointments, and serving as the main papal censor for the index of prohibited books.[147]

Also in an influential position was Monsignor Ferrante Torres, who held the title of vicar of Saint Peter's and was named as the member of the Curial office in charge of Roman streets in 1574.[148] He worked in Rome for more than twenty years, from roughly 1569 to 1590, and was known as an agent of the king's who had been given a 1,000-ducat pension by the monarch in 1571.[149]

Cristóbal de Cabrera was yet another influential Spanish priest from Palencia who served the papacy as a biblical scholar until his death in 1596. He had lived in the "Roman court" for "many years," according to his last testament, where he was attached to the papal palace as a master of sacred theology.[150] Cabrera demonstrated a deep affection for the city of Rome and the papacy and had become a Roman citizen. As a sign of this affection, he left his library, which he called "the treasure I valued most in this life," to the Vatican along with his own commentaries on the Scriptures. He also requested to be buried in the chapel of the Immaculate Conception, which he had caused to be built in the church of Saint Michael the Archangel, next to Saint Peter's.[151]

Even with this strong attachment to Rome, Cabrera remained devoted to the Spanish nation and to his family in Castile. Although he left his house in the Borgo to the Roman Confraternity of the Most Holy Sacrament to use as a pilgrims' hospice, along with 2,000 silver scudi he had invested in the monti, he stipulated that Spanish women be given preference in the hospice. And be bequeathed the valuable royal tax privilege from the city of Toro to his family and to several confraternities and churches in Castile.[152]

Although it is difficult to know exactly what role men like Cabrera played in advancing a distinctly Spanish agenda in Rome, it would be a mistake to underestimate their value as eyes and ears for the Spanish ambassadors, cardinals, and kings. Their proximity to the daily business of the court was a great asset simply for the information they could gather, while they also enhanced the reputation of the Spanish nation generally because of their attachment to the pope.

This was certainly also the case with the substantial number of Spanish clerics who served in lesser positions, such as Gaspar de la Peña from Avila, who appears in Roman records in 1567 as one of the many *scrittori*, or scribes, responsible for the original production and copying of papal briefs, bulls, and proclamations,[153] and Monsignor d'Avila, who was put in charge of the Cancellaria Apostòlica of the Correttorie delle Bolle (the office in charge of issuing bulls) in 1581.[154]

Together with these functionaries in the papal bureaucracy, moreover, were the numerous Spanish *camereros,* or stewards, who served in the papal palace in the 1560s and 1570s. Francisco de Reynoso,[155] Diego Jorge, a cleric from Seville,[156] Sylvestro de Guzmán,[157] and Don Gaspar de la Concha [158] all appear in the records in this capacity. Another Spaniard, Francisco de Soto, held the positions of cantor and chaplain for the papal chapel in the 1560s.[159]

Like these less powerful but well placed men, there was another group of clerics who served to enhance the reputation of the Spaniards in Rome, namely the many members of religious orders who spent years or decades in the city. While it is not my purpose here to trace all the Spanish Jesuits, Franciscans, Dominicans, and Carmelites who came to Rome in this period, it is possible to identify some of the more prominent members of this group, who were well known to contemporaries for their learning, piety, or charity. Generally speaking, the members of the religious orders played a more neutral role politically, but their presence has to be seen as having a substantial social and religious impact on the city.

The religious congregation that had the strongest ties to Spain through its founder and early members was the Society of Jesus. With its local power and reputation growing throughout the period and with Spaniards serving as the generals of the order until the late sixteenth century, it would be tempting to assume that the Jesuits were a base of Spanish political power and influence in Rome. This was not the case, however, owing to a combination of factors: the international membership of the order in Rome in the early years; the increasingly Italian population in the late sixteenth and early seventeenth centuries; the Jesuits' devotion to the papacy and their frequently rocky relations with the Spanish monarchs; and the order's preoccupation with its primary apostolates of teaching and evangelization, especially in its first century of existence.

Still, this did not keep the Spanish Jesuits from playing a significant role in Rome through their work. We have already seen this with the most prominent of the Jesuits of this period, Francisco Toledo, but there were also many others who had successful careers as professors and administrators in the Collegio Romano and who published numerous scholarly works with Roman presses. The "Catalogue of Superiors and Professors of the Collegio Romano, 1571–1773," for example, reveals that Jaime Ledesma was a lecturer in theology beginning in 1557 and the prefect of students from 1563 to his death in 1575.[160] He published eight works during these years, including a grammar, a general treatise on Scriptures, a catechism, and a manual on how to teach the catechism.[161] Other Spaniards working at the college included Jerónimo Torres, a professor of metaphysics and mathematics in 1560 and 1561; Cristóforo de Madrid, the superintendent from 1568 to 1570; Juan Fernández, a lecturer in church law from 1572 to 1574; Francisco Suárez, a lecturer in theology from 1581 to 1585; Gabriel Vásquez, a lecturer in theology from 1570 to 1600; and Miguel Vásquez, the prefect of students from 1595 to 1600.[162]

Of these, Francisco Suárez was the most famous in his own day after Toledo. He was trained in Salamanca and taught philosophy in Paris, Segovia, Valladolid, Alcalá, Salamanca, and Rome before being asked by Philip II to teach and direct theological studies at the University of Coimbra. He was a prolific writer, and his commentaries on Aquinas and a variety of other theological treatises eventually numbered twenty-three volumes and were published from Venice to Brussels to Coimbra. This edition was widely used for theological training into the eighteenth century, when a new edition of his collected works was published.[163]

Certainly the presence in Rome of men like Suárez, even if they stayed only for five years, did a great deal for the reputation of the Spaniards. And there were others, like Gabriel Vásquez, who taught much longer (twenty-nine years) and trained at least two generations of predominantly Italian students in the college. Vásquez became so well known for his theological lectures that his contemporaries in Rome dubbed him the Augustine of Spain.[164]

Besides the Jesuits, members of other religious orders also contributed to the prestige of the Spanish nation in the city. The Dominican Alonso Chacón, for example, has already been mentioned, but there were others, like the Franciscan Angelo Paz. He was well known in Rome in the late sixteenth century for his piety and pious writings, and lived in the monastery that Ferdinand and Isabella had paid to rebuild, San Pietro in Montorio. Although he appears infrequently in the political or institutional record, his local fame as a holy man was widespread, and upon his death the crowds who came to view his body tore pieces of cloth from his habit as relics, forcing it to be replaced three times.[165] As a sign of honor and respect, the duke of Sessa paid for a lead tomb for the friar.[166]

Moving beyond famous friars, Jesuits, and clerics who enjoyed direct affiliation with the papal court, we find another large group of Spanish priests living in Rome off the considerable revenues they received from Spanish church income either in the form of benefices or as a salary for services performed in Rome for churches in the Spanish monarch's realms. This middle group of clerics was primarily composed of ranking members of religious orders or dioceses in the Spanish Empire who most frequently acted as procurators (*procuradores*), or ecclesiastical lawyer-solicitors, working for their orders or for the king.

There were an estimated 180,000 men and women "in religion" in the Kingdoms of Castile and Aragon in the late sixteenth century, and with the papacy still exercising a great deal of institutional as well as spiritual authority over them and their revenues, it was essential that there be representatives on the ground in Rome to speak for their interests. Thus, we find a host of ecclesiastical procurators, trained in canon law and most often holding the title of *licenciado,* descending upon Rome from all over the Spanish Empire.

A brief sampling from the notary records, for example, reveals the following men in that role: Diego de Medina and Juan Morán from the diocese of Toledo;[167] Juan de Salazar from Salamanca;[168] Juan Fernández for the bishop of León;[169] Cristóbal de Caballos, the *fiscal* of the Order of Alcántara and its procurator general in Rome;[170] Juan Pérez de Calabijo from the diocese of Cordova;[171] Friar Diego de Chávez, a Dominican professor and procurator for his monastery in Seville;[172] Hernando de Torres, procurator for his brother Luís, archbishop of Monreale;[173] Friar Francisco Becerra, the procurator general for all the military orders of the king;[174] Benedicto Girgós, the king's secretary from Gerona;[175] Rodrigo de Olea, procurator from Calahorra and intermediary for numerous religious houses in Spain; and Juan Pérez Muñoz, a procurator for *señores temporales* (secular lords) as well as for the chapter of the cathedral in Toledo.[176]

Many of these men settled in Rome and left wills that give us some idea of their wealth and social connections, while others went back to Spain. Of those who clearly made Rome their home, Juan Pérez Muñoz was one of the most successful. Like a secular lawyer with a thriving practice, Pérez Muñoz was able to maintain a sizable household that included five servants; he also owned five houses in Rome and a library of more than three hundred volumes. His estate was worth over 10,000 silver scudi when he died in 1594. Cardinal Mendoza served as one of the executors of his will, and the many people who benefited from it included a brother, a sister, nephews, and cousins in Spain as well as the church of Santiago, the Confraternity of the Most Holy Resurrection, and all his servants in Rome, who received a year's salary and a new set of clothes.[177] Clearly, ecclesiastical law was a good profession for sixteenth-century Spaniards in the eternal city.

Rodrigo de Olea also did well at the profession, and his will reveals that he served as an intermediary for many procurators and *racioneros* (business managers) in Spain. He had performed unspecified services for the convent of the Madre de Dios in Seville, for instance, although the convent owed him 170 gold scudi, and he had also handled some business for the nuns of the convent of Saint Ildefonso in Burgos, for which he had received 100 gold scudi. He also declared on his deathbed in 1599 that he had served the nobleman Lope García de Murza for many years in Rome but had never been paid the 100 scudi owed him, even after he had "won a sentence in his favor in the dealings that he had with the Rota." With a considerable amount of ongoing and unsettled business, Olea entrusted his books and accounts to Juan Fernández Cornejo, the *espeditor* (lawyer) of the church of Santiago in Rome, for final resolution.[178]

The many priests like Olea who served in Rome as representatives of orders and dioceses throughout the Spanish Empire numbered in the hundreds, if not thousands, during the reigns of Philip II and Philip III; the notarial records are filled with their affairs. In general, they bolstered the Spanish presence in Rome, enhanced the reputation of the Spanish Empire, and gave generously to Spanish charities and organizations in the city.

On the other hand, many of these same priests actively lobbied on behalf of their orders or bishops against the king when their interests clashed, and, like other groups in the Spanish faction, they demonstrated what Ronald Weissman has called the social ambiguity inherent in patronage systems.[179] This was virtually always the case when the king tried to impose a new tax or renew an old one on ecclesiastical revenues. We know from surviving letters that Philip II frequently urged the pope to require all Spanish priests holding benefices in Spain to return home during tax negotiations.

In spite of these occasional signs of resistance and divided loyalties, the Spanish clergy in Rome most often appear as loyal servants of the monarchy and proud members of the Spanish nation. They, like other Spaniards, were conscious of forming part of Christendom's strongest "nation" as the self-fashioned heirs of the Christianized Roman Empire, and they were proud of their shared traditions, even in matters of fashion. (When Pius V wanted to impose a rigorous dress code on all clergy living in Rome, the Spanish priests—especially the courtiers—asked the Spanish ambassador and cardinals to intervene so that they could continue to wear the distinctive Spanish cape.)[180]

The final group of Spanish clergy were clerics who had traveled to Rome in the hope of receiving one of the thousands of Spanish church benefices that the pope had the right to dispense. Going back to the period of Alexander VI, the papacy had claimed the right to give out benefices of Spanish churches during times of episcopal vacancy. Almost always a matter of dispute and negotiation, the fact remains that throughout the sixteenth and seventeenth centuries the papacy, through the branch of the Curia known as the Datary, retained this right.

Individually, these benefices were often small compared to those of bishops and cardinals, averaging around 100 ducats per year. In an age of unpredictable income, however, this was still an attractive sum that enabled a "middle-class" lifestyle, and it drew thousands of Spaniards to the city to personally appeal for a pension. Once secured, many priests chose to stay in Rome. Perhaps more than any other practice, it was the distribution of the small pensions that accounted for the largest single group of Spaniards in Rome, as well as the largest percentage of Spanish wealth that flowed into Rome during this period. It was also a practice that bred resentment in Spain.

More specifically, by the late 1620s, economically hard-pressed Spanish bishops in Iberia were increasingly indignant when they saw revenues from their depressed lands being spent on an ever more splendid

and opulent Rome. This reached a new height in 1633 when Domingo
Pimentel, the bishop of Córdoba, went to Rome as a representative of the
Spanish clergy to protest the "offenses committed in that court against
the natives of Spain."[181] In a lengthy printed treatise, the Spanish bishop
complained that it was reprehensible that bishops in Spain should send
their revenues to Rome, which he described as "so much richer, as they
show through their luxury, opulence, palaces, and gardens." How much
less, he continued, did the Spanish church owe to the many courtiers,
architects, musicians, and other secular people who were supported by
Spanish pensions?[182]

     This complaint typified the criticism that had been building for de-
cades from Spanish clerics who resided in Iberia. As the economic de-
pression of the early seventeenth century deepened, moreover, so too did
their resentment. But in a response to this criticism, a Spanish lawyer and
cleric living in Rome, Doctor Juan Pablo Frances, wrote to the king to defend the practice. He argued that while it was true that roughly 800,000
ducats from Spain came into Rome every year in the form of smaller
ecclesiastical pensions and incomes, it was also true that this income supported some four thousand Spaniards who were in Rome seeking other
offices, and another four thousand who were already working in Rome
in cardinals' households, churches, monasteries, and the papal bureaucracy.[183] The implication was that this money was well spent since it supported an important Spanish faction in the papal court that represented
broader Spanish interests.

     In the availability of income, then, we see one of the most impor-
tant explanations for the large Spanish presence in Rome. Moreover, this
makes the earlier estimate of a combined population of thirty thousand
more plausible. A priest living on an income of even 100 ducats per year
could afford at least two or three servants, and these would frequently
be Spaniards, as we shall see in the pages that follow.

THE SPANISH NATION: THE WEALTHY
AND MIDDLE CLASSES

A sizable middle and upper-middle class of Spaniards constituted another important component of the Spanish nation in Rome. These
included merchants, bankers, blacksmiths, painters, educated laymen
who worked as notaries and lawyers, and a considerable group of inde-

pendently wealthy Spaniards who had settled in Rome and invested their income in the profitable papal monti. Thanks to the notarial records and wills preserved in large part by two Spanish notaries working in Rome, Alonso de Avila and Jerónimo Rabassa, we know a good deal about the business dealings, wealth, and piety of this group.

The extended Fonseca family, which included the cousins Jerónimo and Antonio and Antonio's son Manuel, are representative of the wealthier members of this group. With family roots in Portugal, the Fonsecas were merchants with extensive business contacts throughout Iberia.[184] By the early seventeenth century, Manuel had become a highly visible member of Roman society with a large palace in the Piazza di Santa Maria Sopra Minerva.[185] His estate was worth well over 100,000 gold scudi in 1600, and the whole family appears in the social records as prominent members and generous benefactors of the broader Spanish nation in Rome.

Jerónimo Fonseca was apparently the first to settle in Rome,[186] and he had urged another brother in Portugal to move to the city around 1580 to take over his business since Jerónimo and his "very dear and loved wife," Violante, had no children. In a statement that is revealing of the great fondness many Spaniards felt for Rome, Jerónimo explained in his will why he was asking his brother to move his family to the city: "Because of the great affection that I have for the people of Rome, [the city] in which God has done many favors and good deeds for me, helping me in my business, I wish, and it is my will, that my brother Antonio Fonseca come to live [here] with his family . . . to begin to work and continue the business and correspondence that I have had and have, and through the help of God to be able to sustain his family honorably."[187]

Although the Fonsecas were Portuguese, they serve as excellent examples of Iberians from kingdoms other than Castile who also considered themselves part of the broader Spanish nation, loyal subjects of the Spanish monarchs, and prominent members of the Spanish faction in Rome. The cousins Jerónimo and Antonio were early leaders of the Confraternity of the Most Holy Resurrection, and both gave generously to the confraternity and the church of Santiago. Antonio, for instance, left 400 silver escudos for the construction of a chapel dedicated to the Resurrection in the church of Santiago where he, his wife, and his son Manuel were all buried. He also gave 300 silver escudos to establish an endowment to pay the dowries of six poor Spanish women annually.[188] Jerónimo, for his part, was the prior of the confraternity in his lifetime and left the group 300 silver escudos as well as a house in the Campo dei Fiori, whose rent was to pay for the dowries of four Spanish women.[189]

At the same time, however, the Fonsecas also demonstrated continuing allegiance to Portugal: Antonio and Jerónimo both left small sums to the Portuguese church of San Antonio in Rome and also stipulated that the money for dowries be given to deserving Portuguese women first and foremost.[190] Their patterns of giving reveal the various levels of identity and allegiance that marked many of the wealthy and middle-class Iberians in Rome. On the one hand, there was no question that they saw themselves as part of the larger Spanish nation and loyal servants of the crown—Manuel Fonseca, for example, presented Philip IV's pledge of obedience to Pope Gregory XV in 1622[191]—but they also remained loyal to their smaller nation of Portugal.

Moreover, they developed a strong attachment to the city and people of Rome that manifested itself in charitable giving and made them Roman patrons in their own right. Roman establishments that benefited from the Fonsecas' charity included the Confraternity of the Immaculate Conception, the hospital of San Giacomo degli Incurabili, the Fate Bene Fratelli, the Orfanelli, the church of Santa Maria Sopra Minerva, and the Confraternity of the Rosary, all of which received sums ranging from 10 to 50 gold scudi. This was a common pattern among wealthy Spaniards which served to build ties and allegiances with dozens of Roman churches, monasteries, hospitals, and charities.

The goodwill and influence of the Fonsecas did not go unrecognized or unrewarded in Rome. Possibly the most noticeable sign of appreciation came when Pope Gregory XIII legitimized Antonio Fonseca's son, Manuel.[192] This was no small favor since it allowed Antonio's only son to inherit most of his father's estate and to continue the family line in Rome.

Papal favor and financial good fortune also characterized the experience of another prominent Iberian family in Rome, that of Juan Enríquez de Herrera, a wealthy Castilian banker from the bishopric of Palencia who spent most of his professional life in the city and died there around 1602.[193] Herrera owned a bank in partnership with Octavio Costa and, as noted in Chapter 3, had acquired the lucrative papal bureau of the *depositeria generale* in 1591. A well-connected member of the Spanish community in Rome, he was a benefactor of the national church of Santiago, to which he gave a chapel dedicated to the newly canonized Spanish saint Diego of Alcalá.[194] He also financed the luxurious lifestyle and expanding network of dependents of the Spanish ambassador, who was constantly borrowing against the future incomes of his estates and benefices to keep afloat. Between 1592 and 1595, for instance, the duke of Sessa borrowed 44,849 silver scudi from Herrera and Costa.[195]

As with many other wealthy Spaniards, Herrera had an extended household in Rome that included family from Spain who were wealthy in their own right. Juan's cousin Alonso Enríquez de Herrera, for example, also lived in the city and eventually died there. He and his wife, Beatriz López, lived comfortably off the rents of his land in and around the city of Cuenca, which brought in more than 10,000 ducats in 1580. He also had income from an inheritance that he invested in the monti of Rome and which yielded good interest.[196]

It was not only very wealthy businessmen or moderately wealthy churchmen who were able to thrive in Rome and leave substantial or at least moderate estates. Middle-class Spaniards also did well in the city through a variety of occupations, trades, or investments, and this group included such diverse professionals as notaries, blacksmiths, and painters.

Toribio de Escobar, for example, was a blacksmith from Palencia who had a shop "in front of the Illustrious Cardinal Farnese's palace" that also included a stable of twenty-four horses and mules. When he had his will drawn up in 1571, his accounts showed twenty-five people owing him a combined sum of almost 1,500 scudi of silver. He, on the other hand, only owed thirteen scudi to one Doctor Navarra for a mule purchased from the latter.[197]

Toribio's more intimate ties in the city included a daughter, Aurelia, from "his wife Madonna Diamante." Aurelia received 66 silver scudi from his estate, while Salvio Florentino, who had worked for him for seven years, received 10 silver scudi. The blacksmith requested to be buried in the church of Santiago and, like many wealthier or better-placed Spaniards, gave money to the Roman hospital of San Giacomo degli Incurabili and the Confraternity of the Holy Sacrament. This was a common practice among Spaniards of all social ranks.[198]

Similarly, Domenico Trizeno, a "Spanish painter from Valladolid," requested that his cassock and beretta be sold and the proceeds given to the poor; he also asked to be buried in the church of Santiago. He was not as wealthy as the blacksmith, but he did leave his wife 33 gold scudi and a number of paintings and art books as well as some other money owed him, including 15 silver scudi from the Franciscans of San Pietro in Montorio for a painting.[199]

Trizeno is an interesting example of a Spanish artist attempting to break into the Italian art scene, with limited success. He apparently was able to make at least a moderate living, predominantly from Spanish clients like Jerónimo Francés Spagnolo and Señor Aguilar, who both still owed him money for paintings in 1581, when the will was made. But he obviously aspired to greater things; among his possessions were books with "many sketches" by Michelangelo and Raphael. He also counted among his paintings a Madonna that he had copied from Titian, a portrait of Michelangelo, and a painting of Christ.[200]

Yet another example of a member of the Spanish middle class in Rome was Alonso de Avila, a notary whose education in Spain and connections to Spanish institutions in the city allowed him to make a good living. Avila lived in Rome from the early 1560s until his death in 1604, and his primary work was as the notary in Rome for the Spanish nation.[201] Over his four decades in Rome, which neatly corresponded with the rise of the Spanish faction, he worked almost exclusively for the nation and was also the secretary of the church of Santiago, where he requested to be buried.[202] In the years from 1562 to 1586 he produced twenty volumes of notarial records (many of which have been drawn upon in this chapter), which represented thousands of transactions, primarily among the Spaniards in the city.[203]

Avila was a married man with three daughters, Deodata, Christina, and Cecilia. Deodata had entered the convent of Santa Susanna in Naples and risen to become the prioress there. In his will, Alonso left her 215 silver scudi with which to do good works, and a house and vineyard in Rome. His other daughters were to receive the rent from a house that was actually owned by the church of Santiago. Avila had the right to rent this house at the set price of 54 silver scudi. (In fact, he paid only 38 silver scudi per year for the house because he earned 16 scudi for his secretarial work for the church.) But in 1604 the house, which was located next to the church and included a street-level shop, was actually rented back from Avila by the church for 130 scudi. Thus, the right to rent the house at the lower price given him in the 1560s and then to rent it back to the church earned him roughly 80 scudi, and he secured these rights for his daughters even after his death.[204] Such was the complicated exchange of property and property rights that often kept Roman property in Spanish hands.

Avila was just one of many Spanish notaries who did well in Rome. Others include Blas de Cassarubios, a native of Toledo, who was a notary for the Curia.[205] When he had his will drawn up in 1561, he left his house next to the convent of Santa Maria del Popolo to his wife, Gracia Sánchez, but stipulated that after her death it should go to the church of Santiago. He also gave more than 200 scudi to various Roman churches, convents, and charities, including a share in the monte da Fe worth 100 silver scudi to the church of Santiago to say masses for his soul, 50 to the hospital of the Incurabili, 20 to the hospital of the Consolation, 20 gold scudi to the Jesuits to say masses for his soul, 30 scudi each for a silver chalice to the churches of Saint Peter and Saint Eulalia, and lesser amounts to the monastery of Saint Augustine and the monastery of the Trinity.[206]

When Gracia Sánchez de Cassarubios followed her husband to the tomb, moreover, she left 300 more scudi to the church of Santiago and placed 2,700 silver scudi in an endowment for the dowries of poor Spanish girls who wanted to enter convents.[207] Characteristic of wealthier Spanish women in Rome, Gracia Sánchez showed a particular empathy with the plight of the poor Spanish women of the city. Indeed, among the many Spanish women who left an estate and accompanying will, most bequeathed something to their own female servants and often to a general endowment for dowries.

Among the numerous Spanish women who left substantial property in Rome to benefit other Spanish women was Isabel Perez de Peramato, the unhappy estranged wife of the Italian courtier Reale Fusoritto de Narni. The case of Isabella, who had met and married her husband in Spain in the late 1560s when he was attached to the papal nuncio in Madrid, illustrates the benefits of being associated with the Spanish nation and its institutions, as well as the potential economic hazards and exploitation that even wealthy Spanish women faced.[208]

Isabella, originally from Salamanca, had accompanied her husband to Italy upon the return of his patron, Monsignor Castagnio, from Spain. Domestic life with Narni was anything but bliss, however, and she complained bitterly in a notarized letter excluding him from her will that he had paid for nothing in their house, that she only saw him at mealtimes, and that he had all but stopped living with her once he became a part of the household of Cardinal Farnese. Moreover, she claimed that "he treated me very badly both with his hands and his words, both he and his brothers . . . and he has never respected my honor, . . . and he took delight in robbing me of everything that I have and in giving it to his brothers and dishonorable women."[209]

She subsequently decided to give him nothing of her considerable remaining wealth, much of which had come from her dowry. More specifically, her will reveals that her estate contained 2,500 scudi and a vineyard in 1586. The 2,500 scudi, moreover, were invested in seven different Roman bonds that yielded 7 or 8 percent annually.[210] Not surprisingly, Narni contested the will, stating that he was entitled to the money as her husband, and the matter went to court.

Peramato, however, had named as her universal heir the church of Santiago, with the bulk of her money specified for dowries for poor Spanish girls. It was thus the church that Narni was fighting in court, and he quickly lost; a result that would quite likely not have occurred had Peramatto's heirs been other than the powerful Spanish church.[211]

Like Peramato, many wealthy Spanish women who lived and died in Rome had independent wealth that they controlled until their death.[212] María Flores, for example, was a nun in the order of Our Lady of the Immaculate Conception who maintained her own house in Rome until her death in 1583. The circumstances that brought her to Rome from her native Cuenca are unknown, but her sister, María Anna López, had also died in the city, and Flores asked to be buried next to her in the church of Santiago.[213]

With an estate worth approximately 1,500 silver scudi, this woman was a minor patron in her own right, with at least four servants (*criadas*) in her household: Catalina Muñoz, and three others identified only by the first names of Violante, Lucretia, and Perpetua. The last had become a nun in the convent of the Convertida. All these women received 6 to 10 scudi from the estate of Flores, while the major heirs of her will were the church of Santiago, which received 150 silver scudi, and future generations of poor Spanish girls in Rome who were to benefit from a dowry endowment established with 900 silver scudi. Francisco Naxo, whom Flores identified as the "oldest Spanish courtier who resides in this court," was named executor of her will.[214]

Marina Vásquez, a native of Galicia, serves as yet another example of a Spanish woman who had married an Italian, Don Giovanni Dominica Casareo, but continued to control her own wealth and to remain deeply attached to the Spanish community and church. More specifically, Vásquez asked to be buried in the church of Santiago in the same sepulcher that held her daughter Elonore; in recompense she left her house in the neighborhood of San Eustachio to the church. The rest of her wealth, which consisted of 856 silver scudi invested in the monte di Popoli Romani, was distributed among her husband, grandchildren, and nephew.[215]

Examples of similarly wealthy Spanish women in Rome could be cited many times over, but the general pattern of their relationship to Rome and the Spanish nation would be similar to that already established with the examples above. Most women remained deeply attached to the Spanish church even if they married Italian husbands, and many maintained some financial autonomy. When this was the case, they invested their wealth, much like their male Spanish counterparts, in the numerous Roman monti, thereby helping to bolster public finance in the city. At the same time, they gave proportionately more often than the men to endow dowries for poor Spanish women, gave money equal to that of men to the church of Santiago, and just as frequently requested to be buried there. They subsequently constituted a formidable part of the Spanish nation, playing the role of patronesses and taking part in many of its other charitable activities.

THE WORKING CLASS

Together with the wealthier women, families such as the Herreras and Fonsecas and the high-ranking clerics were largely responsible for the presence of another group of Iberians who gathered in Rome, the working-class Spaniards who served in their households, drove their coaches, cooked for them, and provided a variety of other services. The Spanish faction was largely an ethnic economy, and when poor Spaniards were not directly taken care of by a patron it was the confraternity that would bring the various classes together and provide the social insurance or safety net for this group. More specifically, the confraternity provided prison aid, hospital visitation and aid, pilgrim assistance, general charity, burial assistance, and dowries, which were endowed by wealthy Spaniards.

The records associated with this last charity, the giving of dowries to poor Spanish women, gives us information about this group of Spaniards, who were not usually wealthy enough to leave personal wills. By 1600 roughly thirty Spanish dowries were awarded each year on the feast of Immaculate Conception. A few months before the procession and mass held to celebrate the event, officers of the confraternity would go to the various *rioni* (neighborhoods) of Rome to interview potential recipients. The questions asked of the women were known as the *scrutinos,* or scrutinies, and the records of those interviews, preserved in varying degrees of detail, often reveal the woman's neighborhood of residence in Rome as well as her father's occupation and parents' place of origin in Iberia or Italy.[216]

From a study of 1,205 of these records over the period from 1578 to 1628, we can make the following general conclusions:

- Working-class Spaniards were present in all the neighborhoods of Rome, with the greatest concentration (26 percent) residing in the rione of Campo Marzio, also the neighborhood of the Deza palace. Another 26 percent lived in the three adjacent rioni of Ponte, Parione, and San Eustachio, where the ambassador's palace, Fonseca palace, and church of Santiago were also located.
- Members of the three major Iberian kingdoms of Castile, Aragon, and Portugal accounted for roughly 65 percent, 20 percent, and 5 percent, respectively, of the parents of girls receiving dowries. The cities of Toledo, Zamora, Seville, Burgos, Barcelona, and Cordova had the largest contingents.
- Fourteen percent of the girls had a Roman mother or father.
- Working-class Spaniards were engaged in at least 28 identified occupations. These included cooks, soldiers, tailors, painters, builders, tavern keepers, blacksmiths, sculptors, gold- and silversmiths, fishermen, and coach drivers. No particular trade was the special preserve of the Spaniards.

Briefly summarized, this information underlines the pervasive presence of the Spaniards from all regions of Iberia in the neighborhoods and workplaces of Rome, and also reveals the significant amount of intermarriage between Spaniards and Romans. This last point provides yet another indirect example of the ways by which the Spaniards built up ties with the native population but also invites speculation about the impact of Romanization on the Spanish population. While most of this chapter has focused on the cohesion and common projects of the Spanish faction and nation and the various factors that drew them together, it is also clear that loyalties could be mixed and conflicting. In the case of the working-class Spaniards in Rome, intermarriage with Romans may have diluted loyalties to the Spanish community; and the children of these unions

most certainly grew up speaking Italian and thinking of themselves as
Romans. Many Spaniards probably went native.

Nonetheless, the fact that the Confraternity of the Most Holy Resurrection and church of Santiago continued to take care of those who
claimed their Spanish ancestry even after one or two generations in the
city helped to keep Spanish identity strong long after their monarch's
political power was on the decline and large-scale Spanish immigration to
the city had stopped. The dowry records reveal, for example, that by 1630
the great majority of Spanish women receiving dowries from the confraternity and church were the grandchildren of Spaniards rather than
immigrants or their daughters.

Charity thus helped to ensure a continuing Spanish presence and
identity in Rome and also protected and furthered the reputation of the
community. As one of the most public expressions of Counter-Reformation piety, charitable giving was essential to Spanish piety and patronage
in the city.

CHAPTER 5

THE PIETY OF
SPANISH ROME

As Spanish writers, monarchs, and the Spanish faction in Rome appropriated the history of the ancient city and empire, won a dominant political and economic role in the papal court, and staked a claim to the streets and institutions of Rome itself, they also sought to capture one last major prize that the papacy had the unique right to control and dispense: the spiritual rewards and reputation of Roman Catholicism — most particularly, the celestial city of the saints whose gates the Roman canon controlled. Just as the struggle for political influence, control, and spoils in Rome was largely conducted within the boundaries of a complicated patronage system, so, too, was the competition for pious reputation, spiritual benefits, and saints. And Spaniards, both locally and internationally, were eager to prove themselves the most pious patrons among the many peoples of Christian Europe and to have their piety acknowledged both in Rome and in heaven itself. Similarly, they were anxious to gain the religious rewards such piety brought with it.

It is important to recall that the meaning and practice of Roman Catholic piety remained closely connected to social patronage systems, just as it had in classical and Christian antiquity. Central to the meaning of *pietas,* the Latin root for *piety,* was dutifulness toward family, patron, country, and the gods. It was this understanding of piety as duty within a patronage network that also occupied a central role in the religious sensibilities and mentality of the Roman Catholic world in the early modern period. Rather than attempting to examine the wide range of religious practices and beliefs that might fall under a more loosely defined piety, I shall let this more restricted, but precise, definition of piety be the one that defines the boundaries of analysis here.[1]

SPANISH CHARITY IN ROME

On July 30, 1568, the vigil of the feast of Saint James, the wife of Juan de Zúñiga, ambassador to Rome, prepared a dinner for poor mendicants in the city. She personally served the meal with the help of her two children, and when it was finished, they washed the hands of their guests and gave them alms. All this was reportedly done to fulfill a vow made by the ambassador's wife when her husband was in danger.[2]

A week later, on the feast of the Assumption, another public act of Spanish charity took place when fourteen young women were given dowries in the church of Santiago, a ritual that included a procession in the Piazza Navona. The dowries were made possible by the charitable donation of Don Constantino de Castillo, who started the Spanish tradition of endowing dowries in Rome by offering for this purpose the annual rents of three houses he owned in the city.[3]

These charitable acts, while unremarkable in themselves, were nonetheless noted by the Avvisi writer in some detail and point to both the increased frequency and the rising visibility of Spanish charity in the city beginning in the late 1560s. We have already seen that a wide range of Spaniards, including kings, ambassadors, cardinals, churchmen, and merchants, gave in varying degrees to a variety of charities, particularly during the later decades of the sixteenth century, an increase in Spanish pious bequests and charitable activities that paralleled the rise of Spanish political power, local patronage, and influence generally.

Some of this charity, such as the distribution of bread and alms to the population by the Spanish ambassador in 1605 during a time of food shortages, was certainly driven in part by political motives. The desire to build and maintain popular support for the king clearly inspired some of the more dramatic and official displays of Spanish largess that we have already noted. Similarly, concern for local Spanish reputation in Rome also played a large role in the formation of ongoing charitable institutions specifically aimed at the needs of the Spanish community. Another powerful motive — the desire to attain spiritual rewards on earth and ultimately the salvation of one's own soul — was also apparent in the charitable acts of individuals. Although judging the complicated motives of living people, not to mention those long dead, is probably best left to their confessors or their own consciences, particularly when the evidence is thin, it is clear from the wills of many Spaniards of this time that they left money to religious institutions or individuals with the specific, stated requirement that masses be said for their souls. In the most extreme cases, some Spaniards even named their own soul as the only heir of their estate, and gave all their money and property to churches that would agree to say these masses.

This, of course, was a common practice throughout medieval Europe that appears to have increased after the Council of Trent,[4] and it does not preclude the more altruistic intentions many donors may have had in making their contributions. Many Spaniards undoubtedly gave to hospitals, orphanages, churches, religious communities, poor women, and imprisoned men because of a sincere desire to help their fellow human beings or because such actions were considered their pious duty. Nonetheless, as with most duties performed in a patron-client network, there was a reward or exchange of services assumed or explicitly written into most charitable giving. The recipients of the benevolence of wealthy Spaniards were virtually always required to attend the funeral, say masses for, or privately pray for the souls of their benefactors.

Whatever the motive, the frequency and size of their charitable acts meant that the people of the Spanish faction in Rome contributed to the justifiably high reputation its members generally enjoyed in the city — even if building up that reputation was not an explicit purpose or motive of their charity, as it was in the case of more official acts of Spanish generosity. While personal memoirs or spiritual diaries that might give us more extensive insight into the religious mentalities and motives of Spanish benefactors in Rome are scarce, surviving records of the Spanish Confraternity of the Most Holy Resurrection, the church of Santiago, and Spanish notaries in the state archives provide the raw material needed to make at least an impressionistic assessment of the amount of charitable activity in Rome and its connection to the actual institutions and people of the city.

The Church of Santiago

Many acts of individual Spanish charity in Rome were noted in the previous chapter, and the fact that wealthy Spaniards frequently gave substantial sums to a variety of institutions and individuals has, by now, been clearly shown. The general pattern, or patterns, of Spanish charity in Rome, however, are less clear.

Based on an analysis of the information provided by a hundred wills of wealthy Spaniards who lived and died in Rome between 1559 and 1625, the first major conclusion that can be drawn is that of all the institutions that benefited from Spanish charitable bequests, the church of Santiago received the lion's share of donations in return for burying and saying masses for its benefactors.[5] More specifically, among the sample group, more than 60 percent left money or property to the church, including roughly 30,000 scudi in cash and seven houses, whose rents were paid to the chaplains of the church for various designated charities. Fourteen of the donors made their bequests in the form of bonds held in the various monti of Rome. Typically, the interest earned on these bonds was designated for the saying of a certain number of masses each year.

In fact, we know more definitely from a document entitled *Libro de Rentas* from the church of Santiago's archive that the amount of income the church received from bonds, houses, and other cash bequests tripled between 1560 and 1590, during the period of greatest Spanish influence and social prominence in Rome. While the church claimed an income of 20,000 scudi from "houses, interest income, and cash" in 1560, by 1590 it was claiming 60,905 scudi of income. Moreover, in 1585, when Cardinal Deza made an official visit to the church to monitor its finances and general administration, the church was collecting income from ninety-seven houses acquired in the city through bequests and its own investments.[6]

This considerable endowment came with a great many strings and stipulations attached as each individual donor made different requests. When Don Juan de Landa, a canon from Palencia, left the church 800 scudi invested in the monte Julio, for example, he stipulated that the annual interest of his investment should pay the salary of a new chaplain for the church, who would receive 84 scudi a year. This new chaplain (who would bring the number of permanent priests working in the church of Santiago to twenty) was required to say masses on Monday, Wednesday, and Friday at the privileged altars of the churches of the Orfanelli, Santa Maria in Aracoeli, and the hospital of San Giacomo degli Incurabili, for himself, the souls in Purgatory, the commemoration of the Cross, and the commemoration of the Trinity. On Tuesday and Sunday he was to say masses with special intentions for the church and hospital of Santiago.[7]

Similarly, when the *scriptor apostólico* (papal notary), Alonso de Avellano from Toledo, left a vineyard he owned outside of the Porto del Popolo to the church, he specified that the money from the sale of the land be used to build and maintain a chapel dedicated to Saint Peter and Saint Paul in the church of Santiago. Along with this gift, which was valued at 1,000 scudi, Avellano also left the church 847 scudi invested in the monte Pio of Rome and 200 scudi in cash on condition that the priests of the church say one mass for his soul every day and one solemn requiem mass annually.[8]

This request for a daily mass in perpetuo with the high payment of more than 1,000 scudi was also made by Magdalena de Palma in 1596,[9] but such sums were rare among the Spaniards. Rather, requests for weekly masses were more the norm among those who could afford it. Gracia Sánchez, for example, designated 300 scudi for a weekly mass in 1575;[10] Fernando García de Oxeda gave 500 for a weekly memorial mass and an annual sung mass on the anniversary of his death in 1579;[11] Pedro Chacón gave 872 for a weekly mass and two annual sung masses in 1581;[12] Guillermo Ferrante from Portugal gave the church a house in return for five monthly masses in 1598;[13] the banker Juan Enríquez de Herrera paid to build a chapel dedicated to San Diego of Alcalá in 1601 and endowed it with a bond on condition that he and his family be buried in the chapel and weekly masses be said for them;[14] and Gaspar de la Concha gave the church his coach, horses, and household goods worth a total of 319 scudi for a weekly mass in 1604.[15] These examples could be multiplied many times, and there were even more Spaniards who requested that fewer masses be said for them during the year with accompanying donations to the church.

For those who requested smaller numbers of masses, moreover, the records provide a revealing look at the devotional preference of the donors because they often specified the feast days on which the masses were to be said. The Spanish priest Don Francisco de Viedo, for instance, left the church 360 scudi in 1571 with the request that sixteen masses be said for him annually on the following feast days: the Nativity, Transfiguration, Ascension, and Resurrection of Christ; the Purification and Assumption of Mary; Saint Paul, Saint Peter, Saint John, Saint Ann, Saint Michael, and Saint Francis.[16] Similarly, Diego of Sahelizes from Segovia gave the church 100 scudi in 1603 with the obligation to say eighteen annual masses; six of these were designated for the feasts of Saint Peter, Saint Paul, San Lorenzo, Santiago, the Nativity, and All Saints.[17] Doctor Jerónimo González gave the church an annuity in the monte Sisto in 1609 with the obligation that ten annual masses be said for him on the feasts of the Nativity, the Resurrection, the Holy Spirit, Corpus Christi, the Conception and Assumption of Mary, Saint Michael, Saint Jerome, and All Souls.[18] One year later, Felice Perez, from Alcalá de Henares, specified that five masses be said for her on the five Marian feasts of the Conception, Nativity, Annunciation, Purification, and Assumption;[19] and in 1617, Alonso Rodriguez de Escobar, a priest from Placencia, gave the church 120 scudi in return for twelve annual masses to be said on the feasts of All Souls, All Saints, Saint Joseph, Saint Ildephonso, and the eight Marian feasts, which include the five listed above and the Presentation, Visitation, and Expectation.[20]

Again, these examples could be multiplied many times, and the pattern they establish points to some general facts about Spanish devotional life in Rome among the upper and upper-middle class. First devotion to and trust in the intercessory power of Christ, Mary, and the major saints characterized the piety of this group. Following a pattern noted by William Christian in late sixteenth- and seventeenth-century Spain, devotions centered on the life of Christ were on the rise, Marian devotions remained strong and took on an even greater prominence, and devotion to the broader pantheon of saints decreased.[21] Still, devotion to the major saints of Rome, Peter and Paul, remained strong, as did trust in the intercessory power of Santiago, Saint Joseph, Saint Francis, and a few others.

Another related fact about Spanish piety that the Spaniards' charitable giving makes clear is that the majority of Spanish donations to the church of Santiago were dependent upon help for the donor's own soul in the afterlife and a general fear of divine judgment. Most Spaniards clearly thought that they would be spending a considerable stretch of time in Purgatory, and the masses they secured with their donations were meant to make the transitional time from Purgatory to Paradise as short as possible. Masses said on specific feasts at altars that had been given a special indulgence or dispensation by the papacy were meant to honor the heavenly patron and invoke his or her intercession on the donor's behalf in order to shorten the sentence. Similar to the religious and social mentality of late antique Christianity described by Peter Brown, it was still "this hope of amnesty that pushed the saint to the forefront as *patronus*" in the minds of many Spaniards in Rome.[22] It was this same mentality, moreover, that motivated the Spaniards to have their own holy men and women officially declared saints so that they could be assured of celestial patrons from their own lands.

Dowries

After the church of Santiago, the next largest group of recipients of charitable bequests was poor women from the Spanish faction and nation who were given dowries. The dowries mentioned previously were a clear example of a Spanish charity that was deeply tied to Spanish reputation in the city. A practical concern that certainly contributed to the popularity of dowries as a charity was the desire to keep Spanish women from practicing the oldest profession and tarnishing the collective image of Spaniards. The stereotype of the Spanish whore in Rome, already present in the literature of the 1520s as Delicado's *Lozana* amply portrays, was a blemish on the collective Spanish reputation. Moreover, legal records and Avvisi accounts of the late sixteenth century provide real-life counterparts to Lozana. The Spanish courtesans that Clement VIII wanted to expel from Rome in 1592 along with Italian whores, for example, were reportedly being driven from the city in part upon the insistence of Spaniards, for whom they were an embarrassment.[23] The nineteen women eventually stayed in Rome after begging the pope for a pardon and proclaiming their desire to marry or otherwise repent,[24] but they, or other Spanish women, such as Francesca de Avila, continued in their profession well into the seventeenth century.[25]

Together with this practical concern of keeping Spanish women from harming both their own reputation and the collective reputation of the Spaniards, giving dowries also had the effect of displaying the generosity and charitable piety of the Spaniards not only toward their own but to the broader Spanish faction and population of Rome. The practice of giving dowries to poor and working-class women in Rome was a well-established charity of the papacy by the late sixteenth century.[26] The annual distribution of the papal dowries — initially under the administration of the Confraternity of the Gonfalone but by the early seventeenth century under the direction of the Confraternity of the Annunciation — took place in the church of Santa Maria Sopra Minerva and was a major public event noted by court observers.[27]

The Spanish monarchy, too, was known to practice this charity on a large scale when trying to win over newly conquered populations as, for example, when Philip II was reported to have promised Portugal 50,000 ducats annually for dowries after annexing the kingdom in 1580.[28] Although it is difficult to establish a direct tie between this practice and the endowment of Spanish dowries in Rome, it is important to note the various motives involved in the endowment of dowries in the period and how the dowries fit into a broader pattern of piety, patronage, and social control.

In the case of the young women and their families in Rome who benefited from the Spanish dowries, the charity certainly had the effect of underlining their dependence on, and connection to, the Spanish community. At the same time, the Spanish nation, and especially the church of Santiago and the Confraternity of the Most Holy Resurrection, gained religious reputation from the annual distribution of the dowries. The event was usually noted by the Avvisi writers, and even a popular pilgrims' guide to the churches of Rome, first written in Italian during the reign of Sixtus V and later translated into Spanish, described the event: "On the day of our Lady in August a very solemn procession is held in the said church, in which twenty or twenty-two poor virgins take part, who are given a dowry sufficient to allow them to marry."[29]

Apart from the papacy, the Spanish nation was the only major faction or foreign nation in Rome that distributed dowries on an annual basis on such a large scale, and the event further demonstrated its wealth and social power as well as its piety. Moreover, the numbers of dowries continued to rise with the growth of various endowments so that by 1600 more than thirty dowries were typically distributed each year. Table 3 shows the numbers of women receiving dowries in the period from 1567 to 1625.[30]

The growth in this particular charity was directly attributable to the growing numbers of Spaniards who gave considerable parts of their estates to the church of Santiago or the Confraternity of the Most Holy Resurrection to endow and administer dowries. More specifically, between 1566 and 1624 ten primary benefactors made the contributions that would constitute the majority of the capital for the endowment: Constantino de Castillo, Isabel Perez de Peramato, Fernando García de Oxeda, Blas de Cassarubios and Gracia Sánchez, María Flores, Antonio Fonseca, Jerónimo Fonseca, Don Pedro de Foix Montoya, and Manuel Mendez de Paz.

The endowments, which were administered together by the Confraternity of the Most Holy Resurrection and church of Santiago, varied in size and stipulations attached, but they usually came in the form of either a house whose rents were designated for the dowries or capital invested in the monti of Rome, the interest of which was used to pay

TABLE 3: NUMBER OF DOWRY RECIPIENTS IN THE
SPANISH COMMUNITY IN ROME

1567	10	1587	20	1607	16
1568	14	1588	12	1608	27
1569	10	1589	16	1609	19
1570	10	1590	28	1610	33
1571	10	1591	23	1611	29
1572	10	1592	17	1612	29
1573	14	1593	21	1613	27
1574	11	1594	26	1614	26
1575	21	1595	29	1615	36
1576	14	1596	30	1616	34
1577	16	1597	31	1617	31
1578	16	1598	37	1618	25
1579	26	1599	31	1619	31
1580	28	1600	30	1620	34
1581	19	1601	35	1621	32
1582	20	1602	38	1622	26
1583	21	1603	35	1623	25
1584	16	1604	41	1624	31
1585	17	1605	20	1625	30
1586	22	1606	no record		

for the dowries. By 1625 five houses and roughly 12,000 scudi made up the permanent capital that funded the charity, and the fluctuation in the number of dowries coincided with the changing yield of the annuities. Although the records do not provide the exact sums given out each year, they do contain scattered annual figures, which ranged from a high of 1,600 scudi (thirty-six dowries) in 1615 to a low of 988 scudi (twenty-five dowries) in 1618. The actual amount of the individual dowries by 1600 was roughly 45 silver scudi.[31]

A closer look at the individual bequests reveals that three houses came from Constantino de Castillo[32] and one each from Blas de Cassarubios[33] and Jerónimo Fonseca.[34] Large bequests from investments in the monti, on the other hand, included 2,700 scudi from Gracia Sánchez held in the monte da Fe;[35] 2,000 scudi from Isabel Perez de Peramato;[36] 1,100 scudi from Fernando García de Oxeda;[37] 900 scudi from María Flores;[38] 2,000 scudi from Antonio Fonseca;[39] 300 scudi from Pedro de Foix Montoya;[40] and 2,700 scudi from Manuel Mendez de Paz.[41]

The distribution of the dowries, possibly more than any other Spanish charity, touched a broad range of people in the Spanish nation and faction, as well as in the city of Rome at large. Each year as many as twelve official visitors from the church and confraternity were sent out to the neighborhoods of Rome to examine poor families to determine who would qualify for a dowry. The visitors asked specific questions about the women's place of birth, the parents' economic and marital status, and the reputation of the woman and her family. More specifically, the visitors were to make sure that the women were not illegitimate, that they were held to be virgins, that they were at least fifteen years old, that they had no dowry, and that their parents were "wretched and poor people who do not have anything to marry them with."[42] They were also required to be born "of Spanish parents, Castilians being those who come first and after them Valencians, Aragonese, Navarras, Catalans, Portuguese." Lacking enough women from these places, women from Burgundy, Germany, Flanders, Siena, Naples, and Sardinia could be considered, in that order.[43] Finally, among those who met these prerequisites, priority was to be given to orphans and to the oldest women of the poorest and most reputable parents.[44]

With these basic qualifications serving as the criteria, women were chosen by the officers of the church and confraternity in a secret ballot held in the chapel of the Immaculate Conception in the church of Santiago. Four days before the feast of the Immaculate Conception, those who were to receive dowries learned the good news when they were secretly brought the white cloth needed to make the dress they would wear during the ritual, along with money to buy white shoes and a veil.[45]

One can only speculate about the effect this highly ritualized annual event had on the people of the Spanish faction and nation, as well as on the city of Rome. Certainly the season of the visits would have been one of high anxiety and expectation for the many poor women who had a chance of receiving their passport to a good marriage. More important, for those chosen the week of the ritual would have been one of busy, happy activity that culminated in the walk through Rome to the church of Santiago, where the dowries were formally presented.

This annual spectacle of women dressed in white dresses and veils walking through the neighborhoods of Rome and converging in the Piazza Navona was good press for the Spaniards, and we can safely assume that it was an event that most of Rome knew about. It is no sur-

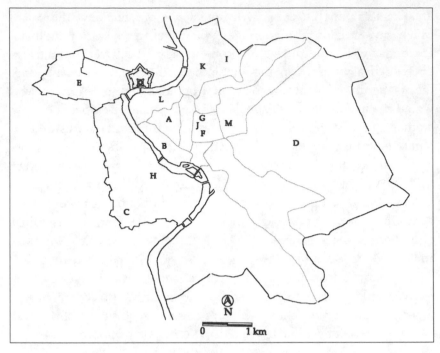

(A) Church of Santiago; (B) Santa Maria di Monserrato; (C) San Pietro in Montorio;
(D) Santa Maria Maggiore; (E) Saint Peter's (F) Church of the Gesù; (G) San Ignazio;
(H) Santa Maria della Scala; (I) Palazzo di Spagna; (J) Palazzo Fonseca; (K) Palazzo Deza
(Borghese); (L) Palazzo Avila; (M) Palazzo Colonna

prise, then, that the Avvisi writers took note of the celebration almost
every year, as they did with many major civic and religious rituals and
processions, and that the event reinforced the image of the Spaniards as
important charitable patrons of the city.

SPANISH SAINT-MAKING

While wealthy Spanish individuals and powerful institutions like the
church of Santiago played the role of generous Christian patron
to the people of Rome, a simultaneous, well-orchestrated effort was
being undertaken by the Spanish monarchs, the religious orders, and
their agents in the city to have the papacy officially acknowledge the piety
of the people of Iberia both past and present by canonizing the most holy

among them—by making Spanish saints. Just as the celestial patronage of the saints mirrored and reinforced the terrestrial power of the political patrons in late antiquity and the medieval period, so too did the new saints of the Counter-Reformation reflect and bolster the political power of the absolutist monarchs of Spain. This was an integral part of the Spanish program in Rome, and it, too, involved gaining reputation and rewards that had been largely denied to the Iberian peninsula during the previous four centuries.

The importance of having Iberians included in the Roman calendar must be seen against the relatively barren medieval backdrop that André Vauchez has described in great detail for the period from 1198 to 1431.[46] During those years only one Iberian—Dominic, founder of the Order of Preachers—was canonized, and his cause was pushed primarily by his followers in Italy and France, where he had spent most of his adult life.[47] This dismal record was not for want of trying, however, since the kings of Aragon, in particular, had often lobbied the papacy on behalf of their most pious subjects. The case of Raymundo of Peñafort, the famous Dominican from Barcelona, was one of the most notable (see below); but all the royal efforts were in vain, and the medieval papacy failed even to initiate a process of canonization at the request of an Iberian monarch in this period.[48] This snubbing from Rome was taking place, moreover, at the same time that canonizations of new saints from France, England, Germany, Italy, Eastern Europe, and even Scandinavia were multiplying.

The fact that the lack of official saints constituted an international failure on the part of the Iberian monarchies and church was not lost on Philip II nor on Iberian religious orders and bishops, who set out to correct the historical imbalance. Not surprisingly, in this area Philip was again a tenacious driving force, and he was largely responsible for both the first Catholic Reformation saint and the first Iberian saint to be added to the Roman calendar in more than a century.[49] The long process that eventually led to the canonization of Diego of Alcalá stretched out over twenty-five years, and its successful culmination was possibly the strongest symbolic testimony to that time of the growing power and influence of the Spanish monarch in Rome.[50]

Although the canonization did not occur until 1588, the process began decades earlier, when the king and high-ranking magistrates and churchmen from Alcalá first began writing to Rome to push the cause of the fifteenth-century Franciscan Diego of Alcalá (1400?–1463).[51] According to a long account of the process written by the auditor of the Rota, Francisco Peña, who himself reviewed all documents concerning the canonization along with the other auditors, letters advocating the cause began coming to Rome in 1562 and 1563 from the archbishop of Toledo; the magistrates and noblemen of Alcalá; the abbot and chapter of the church of Saint Justin and Pastor in Alcalá, where Diego had lived; the Franciscan provincial of Castile; the rector and faculty of the university of Alcalá; and the king.[52]

Although this significant number of powerful religious and civic advocates points to a relatively widespread Castilian effort for the canonization, it was an effort initiated and carefully orchestrated by the monarchy. From the perspective of an early Italian account of the events leading up to the canonization, it was "the church of Toledo, the magistrates of Alcalá, the religious congregations, and all of Spain, following the example of their great king," who eagerly sought the canonization.[53] In fact, the event that precipitated this sudden outpouring of support for Diego was the healing early in 1562 of Philip's son Prince Carlos, which was attributed to the intercessory powers of Diego. More specifically, the healing was attributed to the power of Diego's corpse, which had been brought to the prince's room when all medical interventions had failed to cure him of injuries "judged by the doctors grave and fatal" suffered when he slipped and fell down the stairs at the royal palace in Alcalá. The king himself had ordered the body of the saint brought to the prince's bedside, and it was reported that as soon as the boy's attendants placed his hand on the holy man's body, the illness left him and he quickly recovered.[54]

The central piece of testimony in the process, moreover, was a series of letters written by the king testifying to this "well-known miracle" performed by Diego.[55] According to the king's first letter in 1563, the prince had been close to death and without any further hope of human remedy, when God, through the intercession of Diego, saved him. It was in recognition of this miracle and to thank God for such a gift that Philip was now asking the pope to canonize the saint.[56] To that end, he had instructed his ambassador to collect and present all the supporting testimony and proof for the cause of Diego.

These early efforts of the king and the other Castilian churchmen and magistrates moved slowly, however, and no fewer than three popes — Pius IV, Pius V, and Gregory XIII — delayed the canonization and continued to ask for more documentation and testimony. This papal caution

was certainly due in part to the general criticism aimed at the entire cult
of the saints and the veneration of relics which had reached a peak in
the early sixteenth century. Although the third session of the Council of
Trent in 1563 had clearly supported the veneration of the saints and their
relics and reaffirmed that it was the pope who was uniquely endowed
with the power of canonization, the first popes after the end of the council
proved themselves reluctant to act on these powers.[57]

In the case of Diego of Alcalá, this reluctance was probably compounded by the fact that the life of the Franciscan friar was not well
documented. His parentage and date of birth remained unknown, for example, and originally there was no detailed biography, or vita, on which
to build a case for canonization. In 1566 the Spanish ambassador in Rome
wrote to Prince Carlos notifying him that the pope was asking for the life
story (legenda) of Diego together with his death date and the records of
the process undertaken in Spain.[58] Since no written legenda existed, the
prince ordered the royal historian and professor of rhetoric from Alcalá
de Henares, Ambrosio Morales, to write one.[59] Morales was also named
an official procurator for the cause of the saint in 1567.[60]

In what remains the earliest official life, Morales was able to produce
no more than six pages, or nine paragraphs, of text giving only a rough
outline of the life of Diego. This brief sketch includes a description of his
humble but uncertain origins in the diocese of Córdoba, his early life as
a hermit, his love of poverty and entrance into the Franciscan order, his
piety as a Franciscan, his missionary work in the Canary Islands, his journey to Rome for the Jubilee year of 1450, his last years and death in Alcalá
in 1463, and the exhumation of his body in the sixteenth century.[61] This
was hardly a detailed biography or a heroic epic, but it reflected the extent
of the historical knowledge that formed the core of the subsequent legen-
das by Francisco Peña and Pietro Gallesini. It also revealed how little was
actually known about Diego that could be attributed to solid historical
evidence, such as memoirs or testimonies by Diego's contemporaries.

Although they lacked a more richly documented life which could
overwhelmingly establish the first prerequisite for canonization, sanctity
of life, Diego's advocates built up the second area that was essential for
sainthood: miracles performed either during his life or after his death
which were attributed to his intercession. The healing of Prince Carlos
was the most important of these, but other pieces of supporting testimony supplied by the commission of bishops in Spain appointed to over-

see the collection of information for the cause included a collection of 130 examples of miracles attributed to Diego.[62]

Among these, the first was not actually caused by the intercession of the saint but rather was a miracle attributed directly to God that pointed to the holiness of Diego. This was the preservation of the body of the holy man in a state of incorruptibility. The abbot of the monastery of Saint Hilary in Alcalá, where the body of Diego was kept, testified to its state when it was exhumed in the mid-sixteenth century, roughly a hundred years after its original burial. According to Gallesini's account, an "odor of marvelous sweetness" came from the body when the tomb was opened.[63] Moreover, the body that originally had become "black by fasting, abstinence, and the lack of nourishment, after death had become white."[64] This extraordinary claim, with its implications about the origins of Diego—could he have been of Moorish extraction with darker skin?—and its convenient transformation of the dark man into a white saint, was yet another step in the creation of a Counter-Reformation saint palatable to both the Spanish plaintiffs and the Roman judges of the case.

Other miracles attributed directly to the intercession of the saint were primarily cures of a variety of illnesses: Constanza de Mendoza was cured of a fever; an unnamed man "of noble blood" was cured of leprosy after drinking water from the place where the saint had washed his hands; Catarina Martinez, a paralytic, was cured after praying at his tomb; Maria Flores from Toledo, who had "gone mad" for two months after giving birth, was cured after her husband made a vow to the saint; Juan Martinez, who had not been able to urinate for thirty days, passed a great stone "that could not have passed naturally" while praying at the tomb of the saint one night; and Alfonso Cardero, who had suffered lance wounds to the face and body at the Battle of Navarre that had left his mouth and eyes deformed, was returned to his former "beauty" after praying to the saint for nine days.[65]

In his account Gallesini stressed that he was recounting only those miracles that had been verified by "the voices of almost all of Spain" and "confirmed with notarized documents."[66] This concern with the official appearance and authenticity of the testimony, as well as with the status and number of witnesses, was especially common after 1588, when the Congregation of Rites was formed to oversee all canonization processes. But the case of Diego of Alcalá revealed how the Spaniards had already begun to develop the practice of authenticating in their own right. With

Philip II, a master of bureaucratic process and the use of documentation as a tool of statecraft, pushing the cause, this was to be expected; and it was certainly due in part to the king's ability to work the machinery of papal bureaucracy personally and through his agents that the cause of Diego was brought to a successful end.

It was not simply a matter of mastering the process, however. As with many other aspects of the relationship between king and papacy, saint-making was an area marked by the reciprocal exchange of favors or gifts. In the case of Diego of Alcalá, it was by no means clear that the Spaniards would succeed in getting the Franciscan into the Roman calendar, given the sketchy details of his life, the lack of living witnesses to most of his reported miracles, and the general reluctance of the papacy to canonize. While the Spaniards had done everything they could to present as strong a case as possible, three popes postponed the matter, possibly because of serious doubts about the strength of the cause. By the time Sixtus V came to power, then, it was clear that everything the Spaniards could do had been done, and the ultimate decision rested with the pope. The act of canonization, in a word, had become by that point a favor that only the pope could dispense, and Sixtus V knew well how to use his favors.

Although it is difficult to trace the multiple motives of Sixtus in making the decision to canonize Diego—it almost certainly helped that both Diego and Sixtus were Franciscans—or what precise exchange the pope may have had in mind, the political context and pressures of the 1580s provide some clues. It should be remembered, most noticeably, that from the beginning of his reign in 1585, the pope had been urging Philip II to invade England.[67] Although he personally pledged a million scudi to the campaign, Sixtus was well aware that only the king of Spain could undertake such an expensive war. Thus, when Philip finally made the commitment to this favorite cause of the pope's, it was perceived as an act that deserved a substantial papal response and favor, such as the long-sought canonization of Diego of Alcalá.

While this juxtaposition of the famous expedition of the Spanish Armada in 1588 and the canonization of the first Counter-Reformation saint may appear hard to substantiate at first sight, it was clearly the view of some contemporary observers, including one of the major contemporary historians of the canonization. According to Gallesini, Sixtus "wanted especially to gladden Spain with the joy of such a great gift, and above all others, King Philip" since "the difficult and dangerous war with

England was near."⁶⁸ The pope, according to this view, saw that the king had justly decided to wage war with the Protestant Elizabeth because of her heresy and tyrannical rule. Although the Catholic King had assembled a great number of ships and soldiers, Sixtus wanted to provide the expedition with the "help of God" and knew that they "needed above all else celestial defenders." It was this pressing need, finally, that led the pope to canonize Diego.⁶⁹

Thus, on July 2, 1588, the still unfinished basilica of Saint Peter was elaborately decorated for the first canonization of a Roman Catholic saint to take place in more than sixty years. A large platform had been built just inside the main doors and was covered with richly brocaded cloth and silk tapestries embroidered in gold that included a centrally placed piece showing the descent of the Holy Spirit on the apostles. In the center of the platform was a newly crafted wooden altar covered with velvet and sheltered by an ornate baldachin. On the four corners of the platform hung four large standards that had been painted with the image of the new saint, the coat of arms of Pope Sixtus V, and the coat of arms of King Philip II. Immediately in front of the altar and platform another large image of the new saint's insignia as well as the papal and Spanish royal coats of arms were fashioned out of flowers and plants.

People had begun filling the church and the piazza of Saint Peter's the day before the event so that by the morning of the canonization the crowd spilled out all the way to the street of Borgo Nuovo. Early in the morning the pope gathered in the Sistine Chapel with forty cardinals and a number of Roman noblemen, high clergymen, and foreign ambassadors. Cardinal Deza, who was officially representing Philip II, had three large white candles, also decorated with the coats of arms of the pope and king, which he and the ambassadors of Venice and Savoy carried at the head of the procession. They moved out of the Sistine Chapel, through the piazza of Saint Peter's, and into the church. A choir of clergymen sang hymns, trumpets played, and "the pope, the cardinals, the patriarchs, the archbishops, and all the other prelates who were in the procession in great number carried in their hands candles made of white wax, given to all of them . . . by the ministers of King Philip, at whose urging these solemnities were held."⁷⁰

When the pope was finally seated, Cardinal Deza and Pompeo Arigone, the king's official advocate for the canonization, approached the papal throne and "beseeched the pope humbly in the name of the king for blessed Diego to be declared a saint." The request was made three times, after which the pope read the declaration of canonization. Cardinal Deza thanked Sixtus V "in the name of the king," the Te Deum and mass were sung, and outside in the piazza and at Castel Sant'Angelo cannons fired to herald the event and start the day of public festivities.[71]

This brief description of the canonization, a ritual that lies at the heart of papal prerogative, is remarkable for the Spanish stamp that had been put on the ceremony. In fact, considered along with the other rituals that have been described up to this point, the canonization stands out as possibly the most important example yet of the Spanish having "arrived" in Rome and at the center of papal power.

The author of the account from which my description is derived was not exaggerating when he stated that the solemnities were undertaken at the insistence of the king, and it was no accident that the Spanish monarch's coat of arms was prominently displayed on the standards, candles, and floral displays that decorated the basilica. Indeed, Philip II's agents in Rome had been largely responsible for the decorations of the church, and the king himself took responsibility for the large bill of more than 20,000 ducats for the cost of the elaborate affair.[72]

The ornate and expensive ceremonies were surely perceived as fitting for what Francisco Peña described as the "supreme honor" the Roman Catholic Church could offer, and the central role that the representatives and representations of the king of Spain had in the ceremony was clearly meant to emphasize to everyone present "that heaven has filled glorious and fortunate Spain with many graces and divine favors." The greatest of these favors, moreover, were the "holy men, who, born there, and practicing every virtue, and a holy and pure life, acquired much grace, and dignity, so that they came to merit in the Roman Catholic Church the supreme honor, being canonized, and proposed to the Christian people as examples to imitate in every holy action, and as intercessors in heaven for those who piously make recourse to them."[73]

With the canonization, then, Philip II had won for himself and the people of his realms pious reputation and the "celestial patronage" of a new saint. Even with the failed expedition of the "invincible Armada," Diego of Alcalá continued to be seen as a personal advocate for the Catholic King. When the old monarch was suffering from a serious illness in 1596, for example, it was reported in Rome that there was still hope for him through the intercession of San Diego, who favored the king and was credited with giving him three victories in battle and close to ten more years of life since his canonization.[74]

While Diego was the only new Spanish saint to be canonized in Philip II's lifetime, he was not the only person from the Spanish Empire to be proposed for the honor. In fact, Spanish efforts, both royal and ecclesiastical, to make more Spanish saints in the late sixteenth century grew continuously and bore their most abundant fruit in the seventeenth. In the words of Pierre Delooz, "The seventeenth century was the century of Spanish canonizations."[75] Diego of Alcalá's canonization can thus be seen as the prelude or test case that sharpened the Spaniards' adeptness at the practice of saint-making and emboldened them to pursue the status for numerous other holy men and women from Iberia.

The next success came in 1601, when the second of six Spaniards to be canonized between 1588 and 1625, Raymundo of Peñafort (1175–1275), was raised to the status of saint. The case for this thirteenth-century Dominican had already been compiled shortly after his death, and King James of Aragon, together with high-ranking Dominicans, had done everything possible in the early fourteenth century to convince Pope John XXII, then residing in Avignon, of Raymundo's worthiness. As noted above, however, the process of 1318 was unsuccessful and the case lay dormant for close to three centuries.[76]

In 1595, however, the cause of Raymundo was again taken up by Philip II and the Dominican Order, and shortly thereafter it was officially considered by the Congregation of Rites.[77] The Catholic King's personal letter to the pope in 1595 recommending the case was the leading piece of evidence; it was also placed at the front of the official volume of testimony compiled by the congregation together with a similar letter by Philip III.[78] The original process from 1318, which was only 60 folios in length, constituted the core of the 1596 process as well, but the proficient Spanish compilers of saintly testimony had added to the original so that the new, expanded version of Raymundo's life and miracles filled up 332 folios.

The process included much testimony about the holiness of the saint that emphasized his love of the poor, preaching against the Waldensian heretics, teaching among his Dominican brothers, work as a confessor, and purity of example. Ninety miracles were also attributed to the intercession of Raymundo. Of these, eleven had been "authenticated by those who had seen the process and referred to the pope in the consistory."[79]

A few examples of the accepted miracles included the case of a para-
lyzed and mute man named Barcello from Barcelona who, when asked
by Raymundo if he wanted to confess his sins, miraculously recovered
his speech, made a full confession, and then peacefully died; the case of
a fellow Dominican who was cured of the temptations of the flesh when
he prayed to the saint; the curing of a leper on the day of the saint's death;
the curing of Michele Amati of the plague; and the apparent recovery
of a girl named Margarita, who appeared to have died of a bad fever but
returned to life when the saint's intercession was invoked.[80]

Unlike the cause of Diego of Alcalá, that of Raymundo of Peñafort
came to a relatively quick conclusion. The fact that there had already been
a strong history written by the Dominicans in the fourteenth century
probably helped the case, and this saint was also promoted by a pope,
Clement VIII. There were also powerful members of the Spanish faction
on the Congregation of Rites, moreover, such as Cardinals Gesualdo,
Colonna, and Farnese.[81] Francisco Peña, too, was again instrumental in
pushing the case in his role as auditor of the Rota, which reviewed the
process before it was presented to the pope.[82]

In the political arena, moreover, there was again cause in 1601 for the
pope to be pleased with the actions of the king of Spain and predisposed
to reward him with the honor of a new saint, albeit for different reasons
from those that had motivated Sixtus V. Clement VIII's favorable review
of the case of Raymundo of Peñafort coincided with the signing of the
Treaty of Lyons in January 1601 between France and Savoy. The pope had
a personal stake in the matter since papal mediators were responsible for
the successful negotiations, and Philip III's cooperation in the negotiations with France also fed the pope's continued hope for a French-Spanish
alliance against the Turks.[83] The successful negotiations and cooperation
between the two powers thus raised the international political stature
of Rome and the reputation of Clement himself and left him favorably
disposed toward the Catholic King.

The celebrations in which Raymundo of Peñafort became an official
saint again carried a decidedly Spanish stamp and a large price tag: 25,000
scudi.[84] In addition to the ritual in the basilica of Saint Peter's, there was
a large procession from Saint Peter's to the church of the Minerva and
the Catalan church of Santa Maria de Montserrat on the Via de Montserrat. Led by Dominicans who carried the standards of the saint, the other
dominant group in the procession was made up of Spaniards, who fol-

lowed carrying torches. After leaving one standard at the church of Santa Maria de Montserrat, the procession went to Santa Maria Sopra Minerva, where the Dominicans had elaborately decorated the church and piazza for a public feast. The Spanish Dominican Michel Llot de Ribera, who was the king's procurator for the cause, organized all the celebrations, and one of the standards was sent back to the Catholic King.[85]

Like the annual Spanish Easter procession in the Piazza Navona, the procession celebrating the canonization of Raymundo of Peñafort can be seen as an example of Spanish triumphalism played out on the Roman stage. Indeed, successful Spanish saint-making, while not as frequent as the Easter celebration, gave the Spanish nation and its various contingent groups in the city the opportunity to parade the spoils of victory as did few other occasions. Carrying the painted image of the saint from Saint Peter's through the center of the city like a conquering hero, the Spaniards who dominated the procession made it clear that this was their hero, a hero now permanently part of the Roman pantheon of saints, and a powerful celestial patron.

This triumphalism of Spanish saints reached its apex in 1622 during the pontificate of Gregory XV, just as the Spanish nation in Rome was enjoying what was to be its last period of papal favor as the most powerful and privileged foreign faction in Rome. It was in that year, on March 12, that not one, or two, or three Spaniards were canonized, but four: Teresa of Avila (1515–1582), Ignatius of Loyola (1491–1556), Isidore the plowman (1070–1130), and Francis Xavier (1506–1552). Together with one Italian, Philip Neri, they were to join the Roman calendar in what was to be the most extravagant celebration of saint-making in the entire century.

Of the four Spanish saints, the case for Isidore was clearly the hardest to establish in the late sixteenth or early seventeenth century, given the five centuries that had passed since his death in 1130. A humble layman and farmer, Isidore was essentially a local holy man of Madrid whose fame and fortune grew with that of the city. By the 1590s, with the monarch residing in or near Madrid constantly, the king and local clergy apparently thought that the center of the court deserved its own patron saint. Thus, in 1593 Philip II appointed one of his court preachers, Juan Guitierrez, as an official procurator for the cause of Isidore in Rome, and the bishop of Madrid and theologians from the university there began to organize the process.[86]

The body of Isidore was located in the church of Saint Andre in

Madrid, and beginning in 1593 testimonies from people who had been aided through his intercession began to be compiled officially. By 1613, more than 210 testimonies attesting to miraculous interventions by Isidore had been gathered, and Pope Paul V, at the urging of Philip III and the archbishop of Toledo, had ordered the Congregation of Rites to begin a full review of the process from Madrid.[87]

As in the previous cases for Spanish canonizations, the success of Isidore's process was largely due to the tenacity and bureaucratic efficiency of the Spanish saint-makers: the monarchs, the local clergy and theologians, and the Spanish procurators in Rome. The vita of Isidore, after all, was even leaner than that of Diego of Alcalá and lacked any heroic religious background in missionary work, preaching, or priestly ministry. Thus, with only the more recent miracles constituting the foundation of the case, the authority that royal letters and hundreds of notarized documents lent to the various testimonies of cures and other miracles attributed to Isidore was central to the task of establishing the appearance of legitimacy for the Roman judges of the case and succeeded in getting them to rule in its favor.

The same pattern of collecting as much evidence as possible and supporting it with numerous official letters from royalty, high-ranking clergy, and civil authorities held true for the other saints of 1622, but the cases of Teresa of Avila, Ignatius of Loyola, and Francis Xavier were much easier to make because of their fame and the large number of contemporaries who had given official testimony to their sanctity of life.

The case of Teresa, in particular, provides the best example yet of both the extraordinary efforts made in support of a Spanish holy woman or man and of a person who was reconfigured as a saint of the entire Spanish Empire. The records compiled in Spain and sent to Rome to be considered by the Congregation of Rites began with letters from Philip II, Philip III, Philip III's wife, Queen Margarita, and Don Juan de Henestrosa, the secretary for the Kingdom of Castile.[88] Among these, the letter by Henestrosa was the most eloquent expression of both the general importance of saints for Spain and the specific role of Teresa for the empire. He wrote,

> Among the many and great benefits that these kingdoms of Spain have received and receive every day from the hand of God one is the great devotion and reverence that the natives of them have for the saints and

their relics, and continuing these favors, his Divine Majesty has been served to give them in these times men and women who, inspired and illuminated with his grace, have advanced such perfection of virtue and holiness of life that we are able to have them as signs of that by which he is well served. . . . Among them was Teresa of Jesus from the notable and ancient city of Avila . . . and in a space of thirty years, through her labor and holiness herself founded in Spain, and in the Indies, and in Italy a great number of convents of male and female religious that with her holy life and doctrine have been, and are, a great influence for reforming the customs of the lands in which they reside.[89]

This image of Teresa was furthered by the testimony of major prelates throughout the Spanish Empire, including the archbishops or bishops of Toledo, Valencia, Burgos, Zaragoza, Valladolid, Salamanca, Córdoba, Segovia, Tarragona, Palencia, Barcelona, Granada, Santiago de Compostela, and Mexico. The archbishop of Segovia voiced his support by pointing out the great value of canonizations since "in the kingdoms of Spain" they inspired devotion to the saints whom the faithful took as "patrons and advocates,"[90] and the bishop of Lugo emphasized the "great and general devotion that in all of Spain" the people had for Teresa.[91]

The deputies of the crown of Aragon also wrote a letter in Teresa's favor as did the duke of Alba and the duke of Lerma, who stressed "the great sentiment that there is in Spain concerning the sanctity and virtues and miracles of Teresa of Jesus."[92] Further support came from Carmelites throughout the Spanish Empire; from the faculties of the universities of Salamanca and Coimbra; and from the civic authorities in the cities of Zaragoza, Barcelona, Granada, Málaga, and Tortosa. Clearly, almost everyone wanted to get into the act, or, in the words of the queen, "to take part in a work of such glory."[93]

Together with hundreds of testimonies from less illustrious supporters attesting to the holiness of the life and miracles performed through the intercession of the holy woman, this unprecedented outpouring of support bore its first fruit when Pope Paul V beatified Teresa in 1614. Philip III wrote a letter of thanks expressing his "particular joy and happiness," and asking that the pope grant all priests throughout his kingdoms the right to say the office and mass of the new *beata*.[94] Even the king of France, who began to show a new interest in the game of saint-making, asked for the similar privilege of saying the office of Teresa for the Carmelites in his kingdoms, and also pushed for her canonization.[95]

FIG. 12   BERNINI, *ECSTASY OF SAINT TERESA*, CORNARO CHAPEL,
SANTA MARIA DELLA VITTORIA

Coinciding with the canonization campaign for Teresa of Avila were the similarly formidable campaigns for Ignatius of Loyola and Francis Xavier. The procurator for the Jesuits in Spain, Gaspar Petrosa, requested that a process for the canonization of Ignatius be opened in 1595, and three judges were appointed by the papal nuncio in Madrid to begin collecting testimony.[96] Philip II wrote a letter supporting Ignatius, and again letters of support from Philip II, Philip III, and Queen Margarita led the testimonies in the final process that was reviewed by the Congregation of Rites.[97]

In the cases of the Jesuits, as with that of Teresa of Avila, the sanctity of their lives was a much easier thing to establish than had been the case with the medieval saints because of the enormous amount of testimony from their contemporaries. Famous in their own lifetimes and prolific writers, these sixteenth-century saints made the job of their later advocates much easier. It also appears to have been a relatively easy thing to find hundreds of witnesses from throughout the empire who would attest to miracles performed through their intercession. In the case of Ignatius, for example, the Congregation of Rites eventually accepted ten miracles, all from cities in the kingdoms of the Catholic King including Naples, Majorca, Barcelona, and Valencia.[98]

With voluminous testimony by kings, contemporaries, and clergy from throughout the Spanish Empire thus gathered and reviewed by the Congregation of Rites for all four of the Spanish saints, it again rested with the pope to make the final decision. In these cases, it was Gregory XV (1621–1623) who made the exceptional move of canonizing five saints a short time after his election.

A variety of factors probably played a role in this decision, including the pope's early education by, and continuing affection for, the Jesuits. Moreover, the former Cardinal Alessandro Ludovisi was predisposed to favor the requests of the Spaniards as a discreet, but long-time client and supporter who had previously enjoyed a 1,500-scudi pension from the Catholic King.[99] Combined with a strong personal belief in the intercessory power of the saints and a desire to provide models of Catholic virtue in the face of increasing hostilities with the Protestants, the pope made the proclamation in favor of the canonizations during consistories in January and February 1622.[100]

Thus, on March 12, the basilica of Saint Peter's was once again elaborately decorated with a special temporary stage, or *teatro*, designed and constructed by Guidotti Borghese and commissioned for the event by the Spanish nation in Rome.[101] According to at least one contemporary observer, the largess of the Spanish nation in paying for the decorations was motivated in part by a desire to literally set the stage for the event, even though other princes wanted a hand in the affair as well. Designed to Spanish specifications, the teatro was covered with gold and silver embroidered cloth, and decorated with paintings of the miracles of the saints, statues, and the standards of all the saints hanging on columns topped with ornate lamps. The Jesuits also provided silk tapestries, which hung throughout the basilica.[102]

The canonizations themselves were followed by two days of celebrations throughout the city. Fireworks lit the skies above Rome, while closer to the ground torches and candles adorned private houses and the major churches associated with the saints. Charity also abounded, and the Jesuits gave out the more extravagant white bread to the poor rather than the usual dark rye.[103] On the day following the canonizations, moreover, there was a procession wherein the standards of all the saints used in the canonization ceremony were transported from Saint Peter's to the churches most closely associated with the individual saints.

Combined with the canonization ceremony, the procession of March 13, 1622, possibly more than any other ceremony in the previous decades, constituted a synthesis of Spanish and Roman Catholic triumphalism that ritually claimed Rome for the Spaniards and left their heroes firmly ensconced in some of the central temples of the city.

Beginning at Saint Peter's, the large crowd first processed across the Tiber to the Chiesa Nuova, where the priests of the Oratory of Santa Maria in Valicella left the standard of their founder, Saint Philip Neri. The procession then continued past the statue of Pasquino into the Piazza Navona, where the church of Santiago was located. It was there that the "great multitude of Spanish priests" who followed behind the standard of Saint Isidore left his standard and then rejoined the procession behind the standards of Saints Ignatius and Francis Xavier.

From the Piazza Navona, the procession went through the Piazza Madama and the Piazza della Minerva and then down the street that ended directly in front of the Jesuits' mother church, the Gesù. Greeted as they had been at the other two churches by choirs and musicians, as well as by the senators of Rome and the students of the Collegio Romano, the crowd that followed behind the standard of the two Jesuit saints left their standards in the church and then returned to fall in line behind the other groups that were now all gathered behind the standard of Saint Teresa of Avila.

From the Gesù, the procession made its way down the "strada delle Botteghe oscure" until it reached the Ponte Sisto, where it crossed the Tiber again. Once in Trastevere, it was but a short distance to the Carmelite church of Santa Maria della Scala, where the last standard, Saint Teresa's, was left.[104]

For anyone familiar with the topography of early seventeenth-century Rome, the procession just described may sound like a tour of the heart of the city, and that is precisely what it was. The walk from Saint Peter's to the Piazza Navona to the Gesù to Santa Maria della Scala effectively encircled the most densely populated areas of Rome in this period and took the crowd through many of the most important piazzas and social centers. Few people in Rome would have been unaware of the procession and accompanying festivities or of the great honor it represented for the people of Spain.

Much more than a tour, however, this was a triumphal victory parade for the Spaniards that demonstrated to everyone assembled the central position of Spanish saints in the church militant and the triumph of the Catholic Reformation; and it located these saints in some of the most important churches and neighborhoods of the city.[105] As the Spaniards carried the painted images of their saints through the city streets with musicians playing trumpets and choirs singing songs of praise, they made it clear that their heroes were now a permanent part of Rome and the Roman Catholic pantheon of saints.

That the saints and the ceremonies surrounding their canonization were themselves viewed at that time as part of a triumphal, heroic landscape in a Christianized, classical style, is reflected in a series of poems written for the occasion by the Roman writer Mutio Dansa di Penna. Dedicated to Philip IV, "king of Spain and of the Indies," the first of the poems describes the saints as the "splendor of Iberia: invincible offspring of Philip, and of Charles, celestial heroes."[106] In another poem, moreover, Philip IV is called the "great Spanish Jove," and the canonizations are seen as demonstrating to all assembled the "high worth in the great Roman temple" of "invincible Iberia."[107]

These images would certainly have pleased Philip II and his grandson. Although the political and social influence of the Catholic King and the Spanish nation in Rome began to decline after the triumphal ceremonies of 1622, successful saint-making continued throughout the century. Indeed, Spanish saints, perhaps above all else, remained firmly established as a lasting testimony to the creation of Spanish Rome. Moreover, institutions connected to Spanish saints had a deep impact on the city of Rome itself.

CHAPTER 6

URBAN VIII AND THE DECLINE OF SPANISH ROME

I N June 1624, less than a year after the election of Pope Urban VIII, the Spanish ambassador sought to present him with the annual tribute from Naples, along with the chinea, on the feast of Saint Peter. The pope, however, did not wish to receive the dues on the feast day itself. Rather, he instructed that they be presented on the day before the vigil and that the papal treasurer (*camerlengo*) accept the money and horse in his name. This effectively removed the Spaniards from the central role they had enjoyed during the feast of Saint Peter for almost sixty years and sent an early message that the days of special treatment and favor for the Spaniards were drawing to a close. As though it were an omen of the darker days ahead, the white Neapolitan horse meant for the pope was found dead on the morning of the feast, perhaps poisoned—presumably in revenge for the slight given to the ambassador.[1]

The election of Cardinal Barberini, a Florentine, had been won with the help of the French faction in the College of Cardinals, and, as the Spaniards feared from the beginning, he turned out to be the most pro-French pope in sixty-five years.[2] At the same time, the death of Philip III in 1621 and the ascendancy of the young Philip IV to the Spanish throne meant that personal ties to the Spanish monarchy were still weak in Rome. The task of building up a new faction was at an early stage.

The consequences of this shift in papal favor for the stability of the Italian territories of the Spanish monarch and for the papacy became apparent early in Urban VIII's reign, when French troops, with the help of Venice, marched into northern Italy and occupied the Valtelline region that had been under the protection of papal troops according to the conditions of the recently signed treaty between Spain and France.[3] This action seriously threatened the stability of Italy, and for two years a full-scale war between France and Spain in Italy seemed imminent, the first in seventy years. One noticeable consequence for Rome was that during the Jubilee year of 1625 few foreigners remained in the city, as people feared the coming war.[4] Indeed, the return of war to Italy, with the resumption of hostilities between Spain and France, was probably the single most important factor in the decline of the Spanish population in Rome.

Initially, the Spaniards insisted that the pope enter into an alliance with them to drive the French out of Italy, and when he proved reluctant to do this, they began to suspect his complicity in the affair. There were even rumors of a Spanish plot to poison the pope or remove him by some other means.[5] Cardinal Borgia, leader of the Spanish faction of cardinals and later the Spanish ambassador to Rome, revived the old threat that Spanish troops would invade the Papal State.[6] The Avvisi reports of April 1625, in the meantime, noted that to demonstrate their disgust with the pope over the loss of the Valtelline, no Spaniards attended the ritual processions accompanying the papal distribution of dowries at the church of the Santa Maria Sopra Minerva that year.[7] Borgia complained bitterly that from the pope, "the king of Spain could not obtain the smallest concession; everything was refused him."[8]

This was not entirely true. The pope initially continued to grant the various ecclesiastical financial concessions, and in 1625 he canonized yet another Iberian saint, the Portuguese queen Isabel.[9] Rhetorically, too, Urban VIII insisted that he was the loving father of the kings of both France and Spain.

While the eventual peaceful resolution of the Valtelline crisis with the Treaty of Monzon in 1626 removed the immediate threat of war,[10] France had nonetheless established itself once again as a major player in Italian affairs and in Rome itself. The crisis, moreover, severely strained Spanish-papal relations, establishing the suspicious, often bitter relations that prevailed between the two powers for the next twenty years. At the same time, the crisis revealed the declining ability of Spain to control Roman policy and to use the papacy to advance its own agenda in Italy and throughout Europe. The close alliance and the Spanish hegemony in Rome that Philip II had forced upon the papacy in 1557 were clearly at an end. As yet another sign of the new papal autonomy and assertiveness,

Urban VIII began to rebuild fortifications in Civitavecchia and elsewhere, an act that had been expressly forbidden in the 1557 treaty between Pope Paul IV and Philip II.

This new state of affairs was not the result of any sudden decline of Spain's ability to maintain the policies of rewards and threats that Philip II and Philip III had used so effectively in dealing with the papacy. Rather, the gradual decline of Spanish influence and power in Rome occurred because of the rise of French power internationally and the success of the French cardinals Richelieu and Mazarin in challenging the Spaniards at their own game in Rome.

In this sense, the decline of Spanish power in Rome mirrored the general decline of Spanish power throughout Europe in the seventeenth century. France was clearly the most serious cause of this decline in both local and international affairs since it was French economic and military competition that was draining the Spanish coffers and undermining the reputation and influence of the Spanish Empire both in Rome and in Spain itself. It had largely been through French efforts that Urban VIII was elected, and no pope had worked as hard to undermine Spanish power since Paul IV. Throughout Urban's reign Spanish money continued to flow into Rome, but so did French money. Spanish grain continued to supplement the food supply of the Papal State, but so did French grain. Spanish processions and rituals continued to spread pro-Spanish propaganda, but so did French processions and rituals. Most important, while Spain continued to maintain that Spanish military strength alone guaranteed the security of the Papal State, the widely perceived reality was that the French, looking for reasons to march into Italy, were ready to send troops to Rome if the pope chose them over the Spanish. Although Philip II had been able to force the papacy into a dependent relationship and operated in Italy free of serious international competition after 1559, the revival of France as a patron in Rome and a military threat to Italy completely changed the balance of power.

THE CONTEST FOR ROME IN THE 1630s

In Rome itself, the 1630s proved to be a time of violence and instability that had not been seen since the early sixteenth century as the Spanish and French factions fought for preeminence. The Spaniards were not about to give up the city in which they had invested an extraordinary amount of political energy and money. Indeed, Rome, on a micro level, became yet another front in the Spanish-French wars that raged in other parts of Europe. Usually a cold war, at times the contest turned hot, with French and Spanish soldiers battling on the streets and killing one another in the piazzas. To add to the troubles, Urban entertained illusions of grandeur in Italy that went far beyond his military or economic means, considering that he could barely maintain peace in Rome itself.

What Urban could do, however, as the absolute monarch of Rome, was undermine Spanish power locally in a variety of ways. In late 1630, for example, he issued a strict decree against a Franciscan at the church of San Pietro in Montorio, the oldest site of Spanish patronage in the city. Father Innocenzo, a prophet of sorts, had been preaching popular sermons that included "oracles" that offended the pope. He subsequently issued a decree censuring and silencing the friar, even though Cardinal Borgia protested that the friar's words were far better than those of Thomas Campanella, the infamous Dominican priest imprisoned for heretical pronouncements. The pope responded that he was sure that the cardinal enjoyed the oracles but that he would be excommunicated if he attended any further sermons. Urban also issued decrees against the other friars at the church.[11]

In another confrontation, Urban blocked a petition that the Spanish cardinal Sandoval brought to the congregation of bishops concerning a school in his home diocese in Spain. Sandoval complained bitterly about his treatment by the pope, saying that "his nation" had no liking for the path the pope was following, and his king deserved better treatment considering how much he had given the pope. When Urban heard of the grumbling he was reported to have grown agitated and said that Cardinal Sandoval could leave Rome at his pleasure "with all the other Spaniards, whom he had not called" to Rome. The pope went on to complain that he "did not understand why they had come" in the first place. The implication of this last comment was said to have scandalized the city.[12] A month later the pope issued a decree ordering all bishops to return to their residences, a move clearly aimed at the Spanish cardinals. They ignored the order, while Spanish ministers responded that the king might have to withhold the Spanish pensions that were distributed in Rome in response.[13]

This proved to be a mere warm-up for confrontations to come, which included a strict limiting of the influence of the Spanish ambassador. Be-

tween 1630 and 1635, moreover, the pope not only challenged the authority of the ambassador but tried to run the descendant of Spain's only
papal family, Cardinal Gaspar Borgia, out of town.

The symbolic importance and implications of the struggle between
Cardinal Borgia and Urban VIII went to the heart of the transformation of Spanish-Roman relations in this period. A wealthy prince of the
church and member of the family of Pope Alexander VI, Borgia represented continuity with the initial period of Spanish incursions into the
city more than a century earlier. He was well aware of this and also of the
preeminent position that the Spanish kings had held in Rome for many
years. He expected the papacy to continue its alliance with the Spanish
monarch, something Urban VIII had no intention of doing. A confrontation between the two prelates was thus inevitable when Borgia became
ambassador in 1631.

The wars of religion that were raging in Germany in 1631 and 1632
precipitated the first major clash. By then it was clear to everyone that
France was aiding the Protestants against the Habsburgs. Borgia approached the pope in the consistory of January 1632 to present his monarch's request for the renewal of the three gracias, as well as a large tax on
all benefices throughout Iberia, to aid the war effort. Urban refused, pro-
posing instead a onetime tax amounting to far less than the Spanish king
had in mind. This angered Borgia, who saw it as yet another move in favor
of the French. Thus, at the March consistory, Borgia took the extraordinary step of issuing a formal protest against the pope, demanding that he
not only grant Philip IV the requested funds but that he also exhort all
Catholics to fight for the faith, a thinly veiled shot at the French. As the
pope loudly interrupted Borgia, the two Barberini cardinals moved as if
to forceably evict him from the meeting.[14] This widely publicized scandal
shattered all diplomatic pretense: Borgia and the Barberinis were open
enemies from then on.

Relations were thus icy throughout 1632, but the Spanish ministers
advising Philip IV back home held out hope that they could still per-
suade the pope to join them in another holy league against the French.
To this end, an extraordinary ambassador was sent by the king in 1633
to try and sway the pope. According to a report attributed to the abbot
Giulio Cesare Braccini, the offer made to the pope and his family was
quite remarkable.

First, Philip promised to order Cardinal Borgia out of Rome if the

pope joined the league. He also promised that one of the Barberini nephews would be made grandee of Spain, with the title of prince or duke
in one of the king's states. Another nephew would be made a knight of
the order of Tuscon, and Cardinal Barberini would be made protector
of Germany. The pope's brother and his sons would be made princes of
Salerno and dukes of Amalfi with a 150,000-ducat pension. Part of this
pension was originally intended to aid the Catholic cause in Germany.
The pope refused the offer but to prove his goodwill toward the Catholic
league pledged 200,000 ducats per year to the cause.[15]

As for Cardinal Borgia, the pope had other ways of dealing with him.
Late in 1634 he issued a bull ordering all bishops and cardinals to return
to their home countries under pain of excommunication.[16] Unable to resist any longer, Cardinal Borgia departed at the end of 1634, making his
way through a great concourse of people who came to his residence at
the Piazza Santi Apostoli to see him off. At least one report claimed that
many were sad to see him leave since he had "supported many poor families and people in need to such an extent that he spent 2,000 ducats per
month."[17]

The forced departure of Cardinal Borgia, which would have been inconceivable earlier, perhaps more than any other single event marked the
beginning of the end of unchallenged Spanish strength in Rome. In ten
years Rome had gone from being, as Charles V had once said, a virtual
part of the Spanish kingdoms, to an increasingly independent territory
unfriendly to the Spaniards. A sure sign of this was the growing hostilities
in Rome involving the Spanish ambassadors and their new household in
the piazza that would eventually take its name, Piazza di Spagna, from
the ambassador's palace.

The ambassador who had replaced Borgia in 1633, the marquis of
Castel Rodrigo, had rented the Mondaleschi palace near the Villa Medici
and the church of Trinità dei Monti. In 1635 he used the diplomatic immunity of the palace to house a servant of the king, Ludovico Camutio,
who was wanted for murder in Rome. Camutio later escaped with the
aid of the duke of Montalto, an important Sicilian noble, who was stay-
ing at the palace at the time. These actions led to an increasingly tense
series of confrontations between the Spanish ambassador and Cardinal
Barberini, who badly wanted to diminish Spanish power in the city and
began to increase police pressure on the Spanish.[18]

After Camutio's escape, for example, the papal police, or *sbirri*, arrested a woman who was a member of the ambassador's household but lived next door to the palace. They paraded her in front of the palace as a clear provocation, causing one of the ambassador's guards to challenge the sbirri, who restrained him. The ambassador protested but was told that the diplomatic immunity of his palace did not extend to the nearby houses and that he should keep his extended household living in the area from offending the court in the future.[19] The pope also issued a decree in 1635 strictly limiting who could carry weapons because of the rising violence in the city.

As a further example of eroding civic order and increased hostilities, in April 1636 a simple insult thrown at a Frenchman by some Spaniards in the Piazza Navona led to a large confrontation that required the intervention of the governor of Rome with a company of Corsican soldiers. The piazza was described as being full of armed men, and for a number of days afterward the streets of Rome were tense.[20]

The Spaniards, of course, blamed this wretched state of affairs on the pope and his family, and openly hoped for his death. When Urban VIII fell ill in late July 1637, the viceroy of Naples moved six thousand infantry and a thousand cavalry from that kingdom to the border of the Papal State. They were ready to march on Rome in the event of the pope's death and take their revenge on the Barberinis, who had stripped the papal apartments and locked themselves in Castel Sant'Angelo in fear of exactly that.[21]

The pope, however, began to recover in early August, and when he came to his chapel on August 6, his appearance was carefully staged: musicians performed and a crowd of supporters shouted, "Viva Pope Urban VIII" and "Spaniards out." This recovery depressed the entire Spanish nation, which did not hold its normal festivities that year. The French, on the other hand, celebrated theirs with great gusto.[22]

Indeed, the French had double cause to celebrate in 1638, for the future Louis XIV was born that year. Although numerous feasts, festivals, comedies, and other public and private spectacles marked the years of Urban VIII's reign, the festival to honor the birth of the dauphin was the most politicized ceremony, openly expressing the alliance between the French and the Barberini family. More than any previous event, it revealed the dramatic transformation of factional alliances and the shifting political geography of Rome.[23]

Led by the French ambassador, François Annibal d'Estrées, and Cardinal Antonio Barberini, the festivities took place on Sunday, November 21. First off was a cavalcade of horses and carriages, which began at the Ponte Sisto and proceeded down the Via Giulia.[24] It there passed the Farnese palace, decorated to honor the occasion: the arch that traversed the Via Giulia from the palace was richly adorned with torches, and the windows were all lit with white candles.[25]

In the next major display of honor from a Roman noble family, the procession was greeted at the Piazza Navona by the elaborately decorated palace of Giovanni Antonio Orsini. Reminiscent of Cardinal Sforza's actions in 1590, he had hung a large banner with the French monarch's coat of arms out of the balcony that overlooked the piazza. The balcony was illuminated by torches and all the windows of the palace were lit by candles, while the main entrance was also lit by torches.[26] After passing through the piazza, past the Spanish church and hospital, and stopping for a fireworks display in front of the church of San Luigi dei Francesi, the procession made its way to the Barberini palace on Via Quattro Fontane for the culmination of the festivities.[27] There, too, the festival of lights continued: the windows were all lit with white candles, and more than three hundred torches burned on both sides of the palace. These framed the main doors of the palace, adorned with the coats of arms of the pope, the king of France, and Cardinal Antonio Barberini, who rented the palace from his brother Taddeo.[28] A large inscription in gold letters on a blue cloth was hung between the coats of arms of the king and cardinal and underneath that of the pope. Using classical metaphors, the inscription praised Louis XIII as a new Hercules who had suppressed both heresy at home and the impudent Geryon, the three-headed monster king Hercules had slain in Spain—in this context, obviously the Spanish monarchy. It was to the king, who had restored piety and overcome tyranny, that the new dauphin owed a great filial debt.[29]

This homage to the kings of France, and the obvious insult to the Spanish monarchy, spelled out for all that this was French territory. Indeed, as the revelers drank the red and white wine that flowed from the fountains in front of the palace, they were celebrating not just the birth of the new French prince but the birth of the new French power in Rome.

In a space of forty years, then, the Orsini and Farnese families had been brought into the French camp, and the Medici palace that once hosted feasts for the Spanish ambassadors and viceroys was lit up in honor of the French dauphin. The ambassador of the grand duke of Tuscany also illuminated the facades of his palace in Campo Marzo and the palazzo Madama for the event. Other Italian noble families that did likewise were the Frangipanis at their palace next to the Piazza San Marco and the Strozzis.[30] The French were clearly in the ascendancy, as was the violence between them and the Spanish.

In 1639 a Frenchman was killed while walking near the Spanish ambassador's palace, and suspicion fell on the Spanish. Ambassador Castel Rodrigo secretly called in more troops from Naples, and the Barberinis moved to expel the many "Spanish vagabonds" who were in the city. The governor of Rome reported that the prisons were full of Spaniards.[31]

In the meantime, gangs of bandits were making trouble in the Papal State from their base in the Kingdom of Naples. They were suspected of being encouraged by the Spanish authorities, a view that was confirmed when the Spanish ambassador granted the most famous leader of the bandits, Giulio Pezzola, lodging in his palace when he came to Rome over Christmas 1639. An open insult to Urban VIII, this was just one more sign that the Spanish were waging a guerrilla war against the papacy. At the same time the Spanish were helping Pezzola escape early in 1640, it was reported that a band of armed men had been sent by the viceroy of Naples to the mouth of the Tiber. If this were not enough, it was also rumored that there was a death warrant against the pope in Naples.[32]

Not surprisingly, given the hostile posturing of the Spanish, Cardinal Barberini ordered the many Spaniards who had come from Naples to live in the embassy to leave the city. He also arrested two Spanish soldiers in Rome and informed the Spanish ambassador that in Rome there would be only papal soldiers.[33]

Between 1640 and 1644, the year of Urban VIII's death, matters worsened for both the Spanish monarchy and the papacy. With the Portuguese and Catalans rebelling in Iberia, the Spanish monarchy had little appetite for open confrontation with the pope. In fact, Philip IV's favorite, his minister the count duke of Olivares, who had been born in Rome while his father was serving as the ambassador there in the 1580s, worked hard to win a measure of papal support. He continued to secure the ecclesiastical tax concessions for Habsburg military operations that previous monarchs had enjoyed. Any actions that might have opened the door to a French-papal military alliance and a costly war in Italy were avoided. In short, the ability of the Spanish monarchy to back up its threats of military intervention in the Papal State, which always constituted the submerged foundation of Spanish power in Rome, had seriously eroded by 1625 and had become virtually unimaginable by 1640.

In 1641 Olivares wrote to the new ambassador in Rome, the marquis de los Veles, with instructions concerning his main point of business, to gain papal support against the Portuguese rebels. Reflecting the weakened Spanish position and the new autonomy of the papacy, he warned, "To obtain that which you desire from His Holiness you need to dress yourself in the skin of a lamb and put away that of the lion, because today the popes do what they wish, and not what the ministers of princes seek."[34] This was a frank admission of the dramatically altered political landscape in Rome, and Olivares knew that the situation was potentially hostile. He instructed his ambassador to discreetly bring "a good number of soldiers" into the city from Naples in order to protect himself and the "reputation" of the king.[35]

The primary mission of los Veles failed largely because the papacy was more than happy to see the Spanish monarchy weakened through the loss of Portugal. This became obvious when a Portuguese ambassador, Monsignor Lamego, sent by the new Portuguese pretender to the throne, came to Rome in the summer of 1642. Lamego had come to pledge the allegiance of his king to Urban VIII, and the simple fact that he was allowed in the city gave a degree of legitimacy to the idea of an independent Portugal. The move enraged los Veles. The rumor in Rome was that the Spanish ambassador had said that he wanted Lamego "dead or alive."[36] Apparently the Spanish ambassador had decided to put on the old lion skin one more time.

This set the stage for more extensive hostilities between the Spanish and French, for it was the French ambassador who was acting as host and protector of Lamego. The drama unfolded on the summer night of August 20, in the center of the city. At 10 P.M., Lamego left his house in Piazza Navona to visit the French ambassador at his residence in the Ceri palace near the Trevi fountain. Los Veles had spies tracing Lamego's movements, and when he heard of the monsignor's whereabouts, he decided to personally capture his Portuguese rival with a group of his men.

Thus, when Lamego left the French ambassador's residence at midnight, the Spanish ambassador left Cardinal Roma's house in the neighborhood of Campo Marzo with his contingent of men. Lamego, however, had a French escort, and was accompanied by thirty armed soldiers and three coaches filled with men in the French ambassador's service. The two parties met in a narrow side street near the Piazza Colonna. The battle that ensued left five Portuguese and French dead, as well as two Spaniards. In addition, nine Spaniards were wounded, together with six or seven French and Portuguese. Lamego escaped unharmed, while los Veles was slightly wounded.[37]

In response to the battle, Cardinal Barberini sent five hundred soldiers to guard the Portuguese ambassador's house in the Piazza Navona, and others to keep the peace in the Piazza di Spagna. A lengthy trial was also set in motion, with eleven cardinals as jurors and the pope himself presiding. In the end Lamego left Rome without the papal blessing he had sought, but responsibility for the battle was placed squarely on the shoulders of the Spaniards. This gave Urban the justification to expel not only los Veles but also the Spanish cardinals Albornoz and Montalto. The other Spanish cardinal, Queva, was ordered to stay in his house. Thus, with one clean stroke, the pope cut off the head of the Spanish faction, at least for the time being. It was the predictable end to a long cold war.[38]

Although there was never any official break in relations between the Spanish monarchy and Urban VIII, their growing estrangement came with a price. While Urban's policies gave him a local autonomy that few of his recent predecessors had enjoyed, it also undermined the economic and social stability of Rome and the strength of the Papal State. The papacy simply did not have the economic or military resources to act independently.

This became most clear in the disastrous policy Urban pursued in the costly War of Castro with Odoardo Farnese, the duke of Parma.[39] Entertaining illusions of military strength and seeking the expansion of the Papal State, in 1641 Urban occupied Farnese's territory in northern Latium, known as the duchy of Castro. He had weak cause to do so and also threatened to march on the duchy of Parma itself. When both the king of France and the king of Spain protested the action, however, and the French, Venetians, and Tuscans gave financial support to the duke of Parma, the pope found himself politically isolated, and the estimated 50,000-scudi-per-month cost of the war strained the papal coffers beyond their capacity.[40]

The war was the first military venture the papacy had undertaken on its own since the equally disastrous Caraffa War, which Paul IV had provoked with the Spanish almost a century earlier. Like that mistake, the War of Castro, which dragged on for three years, placed a heavy bur-

den of taxation upon the subjects of the Papal State and left the people of
Rome embittered against the pope and his family. It also underlined the
simple economic fact that without outside military support, the papacy
did not have the economic strength or military capability to win even a
modest war against its Italian neighbors. Moreover, the French, whom
Urban had welcomed as a check on Spanish power in Rome, had instead
helped the pope's enemies, thereby proving themselves far less gracious
patrons of Rome than Spain had been.

Thus, when Urban VIII died in 1644, the mood among the cardinals
and people of Rome had shifted against the Barberinis and the French.
With Spanish troops massed along the southern border of the Papal
State and Tuscan troops threatening from the northern border, the conclave was predisposed to Spanish suggestions. Moreover, the leader of
the French faction, Cardinal Mazarin, was in distant Paris, and his protests against the election of the Spanish candidate, Giambattista Pamfili,
arrived in Rome too late.[41]

The new pope, Innocent X (1644–1655), who had served as nuncio
in Spain, faced the difficult task of appeasing the openly hostile French
and Spanish in Rome throughout his reign. Although his election was
itself testimony to the continuing influence of the Spaniards in Rome,
the French were not about to give up the strong foothold they had established in the city under Urban VIII. Mazarin and his agents, moreover,
were intent upon flaunting their strength in Rome, and in 1646 conflict
between the two great powers erupted once more into an armed battle
between French and Spanish soldiers in the Piazza de Gesù.[42] The defeat
of the Spanish in this minor encounter was celebrated by the French both
in Rome and in Paris as a great victory and underlined that even with a
pro-Spanish pope in power, the French could keep the Spaniards from
dominating Rome as they had once done.

This was again apparent when the Spaniards attempted to perpetuate
the traditional symbolic manifestations of their power, such as the Easter
procession in the Piazza Navona. Urban VIII had prohibited them from
holding the Easter procession for some years at the end of his reign, but
after his death they once again put together the elaborate festivities in the
spring of 1646. However, as yet another sign of the changing times, few
people showed up for the event because they feared hostilities, according
to one contemporary observer.[43]

Another factor in the poor attendance—which was not reported—

FIG. 13   DIEGO VELÁZQUEZ, *INNOCENT X*, DORIA PAMPHILI GALLERY

was the simple fact that there were no longer many Spaniards in the city. The confraternity records show a steady decline in membership; only ten or fifteen new members annually were joining by 1650, and by the end of the century only five members attended one annual meeting.[44] Similarly, charitable giving by Spaniards was drying up, and according to information given to the ambassador in Rome during this period, the Spaniards in the city were few in number and concerned only about themselves.[45]

Adding to the general feeling of deterioration was the fact that the Spanish nation in the city could no longer count the Portuguese as their own after 1640.

Rome, in short, was no longer as attractive to Spaniards as it had once been, and although pilgrims and some famous visitors like Diego Velázquez continued to make the journey to Rome, fewer lived there or held prominent positions in the city. Fewer wealthy patrons also meant a shrinking servant class. Adding to the Spanish malaise in this period was the fact that Philip IV had no heir. It looked for a time as though the Spanish Habsburg line might be dying out.

The end, however, had not yet come. Instead, fundamental economic, ecclesiastical, and military ties built up over almost two centuries kept the Spanish monarchy and papacy locked in a tight embrace. This was something that Urban VIII and the French had been unable to destroy, and in the 1650s and 1660s Philip IV sought successfully to strengthen the traditional bonds between the two courts. Defying the prophets of doom, the Spanish presence, albeit much diminished from its earlier glory, continued. In fact, a season of modest revival was about to begin.

SPANISH REVIVAL AND RESILIENCE, 1650–1700

I N 1662 the Piazza Navona was once again decorated for a Spanish festival, this time to celebrate the birth of a successor to Philip IV, Prince Charles. With the revolutions of the disastrous 1640s past, and following the signing of the Peace of the Pyrenees with France in 1659, the Spain of Philip IV finally had cause to celebrate. For many Spaniards both in Iberia and Rome, the birth of a healthy prince seemed almost miraculous, and it was taken as a sign of rebirth for a family and an empire that many thought were on the brink of extinction. Again the myth and site of Rome provided the Spanish with both a story and a stage to reflect on their own destiny as the modern heir to the Roman empire.

The Spanish ambassador in Rome, Don Luís Guzmán, had organized several days of public feasting to celebrate the birth. Included in these celebrations were orations by learned Jesuits in the Collegio Romano, fireworks in the Piazza Navona and Piazza di Spagna, various masses, and a number of processions.[1]

The procession in the Piazza Navona, which took place on February 15, 1662, stood out both for its grandeur and for the classical symbolism it appropriated. The festivities began early in the evening, after sunset, and the piazza was lit by countless lamps and torches. The facade of the church of Santiago on the south end of the piazza was elaborately decorated with tapestries, and over the central door two large angels framed a banner that dedicated the ceremonies to the honor of the new Spanish prince, the "security of the empire" and the "happiness of the world."[2]

With this serving as the preview to the show that would follow, the rest of the piazza was dominated by a large ephemeral construction in front of the church that was meant to represent the city of Troy. In the words of the author describing the festivities, "In all its signs it showed itself to be that Troy, much celebrated for its fire or because out of its ashes Rome was born."[3] The structure took the shape of an octagon with four doors, one of which was graced by a likeness of Aeneas carrying his father, Anchises, on his back, with his son, Ascanius, by his side. The other doors were all closed since the city was at war, but one could see the great towers of the city within the walls.

The stage was thus set, and what seemed to be all the people of Rome were assembled, when the ambassador of Spain, seated on a central balcony with Cardinals Colonna, Barberini, and Aquaviva, gave a signal. From one of the Spanish houses on the piazza rushed a fiery horse that entered the city of Troy. With a great shower of fireworks the walls and towers of the city burned and fell to the earth in ashes. In the middle of the ashes, however, was revealed a giant statue of a beautiful maiden dressed in regal robes. In her right hand she held three scepters and in her left a medallion inscribed with the words *omnibus unus* (from all, one). Was this the symbol of Rome born of Troy's ashes? No. It was the Spanish monarchy, heir to the Roman Empire, which reigned over dominions in Asia, Africa, America, and of course Europe, all of which were represented on the pedestal beneath the maiden's feet.

A theatrical climax to the historical myth of Spanish Rome that had developed over almost two centuries, this was Spain regarding itself in a Roman mirror and holding that mirror up for the world to see. While the empire had suffered painful losses in Portugal and the Netherlands, as well as embarrassing rebellions in Catalonia, Naples, and yes, even Rome, it had emerged from those flames to fight another day. The monarchy was much weakened, to be sure, but Philip IV, like his father, great-grandfather, and great-great-grandfather, was still the most powerful king and patron in Italy, a role he finally began to exercise more effectively in the late 1640s and 1650s.

THE SPANISH REVIVAL, 1644–1665

The election of Innocent X Pamphili in 1644 initiated a process of rebuilding for the Spanish faction in Rome as the monarch and his ministers tried to reestablish the political presence and practices that had served the empire so well in the past. Initially, at least, the results were mixed. First attempting to win back some of the key Roman nobles, Philip instructed his ambassador to offer Cardinal Orsini a 12,000-ducat pension if he would join them. The cardinal refused, and his family hung the French monarch's coat of arms from their palace to emphasize their allegiance. The king of France sent the cardinal a diamond worth 3,000 ducats to express his appreciation for this declaration of loyalty.[4]

The Spanish were more successful with the papal family, which was, as the Barberinis had clearly shown, the key to smooth relations in the papal court. This was especially apparent when the ill-fated duke of Arcos, the new viceroy of Naples, stopped in Rome in January 1646 on his way to his new post. Accompanied by a household of three hundred, the duke and his wife were given a warm welcome reminiscent of visits before the dark days of Urban VIII. The pope held a banquet in their honor, and his sister Donna Olympia welcomed the duchess for a reception. Innocent X also assigned a company of his own Swiss guards to escort the duke around the city during his stay and gave him numerous gifts, including paintings, reliquaries, and crowns. The duke responded in kind, giving the master of the papal palace a gold and diamond chain, and leaving 1,000 ducats to be distributed among the Palatina family, which had hosted him. Finally, Cardinal Pamphili invited the duke and duchess to his palace for a lavish banquet. Afterward there was a "most beautiful comedy by both Spanish and Italian actors" in the Piombino palace.[5]

The visit coincided with the flight of many of the Barberini family from Rome. Fearing for their lives, Cardinals Francesco and Antonio Barberini fled for France, and the secular head of the family, Taddeo, was forced to leave the city disguised as a hunter, with his children dressed as pages.[6] The changing landscape of factional politics could not have been clearer: the Spanish were once again in favor with the pope.

These warm relations were critical in the following year, when the revolt of Masaniello in Naples against the duke of Arcos and the Spanish crown threatened the kingdom. Had Urban VIII been in power there is no question but that he would have tried to claim Naples for himself or given it to the French. Innocent X, however, remained firmly on the side of the king of Spain and was a critical source of support when Naples was retaken in 1648.[7] As Spanish kings had realized since the time of Ferdinand, the papacy was the key to stability in Naples, a point underlined by the events of 1647–1648.

Innocent X's loyalty to Spain extended to other members of his family as well. The pope's nephew Camillo Pamphili held lands in the Kingdom of Naples as a vassal of the Spanish king and was a firm member of the Spanish faction. In 1652 he presented the chinea to the pope on behalf of Philip IV, a move the king enthusiastically supported in a letter to a leading cardinal from the faction.[8]

Besides this successful courting of the papal family, another coup for Spain was the reestablishment and strengthening of its embassy. Most important, the Spaniards managed to purchase a permanent palace, the first embassy actually owned by a foreign power in Rome. The fact that this was allowed was a clear sign of papal favor.

The Spanish ambassadors had been renting the Mondaleschi palace for more than a decade. In 1647 the new ambassador, Iñigo Veles de Guevara, the count of Oñate, bid on the palace through an Italian agent, Bernardino Barber, and then won the approval of the purchase from the Congregation of the Barons of the Papal State, who had the power to approve the sale of major palaces. Barber bought it for 22,000 escudos, and it was then immediately transferred to the count of Oñate.[9] Four other houses next to the palace were bought to enlarge the building shortly thereafter, and in 1654 the king sent 19,000 ducats for its maintenance and repair.[10] The palace, which still serves as the Spanish embassy to the Holy See, and the piazza in front of it, quickly became the new center of Spanish political ritual and display, as well as the center of the Spanish faction.

After the forced removal of los Veles in 1643, the arrival of the new regular ambassador was itself a sign of a normalization of relations. Making a secret entry into the city in July 1646, the count of Oñate had gone quietly to "kiss the foot" of the pope and also to visit Cardinal Pamphili. Two months later, he made a more formal visit, accompanied by a large following of a hundred coaches carrying cardinals and nobles of the Spanish faction. A respectable show of strength, the procession and entry of Oñate were nonetheless subdued and lacking the triumphal trappings of power of years gone by.[11]

The pontificate of Innocent X was generally marked by a more subdued Spanish presence in the city as the king and his ministers simply tried to ensure that the traditional favors and support of the papacy continued both in Rome and at home. The three gracias were granted on a regular basis throughout the period, and Spanish pensions were distributed in Rome, albeit on a smaller scale. At the same time, the Span-

FIG. 14   TEMPESTA-ROSSI PLAN OF ROME, 1693, DETAIL SHOWING
PIAZZA DI SPAGNA

ish cardinals and ambassador tried to keep the Spanish nation in Rome from fragmenting further. They kept a close watch on the Portuguese and Catalan clerics, and reported back to Madrid on Catalans who were inclining toward France during the rebellion of the early 1650s.[12]

Philip IV, for his part, showed increasing engagement with Roman affairs as the pontificate of Innocent X progressed and proved himself very attentive when the pope died in 1655 and a new conclave was called. The conclave produced a flurry of correspondence from Madrid that revealed more than any previous event that Philip had entered the game of patronage politics. Writing to his ambassador, the duke of Terranova, in March 1655, the king revealed that he had asked his advisers from the Council of Italy and Aragon to give him a list of all the church pensions at his disposal to distribute to cardinals.[13] A month later he wrote again with the news that he had given another ambassador, the count of Castro, 50,000 ducats' worth of pensions to distribute during the conclave.[14] Among the larger pensions were 4,000 ducats to Cardinals Colonna and de Lugo, 1,100 to Cardinal Sforza, 1,000 to Cardinal Civo, and 2,000 to Cardinal Roseti.[15] The king also wrote to Cardinal Medici with a list of cardinals he wanted excluded from consideration in the election.[16]

When Fabio Chigi was elected Alexander VII in April 1655, it was counted a success for the Spanish faction in the College of Cardinals. Philip IV was quick to send a letter to his ambassador claiming that he had hoped for the election of Chigi.[17] Similarly, he wrote to the pope with his congratulations and pledged to give all his kingdoms as well as his own life and blood to protect the church.[18]

Getting down to practical business concerns, the king instructed his ambassador shortly thereafter to seek a renewal of the three gracias for as many years as possible. The rationale used was the same as always: the king needed the money for the "defense of the holy Catholic faith and the opposition to the Turks, Moors, and heretics."[19] Similarly, Philip was trying to gain more control over the dispensing of pensions, this time from the military orders. The papacy still controlled some of these pensions, and the king wanted all of them in his hands.[20]

On a more local level, Philip wrote in 1656 to the duke of Terranova complaining about the behavior of Queen Christina of Sweden, then in Rome, who apparently did not like Spanish grandees wearing their hats in her presence. The Spanish king took this as an affront to his reputation and told the ambassador to protest such treatment.[21] Hardly a matter of grave diplomatic importance, this small conflict over court etiquette nonetheless serves to reveal Philip's careful attention to Spanish reputation in Rome.

Rome was still at the center of international diplomacy at this point, at least in the minds of the Spaniards. In 1658, for example, Philip was pushing for the Peace of the Pyrenees treaty with France to be negotiated and signed in Rome, a proposal rejected by the French.[22] Moreover, the Spanish monarch also wanted to resurrect the old centerpiece of Spanish diplomacy in Italy, namely, a holy league with the pope. As in the past, this was ostensibly against the Ottoman threat. In the context of 1662, when it was proposed, however, it was also intended to bring Spain and the papacy together in a united front against the French.[23]

The French, in fact, unwittingly played a large role in the rising fortunes of the Spanish in Rome during the reign of Alexander VII. While their strength and success at undermining their rivals had been a central factor in the Spanish decline in the previous decades, the haughty posturing of Louis XIV and his primary adviser Cardinal Mazarin showed the Spaniards in a better light in the 1660s.

An early instance of perceived French arrogance involved one of Alexander VII's most notable arenas of activity: urban planning and the embellishment of Rome. In 1660 Cardinal Mazarin had proposed building, and paying for, a majestic staircase winding up from the Piazza di Spagna to the church of Trinità dei Monti. Alexander was initially happy with the project, and the French asked no less a figure than Bernini to submit plans for the enterprise. Apparently at Mazarin's insistence, the plan included an equestrian statue of Louis XIV in the middle of the staircase. Such a statue was clearly "an implicit claim to sovereignty," and the pope subsequently refused to allow the project.[24]

A more serious incident, which led to a rupture of diplomatic relations, concerned the French ambassador's claim to diplomatic immunity for a large area around the Farnese palace, which he was renting as the embassy. Within a few months of arriving in the spring of 1662, the duke of Créqui, Louis XIV's first ambassador to reside in the palace, went so far as to demand that Alexander instruct his Corsican guard that they could not march near the palace. He also claimed legal jurisdiction in the neighborhood.

Unfortunately for the French ambassador, by August these pretensions had led some soldiers in his service to insult and assault one of the nearby Corsican soldiers, a move that in turn, prompted a military attack on the palace. Not only did the Corsicans surround and fire on the palace, they also attacked the carriage of the ambassador's wife as she returned from church, killing one of her pages. In fear, she fled to the palace of one of the leading members of the French faction of cardinals, Cardinal d'Este. The immediate aftermath of all of this was the temporary transformation of the palace into a fortress, manned by a thousand French soldiers. A few weeks later, Créqui left Rome, less than four months after his arrival.[25]

In the aftermath of this scandal, Louis XIV sent angry letters to the pope, and by 1664 the Spanish suggestion of a holy league was embraced by Alexander VII with Venice and Savoy also joining. In short, the French failed to play by the rules of Roman politics the Spaniards knew so well. Political influence and stature in Rome required a basic respect for the formal status of the pope as absolute monarch in his own states. Spain had generally supported this role, but the French under Cardinal Mazarin and Louis XIV increasingly sought to claim a status and autonomy in Rome that alienated the papacy and undermined their own power.

With France in decline as far as influence in Rome was concerned, Spain began to recover some lost ground. Pope Alexander and a number of Roman nobles began to incline toward the Spanish monarch as a less dangerous and demanding patron. In short, a weakened and humbled but still wealthy and powerful Spain was a far better political ally than the haughty French, who also spent far less money in Rome.

This was the decision of the Barberini family in the early 1660s, when they declared themselves for the Spanish, a real victory for Philip IV. Even the family of his old nemesis Urban VIII became visible supporters of the Spaniards by 1663. In that year, Maffeo Barberini, the prince of Palestrina, had been given the honor, as a vassal of the king with lands in Naples, to present the chinea. Philip had written to tell the prince, who immediately traveled from Gaeta to Rome to thank the Spanish ambassador, Cardinal Aragona, for the great honor.

The procession planned by the Barberinis was equal to any of the most lavish from previous years, and it had certain signs that made it clear to all observers that the Barberinis had become "spagnolizatto." The festive uniforms of the thirty-eight gentlemen who accompanied the prince, for example, were decorated "with many bizarre ornaments" that were described as being "alla Spagnuola."

The prince had first gone to the palace of the Spanish ambassador, where his entourage was met by many other members of the Spanish faction, as well as by the pope's nephew. Many of the major noblemen of Rome had gathered to take part including Duke Altemps, Duke Casarelli, Duke Brancaccio, and Egidio Colonna. According to Marcantonio Nobili, who wrote a description of the event dedicated to Cardinal Barberini, it was the most impressive procession seen in Rome in some years. After moving through the streets to the Quirinal Hill, where the pope awaited them, Prince Barberini presented the horse and 7,000 ducats to Alexander, delivering a speech in Spanish in the name of his sovereign, the king of Spain.[26]

Perhaps the most lavish sign of Philip IV's success at building up loyalty among the Roman nobility, the presentation of the chinea in 1663 stood in stark contrast to the years of Urban VIII. Representing continuity with the Spanish political policy and practice of more than a century, it demonstrated that the edifice of Spanish power in Rome still stood, even if it was less populated than before.

Indeed, throughout the period from 1650 to 1665 the fundamentals of the old relationship between the Spanish monarchy and the papal court remained in place. The three gracias, the courting of cardinals and noble families through the distribution of pensions, the Holy League, the presentation of the chinea, the Easter ceremony and other festivals, and Spain's role as the most loyal protector of Rome, as opposed to France, all continued.

Still, the tone of the correspondence between Rome and Madrid, and the power of the papacy to resist, delay, and challenge, was obviously much stronger in this period. In ecclesiastical matters and local Roman affairs the papacy reasserted itself, and the Spanish presence in Rome itself was diminished a great deal. The French, while out of favor, were hardly gone from the scene. Louis XIV was just coming into his prime. Unfortunately for the Spanish, their king's time was short. Philip IV died suddenly in September 1665, at the age of fifty-six.

CHARLES II, LOUIS XIV, AND THE FINAL YEARS

The Spanish revival, particularly during the last decade of Philip IV's reign, proved to be a brief respite from the old battles of the 1630s and 1640s. The French increased their pressure on both Spain and the

papacy in the 1670s and 1680s. In 1673 open warfare was once more declared between Spain and France, and the political climate in Rome was
again unsettled by the conflict between the two powers. Spain held fast to
its old practices while Louis XIV was relentless in pressuring the papacy
to conform to his own will.

Upon the death of Alexander VII in 1667, Philip's widow, Queen
Maria Anna, followed standard procedure, writing to the heads of the
Spanish faction of cardinals. Cardinals Hesse and Sforza were named protector of Aragon and temporary ambassador, respectively, and they were
urged to pay careful attention to the Spanish interests and faction of cardinals.[27] The election of Clement IX Rospigliosi (1667–1669), a former
nuncio to Spain who had spent nine years in Madrid, was supported by
Spain, and the queen's correspondence revealed a solid knowledge of factional politics in Rome.[28] So, too, did her role in the election of Clement X
Altieri (1670–1676) following Clement IX's early death.

During these years, the Spanish faction in Rome continued its usual
rituals: the chinea, the Easter ceremony, the dispensing of dowries, and
occasional special events.[29] In 1670 they also celebrated the canonization
of two more saints from the Spanish Empire, Francisco de Borgia and
Rose of Lima,[30] and in 1675 John of the Cross was canonized as well.[31]
Other favors, such as the various ecclesiastical taxes, continued to be
granted, and in return Spanish pensions still came to Rome.

Yet there was rising military tension beginning in 1670, when Maria
Anna instructed her ambassador to protest to the pope about the bandits
who were raiding the Kingdom of Naples from the Papal State. This was
widely perceived to be provoked not by the pope but by the French, and
it signaled worse things to come.[32]

In fact, during the 1670s the most serious challenge to, and erosion
of, Spanish military domination in the Papal State in more than a century occurred. Shortly after the 1673 war broke out between Spain and
France, Louis XIV began demanding that the Papal State grant him equal
access to ports with the Spanish and the right to recruit soldiers and pro-
vision ships in the Papal State. This was granted in 1675, and the Spanish
protested bitterly.

The pope responded that to deny the French the right to buy grain
and use papal ports would be to declare them enemies. Still, the Spanish
were outraged. Papal ships were forbidden to enter Spanish ports, a ban
that created the clearest cracks in the Spanish-papal military alliance since

the days of Urban VIII. The Spaniards rightly suspected that the French were supporting rebels in Sicily and Naples with an eye to conquering the territories for themselves. From the Spanish perspective, the papacy was aiding France in this enterprise.[33] In Rome itself, moreover, the news that Rainaldo d'Este, a servant of the French, was coming to town caused the Spanish further anxiety. The queen instructed her ambassador to try to keep him from increasing the strength of the French faction.[34]

By 1677, when Philip's son Charles II had begun to govern on his own, or at least to sign the official correspondence, the tone of communications with Rome was bitter and marked by protest. In a letter dated August 1677, the king bluntly pointed out to the new pope, Innocent XI (1676–1689), that the presence of the French fleet in Civitavecchia meant that "Your Holiness permits the French, enemies of this monarchy, to use your ports as their own against us and for the infestation of our dominions."[35]

This was precisely the case, and it underlined Spanish vulnerability. A French naval presence as far south as Rome had been inconceivable in the years of Philip II and Philip III—such a thing had not even been attempted under Urban VIII. This act increased tension in Rome, as well, and again the possibility of armed confrontation between French and Spanish loyalists hung like a cloud over the city. In 1683 a number of Spaniards were arrested near the embassy by the papal police, an action the ambassador and king protested on the grounds of diplomatic immunity.[36]

Unlike Urban VIII, Innocent XI could not be charged with being overtly pro-French. Rather, he was confronted with an increasingly volatile situation in Rome because of the French and Spanish wars and sought to keep the embassies and their quarters from being used as armed fortresses. To this end, he passed laws in 1687 abolishing the autonomy or diplomatic immunity of the neighborhoods around the embassies.

The new French ambassador protested the act vigorously, and it became an international incident in large part because the French saw it as a grave assault on their rights. Everyone from the king to the parliament to the ambassadors and French faction in the city became involved in the protest. Louis XIV sent a threatening letter to his ambassador accusing the pope of acting in a way that aided his enemies, the Habsburgs, and could lead to war in Europe. He also threatened to take Avignon and Castro from the papacy.[37]

This led to a rupture between France and the pope reminiscent of the breach caused by the Corsican guard incident twenty years earlier. Again the Spanish gained from the overbearing and threatening tone of French diplomacy, and the crisis provided the Spanish monarch with another opening to play the dutiful son. Charles II was quick to do this, writing a letter to the pope in 1689 assuring him of his aid, and letting the pope know that he had instructed his governor in Milan to place his troops at Rome's disposal.[38]

It was a remarkable testimony to the success of two centuries of Spanish political practices in Rome that even though Louis XIV was much the stronger, Charles II was the more successful of the two monarchs in winning favors and the loyalty of central Roman families. The Barberini prince again presented the chinea in 1691, and the Orsini and Colonna families requested the king's intercession on behalf of their families.[39]

With some key cardinals, too, the king retained strong influence. Cardinal Medici was the protector of Castile, Aragon, and Naples, and he also served as head of the Spanish faction during the conclave of 1691.[40] The king showed a close interest in the election and sent numerous letters of instruction to his ambassador, the viceroy of Naples, and the cardinals in the Spanish faction. When Innocent XII (1691–1700) was finally elected, the king expressed his pleasure at the outcome.[41]

The war with France continued to color Roman-Spanish relations throughout the 1690s, and it did not help matters that Louis XIV reconciled with the new pope and won his support in a number of crucial areas. The French king was again allowed to recruit soldiers in the Papal State, for example, and to use the papal ports. So, too, were the Spanish, however, and in 1694 they sent an armada to Civitavecchia, where it stayed for a number of months. The Spanish were managing to hold off the French challenge even if they had lost the dominant position of years past.

Yet by the middle of the 1690s, an adversary far more powerful than the French and beyond the control of popes, kings, or political tradition was looming over the Spanish Empire. Charles II, "the bewitched," was clearly ill and unlikely to produce any heirs to the Spanish throne. Subsequently, maneuvering began between the French and the Austrian branch of the Habsburg family for the Spanish succession.

In Rome the Spanish presence had become a shadow of its former self. No ambassador was present in 1699, and only five men attended the meeting of the Confraternity of the Most Holy Resurrection in 1700. Political anxiety was thick in the air. For the papacy, too, the succession had deep implications, and Innocent XII appears to have advised Charles II to favor French claims to the throne.[42] France was to win after all in the centuries-old battle with Spain for the domination of Italy. But it was death and the extinction of a royal line that brought about this victory, not French military or political acumen.

Indeed, the political strategies and practices of Ferdinand and Isabella, Charles V, and Philip II had survived until the end. Moreover, they had given Rome 150 years of relative peace and prosperity, something the city had not known since antiquity. When Charles II, the last Spanish Habsburg monarch, died in 1700 it was also the end of an era in Rome. No patron would appear who would be as generous to the city. No European power would prove so supportive of the exalted claims of the Catholic Reformation papacy. Instead, Rome would begin a long slide into an increasingly marginal position in Europe. Thus, the end of Spanish Rome also marked the end of one of papal Rome's greatest eras.

CONCLUSION

THE death of Charles II in 1700, and the expulsion of all remaining Spaniards from Rome during the War of the Spanish Succession, marked the end of Spanish Rome. With no monarch to guide policy and no colony to enact it, the elaborate set of political and institutional practices collapsed. Imperialism in the age of absolutism depended on a strong monarch, and for Spain the collapse of the Habsburg monarchy meant an end to the old imperialism. The Bourbon dynasty of Philip V that followed quickly adopted a more Gallican approach to the church and deferred to the stronger French branch of the family with respect to Roman policy.

But two centuries of a strong and often dominating Spanish presence had left deep and lasting marks on Rome. Indeed, the perseverance of Spanish influence constituted one of the great political successes of the Spanish Empire. By fighting off the repeated challenges of France and overcoming the persistent resistance of the papacy to Spanish domination, the Spanish monarchy had fundamentally altered the political landscape in Italy and Europe. By finding and following the formula — a combination of real or threatened military coercion and benevolent patronage — for winning and maintaining stability, the Spanish monarchs were able to claim the leading role not just in Rome and Italy but in the Catholic and Mediterranean worlds more generally.

This was a victory for informal Spanish imperialism. Moreover, as the preceding chapters have shown, the case of Spanish Rome is one of the best examples we have of the development of informal imperialism in the early modern world. It both illuminates early modern imperialism and reveals complexities in the Spanish Empire that need to be understood as part of the larger historical picture.

More specifically, by combining limited military force, constant diplomatic contact, a strong presence of Spaniards in the city, and generous foreign aid, the Spanish monarchs from the time of Ferdinand and Isabella developed a foreign policy strategy in Rome that was unmatched by any other European power. The strategy succeeded generation after generation in cultivating a strong group of loyal Italian followers and a strong faction in the College of Cardinals. Perhaps most important, the policy placed pro-Spanish popes on the papal throne for the majority of the years between 1500 and 1700.

The impact of this policy on the papacy, papal Rome, and the Catholic Reformation was decisive. Renaissance Rome between 1480 and 1560 was frequently characterized by a turbulent political environment created by the local factional feuding among Roman and Italian nobles on the one hand and the international contest between Spain and France on the other. Papal power was unstable in this political landscape. Popes were forced to spend a great deal of time, energy, and money simply trying to protect their local interests and power.

By 1560, however, the decisive victory of the Spanish over the French in the contest for Italy, and the victory of Philip II over Pope Paul IV, made the Spanish monarchy the unchallenged protector and patron of Rome. While this ascendancy was often resented in Rome, the result of this change was that serious local uprisings against the papacy virtually disappeared. Papal power, under the protection of Spain, increased. Moreover, the Spanish monarchy assumed almost in full the costly burden of protecting the shores of the Papal States from the Ottoman threat. Freed from the burden of military spending, the papacy directed its funds more and more to building up Rome as an urban showcase of the Catholic Reformation.

Similarly, papal authority, so important to the reputation and claims of the Spanish kings in their own ecclesiastical affairs, was increased by the strong support of the Spanish monarchy. Although there were numerous conflicts between the papacy and monarchy over the Spanish king's infringement on ecclesiastical rights and privileges, on the larger matter of papal supremacy in the church the Spanish monarchs did not waver. Moreover, they alone among European powers continued to acknowledge papal financial claims vis-à-vis the Spanish church, providing the papacy with much needed revenues. Thus, in matters of both political theory and material substance, the Spanish monarchy was the critical partner in the construction of the early modern papal prince.

It was clear, furthermore, that popes who resisted the Spanish partnership and challenged the alliance and unwritten rules of the financial and political give-and-take between the two powers usually lost in the end. This was certainly the case with Paul IV, Sixtus V, and Urban VIII, all of whom died under a shadow of urban unrest and local threats of violence to their memory, monuments, and families.

That this was the case was largely because Philip II had succeeded in establishing a largely benevolent Spanish hegemony in Rome through the distribution of millions of Spanish ducats to thousands of Italian and Spanish churchmen and noble families. And while the Spanish monarchs established themselves as the most consistent, reliable source of patronage in Rome the Spanish community was doing the same throughout the city. Spanish cardinals and wealthy families built palaces and supported large households; the Spanish confraternities provided dowries, pilgrim aid, and hospital care to the poorer members of their community and other Romans as well. The monarchs and their followers, both Spanish and Italian, thus became a central part of the political culture of Rome.

Spanish money in the form of ecclesiastical pensions from Spanish imperial lands also flowed into the purses of popes, cardinals, and thousands of lower-ranking clerics in Rome. These contributed close to one million ducats a year to the Roman economy by the early seventeenth century, a sizable proportion that benefited everyone from builders to bakers.

The Spanish community itself also contributed to the life and vitality of the city. Living alongside Romans and other residents of Rome, Spaniards painted, composed music, conducted business, cleaned houses, shoed horses, and taught school. Some were counted among the best theologians of their day and others were considered saints.

The Spanish holy men and women who worked in Rome bolstered Spanish reputation through their service to both rich and poor. They, above all others, won a place in the Roman calendar and many places of honor in the Roman churches, where they were memorialized by sculptures and paintings that remain to the present day. A modern visitor to Saint Peter's basilica, for example, is greeted at the beginning of the nave by two monumental sculptures of Saint Teresa of Avila and Saint Peter of

Alcántara. Sculptures of Saint Ignatius of Loyola, Saint John of God and San José Calasanz also look down upon the masses from their places in the nave or around the main altar. Spaniards had given more than 2 million ducats to build the church over the years, after all, and their saints received a number of honored places second only to the Italians.

In short, the creation of Spanish Rome relied above all else on the domination of the patronage politics that characterized early modern political life. Viewed from this perspective, Spanish monarchs, cardinals, ambassadors, merchants, clerics, and saints all played explicit or implicit imperial roles. It was their patronage on many levels that united high and low, international and local, secular and ecclesiastic.

It followed that the Spanish Empire on the eastern edge of its territories came to be characterized not by the heavy-handed conquistador but by the generous patron, not by missionaries converting the natives under the guard of soldiers but by Spanish saints transforming Roman Catholicism through their new institutions and reforms, not by a colony that plundered the wealth of the natives but by a community that built up the economy of the city and became an important part of the social fabric. If Italians described themselves as "hispanized," it was not from force but through choice. The Spaniards had convinced them that Spain had the most to offer.

Rome subsequently became a central player in the history of the Spanish Empire, and it was the key to the broader success of the Spanish monarchy in Italy. By keeping Rome closely allied with them, Spanish monarchs kept their Italian possessions at peace. As Charles V and Philip II stated in their political testaments, Rome was the cornerstone of Italian stability. And the support of the papacy was critical to the political strength of the Spanish Empire as a whole. That support helps explain the repeated resilience of the empire in the face of severe external opposition and internal crisis. That Spain retained papal support and the loyalty of many Roman nobles in the face of a much stronger France testified to the success of informal imperialism, to a form of political domination that relied more on the cultivation of a strong patron-client network than on military strength. In the end, Spain conquered Rome with kindness.

EPILOGUE

IN the spring of Jubilee year 2000, the Bourbon king of Spain, Juan Carlos, visited Rome. At the church of San Pietro in Montorio, he would have seen numerous plaques on the walls next to Bramante's Tempietto commemorating the role of his ancestors in building and restoring the monument. The most recent inscription, dated 2000, noted his own generosity in providing the funding for the modern restoration of the Renaissance masterpiece. Next to the church and convent stand the Spanish Academy of Art, the Spanish embassy to the Italian government, and the Spanish grammar school, all built on that section of the Janiculum Hill to which Ferdinand and Isabella had long ago sent a few thousand gold pieces.

Walking down the hill, the king would have passed the Spanish school; making his way into Trastevere, he would have come to the church of Santa Maria della Scala, where a portrait of Saint Teresa of Avila looks upon the high altar from one of the side chapels. Passing on into the Piazza Navona he might have bought a book in the Spanish bookstore that occupies what was once and still is part of the Spanish church property there. And if he then made his way through and around the neighborhood of the Campo Marzo, past the street dedicated to "the Spaniards" who lived there long ago, the king would eventually have arrived at the Piazza di Spagna and the Spanish steps. There he probably spent a few nights in the seventeenth-century palace that gave the piazza and steps their name. Decorated with Bernini's sculptures, the palace still serves as the Spanish embassy to the Holy See.

If the king had decided to visit a few more churches during his visit he could have gone to Saint Ignatius or the Gesù, where Spanish Jesuits are celebrated and remembered, and in Santa Maria Maggiore, he would have been greeted by a statue of his ancestor Philip IV that stands near the entry.

These, of course, are only a few of the lasting reminders of the Spanish claim to Rome in the early modern period, but perhaps they explain in part the sentiment the king expressed to the local press during his Jubilee visit. "Rome," he declared with innocent enthusiasm, "is my town." How happy his ancestors would have been to hear him.

NOTES

ABBREVIATIONS

AGS	Archivo General de Simancas, Estado, Roma, Simancas
AMAE, AEESS	Archivo del Ministerio de Asuntos Exteriores, Archivo de la Embajada de España cerca de la Santa Sede, Madrid
AOP	Archivo de la Obra Pia, Rome
ARSI	Archivum Romanum Societatis Iesu, Rome
ASC	Archivio Storico Capitolino, Rome
ASR	Archivio di Stato, Rome
ASV	Archivio Segreto Vaticano Processi, Rome
BAV	Biblioteca Apostolica Vaticana, Rome
BCR	Biblioteca Casanatense, Rome
BNM	Biblioteca Nacional, Madrid, Manuscript Section
BUS	Biblioteca de la Universidad de Salamanca, Manuscript Section
HSA	Hispanic Society of America, Manuscript Section, New York
leg.	legajo (folio volume)

INTRODUCTION

1. See Primo Luigi Vannicelli, *San Pietro in Montorio* (Rome, n.p., 1971), for a good general account of the history of the church and convent. He cites an early seventeenth-century manuscript, "Memorie istoriche di S. Pietro in Montorio," which notes (p. 29) the consecration by Alexander VI and also points out that the monarch's coats of arms were displayed in the sacristy and other rooms connected to the church. The title "Catholic Kings" was granted to Ferdinand and Isabella and their successors by the pope.

2. AMAE, AEESS, leg. 87: *Derechos y Patronato de España; Regalías.* Included in this volume is an unfoliated printed pamphlet from 1875 entitled *Documentos relativos a la fundación de San Pedro in Montorio,* which is a compilation of original documents found in the embassy archive. Among the documents are the bulls of Sixtus IV from

1472 and 1481 granting the ruined monastery to the Franciscan P. Amadeo, and the 1480 letter from Ferdinand giving Amadeo 2,000 gold ducats to rebuild the church and convent.

3. *Documentos Sobre Relaciones Internacionales de los Reyes Católicos,* ed. Antonio de la Torre (Barcelona: Consejo Superior de Investigaciones Científicas, 1951). In a letter dated September 1488 from Ferdinand to Cardinal Bernardino Carvajal and Doctor Medina, his *procuradores* in Rome, the king advises them of the annual pledge to the church (vol. 3, pp. 142–143). In another letter from the same month to Lope de Sant Martin, the procurator of the bishop of Cefalu in Rome, the king mentions the 2,000 ducats committed to building the church of San Pietro (p. 150). In June 1493 Ferdinand writes to his viceroy of Sicily ordering him to pay 1,000 ducats to help build the church (vol. 4, p. 212).

4. Jerry H. Bentley, *Politics and Culture in Renaissance Naples* (Princeton: Princeton University Press, 1987), p. 23. Alfonso V of Aragon (1396–58), king of Aragon, Sicily, Sardinia, and Naples, left Naples to his illegitimate son Ferrante. The other realms went to his brother Juan II, father of Ferdinand, who was thus the heir to Sicily.

5. *Documentos Sobre Relaciones Internacionales de los Reyes Católicos,* vol. 4, p. 212. Unless otherwise identified, all translations are my own.

6. AMAE, AEESS, leg. 87: *Documentos relativos a la fundación de San Pedro in Montorio.* In 1523 Charles V confirmed the annual gift of 500 ducats; Philip III gave 3,000 ducats for the restoration of Bramante's Tempietto and the construction of a sustaining wall in 1604; and Philip IV gave 6,000 ducats for repairs and ornamentation during his reign.

7. AMAE, AEESS, leg. 87, f. 160: a copy of the text written on a plaque in the church of San Pietro in Montorio whose obligations the Spanish ambassador, Francisco de Castro, had renewed before a notary in 1611.

8. Peter Murray, *Bramante's Tempietto* (Kent, U.K.: Westerham Press, 1972), p. 6.

9. For the history of Alfonso the Magnanimous in Naples see especially, Bentley, *Renaissance Naples,* and Alan Ryder, *The Kingdom of Naples Under Alfonso the Magnanimous* (Oxford: Oxford University Press, 1976).

10. J. N. Hillgarth, *The Spanish Kingdoms, 1250–1516,* 2 vols. (Oxford: Clarendon, 1976–1978), vol. 2, p. 548. Hillgarth notes that there was general satisfaction with the election except at the Neapolitan and Spanish courts. The account of the five thousand cheering Romans is cited from a document published by M. Battllori in *Atti del Congresso internazionale de studi sull' età aragonese* (Bari, 1968), p. 592.

11. Marino Sanuto, *I diarii di Marino Sanuto,* ed. Rinaldo Fulin (Venice: Marco Visentin, Deputazione veneta di Storia Patria, 1880), vol. 3, pp. 842–847. The same event was recounted by another contemporary, the master of ceremonies of the Vatican palace Johannes Burchard, in his *Diarium sive Rerum Urbanarum Commentarii (1483–1506),* ed. L. Thausne (Paris: Ernest Leroux, 1885), vol. 3, p. 64.

12. Johannes Burchard, *Alla Corte di Cinque Papi, Diario 1483–1506,* trans. of his *Liber Notarum* by Luca Bianchi (Milan: Longanesi, 1988), p. 232. Burchard reports

that "around two thousand Spaniards" attacked the Swiss; this was thought to have been revenge for the robbing of the house of Cesare Borgia's mother during the visit of the French king in Rome in January.

13. Leopold von Ranke, *History of the Popes,* trans. E. Fowler (New York: Colonial Press, 1901), p. 37.

14. Francesco Guicciardini, *The History of Italy,* trans. Sidney Alexander (New York: Macmillan, 1969), p. 185.

15. Edward Said, *Culture and Imperialism* (New York: Vintage, 1994), p. 9. Writing about the two dominant nineteenth-century empires, France and Great Britain, Said defines imperialism as "the practice, the theory, and the attitudes of a dominating metropolitan center ruling a distant territory; 'colonialism,' which is almost always a consequence of imperialism, is the implanting of settlements on distant territory." This definition fits Spain's relationship with Rome quite well as far as it goes. But Michael Doyle's definition of empire as quoted by Said gets closer to the sixteenth-century reality: "Empire is a relationship, formal or informal, in which one state controls the effective political sovereignty of another political society. It can be achieved by force, by political collaboration, by economic, social, or cultural dependence." This last sentence, in particular, succinctly sums up the range of Spanish imperial practices in Rome. Although force, or hard imperialism, was used by Spain, more often than not it was the softer imperial strategies of political collaboration and economic, social, and cultural dependence that marked the Spanish approach to Rome.

16. Montaigne, *The Travel Journal,* trans. Donald M. Frame (San Francisco: North Point Press, 1983), p. 72.

17. Ibid., p. 91.

18. Gregory Martin, *Roma Sancta,* ed. George Parks (Rome: Edizioni di storia e letteratura, 1969), p. 194.

19. Jean Delumeau, *Vie économique et sociale de Rome* (Paris: Bibliothèque des écoles français d'Athènes et de Rome, 1957), pp. 199–200. Delumeau cites a late sixteenth-century source that called the Spanish community "plus riche en hommes que n'importe quelle autre de la ville."

20. AOP, leg. 71, unfoliated.

21. Peter Burke, *The Historical Anthropology of Early Modern Italy* (Cambridge: Cambridge University Press, 1987), p. 49.

22. See Michael W. Doyle, *Empires* (Ithaca: Cornell University Press, 1986), p. 135. Doyle defines formal and informal empire as follows: "Formal empire signifies rule by annexation and government by colonial governors supported by metropolitan troops and local collaborators. Informal empire involves an Athenian pattern of control exercised indirectly, by bribes and manipulation of dependent collaborating elites, over the legally independent peripheral regime's domestic and external policies."

23. Montaigne, *Travel Journal,* p. 79.

24. Vincenzo Forcella, *Iscrizioni delle chiese e d'altri edifici di Roma* (Rome: Tip. delle scienze matematiche e fisiche, 1873), pp. 209–210.

25. Benedetto Croce, *La spagna nella vita italiana* (Bari: Laterza, 1949). It is far from surprising that Croce, who established a different type of Italian cultural hegemony in his own historical writings, would have such an aversion to the hegemony of Spain in this period. For a revealing analysis of Croce's preferred hegemony see Edmund E. Jacobitti, "Hegemony Before Gramsci: The Case of Benedetto Croce," *Journal of Modern History* 52 (1980): 66–84.

CHAPTER 1: FOUNDATIONS

1. Antonio de la Torre y del Cerro, *Don Juan Margarit, Embajador de los Reyes Católicos en Italia, 1481–84* (Madrid: Archivo del Ministerio de Asuntos Exteriores, 1948), p. 5.

2. Ibid., p. 6.

3. Michael Mallet, *The Borgias* (London: Bodley Head, 1969), p. 112. Regarding Ferdinand's attitude toward the junior and illegitimate branch of the Aragonese monarchy, Mallet notes that he regarded them "with mixed feelings of patronizing tolerance and ultimate self interest."

4. Torre y del Cerro, *Don Juan Margarit,* p. 21.

5. See Ludwig Pastor, *History of the Popes,* ed. Ralph Francis Kerr (St. Louis: Herder, 1928), vol, 5, pp. 249–270 for a pro-papal but detailed account of the war.

6. See Mallet, *Borgias,* pp. 94–102. Briefly summarized, the erratic and shifting relations between Ferdinand and the cardinal that marked the entirety of Roderigo's life were put in high relief during this crisis. Before the 1484 conflict, relations between the two men had been very wary. In 1472 the cardinal had been sent as papal legate to Spain, where he met Ferdinand for the first time and presented him with the papal dispensation to marry Isabella that Ferdinand needed because they shared great-great-grandparents. During that trip Roderigo played a minor role in the union of the crowns of Castile and Aragon by promoting the marriage and was credited with helping to end the civil wars in Spain. He presided over the marriage of Queen Juana of Naples at the king's request and in 1478 was invited to be godfather of the monarch's son. Relations chilled, however, in 1484, when Roderigo succeeded in getting the bishopric of Seville, which Ferdinand wanted for his own bastard son. Ferdinand subsequently imprisoned Roderigo's bastard son, Pedro Luís, who was living in Spain, and seized all the Borgia properties. It was only after Cardinal Borgia's successful mediation between the pope and the king of Naples that the breach was mended: and Pedro Luís was given the title of duke of Gandia, and all Pedro's properties restored.

7. J. N. Hillgarth, *The Spanish Kingdoms, 1250–1516,* 2 vols. (Oxford: Clarendon, 1976–1978), vol. 2, p. 551. Also see Mallet, who points out that another agreement worked out between Alexander VI and the Spanish monarchs in 1493 led to the pope's intervention in the New World boundary dispute with Portugal. The famous bull *Inter Caetera* of that same year set boundaries that greatly favored Spain, and in return the Spanish monarchs agreed to push forward the marriage of the pope's son Juan to a cousin of the king, Maria Enriquez (*Borgias,* p. 128).

8. Hillgarth, *Spanish Kingdoms,* vol. 2, p. 552. Hillgarth points out that the war

of 1495 also gave Ferdinand his first military footholds in Naples. It was at that time that the Captain Gonzalvo Fernandez de Córdoba was sent to aid the new Neapolitan king Alfonso II, on condition that Ferdinand be given fortresses in Calabria and Naples in exchange.

9. Pastor, *History of the Popes,* vol. 6, p. 64. The princes accused each other of being usurpers of authority, among other things.

10. Hillgarth, *Spanish Kingdoms,* vol. 2, p. 552. The Treaty of Granada (1500) established the partition, but fighting between the French and Spanish began almost immediately. It continued until the decisive battle of Cerignola in April 1503, when the Spanish army destroyed the French using new methods of war; Naples fell to Spain in May. See Jerry H. Bentley, *Politics and Culture in Renaissance Naples* (Princeton: Princeton University Press, 1987), pp. 37–39, for a succinct synthesis of events leading up to the Treaty of Granada and its aftermath.

11. James Hankins, "The Popes and Humanism," pp. 47–85 in *Rome Reborn,* ed. Anthony Grafton (Washington, D.C.: Library of Congress, 1993). See especially pp. 66–70.

12. Anthony Grafton, "The Ancient City Restored," in *Rome Reborn,* pp. 87–123. See especially page 91: "Antiquarianism, in other words, could have a sharp political edge. But it did not need to aim at radical or subversive ends. Great Roman families, like the Orsini and the Colonna, actually traced their ancestry back to the aristocrats of the Republic."

13. For this and other biographical details see Robert Weiss, "Traccia per una biografia di Annio da Viterbo," in *Italia medioevale e umanistica* 5 (1962): 425–441.

14. *Enciclopedia italiana* (Rome: Istituto della Enciclopedia Italiana, 1949), vol. 3, p. 399. Knowledge of Annius's activities in the papal court comes from Johannes Burchard's *Liber Notarum,* in the series *Rerum Italicarum Scriptores,* vol. 2, pp. 125, 339.

15. The original volume was entitled *Commentaria Fratris Joannis Annii Viterbensis ordinid praedicator, theologiae professoris super opera diversorum auctorum de Antiquitatibus* (Rome: Eucharius Silber, 1498). Two sixteenth-century Italian translations which I refer to here are *I cinque libri delle antichità de Beroso Sacerdote Caldeo con lo commento di Giovanni Annio di Viterbo,* by Pietro Lauro Modonese (Venice, 1550), and Francesco Sansovino, *Le antichità di Beroso caldeo sacerdote . . . , et d'altri scrittori, cosi hebrei, come greci, et latini, che trattano delle stesse materie* (Venice, 1583). See Weiss, "Traccia per una biografia di Annio da Viterbo," p. 435, for details on the publication history.

16. Anthony Grafton, *Forgers and Critics* (Princeton: Princeton University Press, 1990), p. 61. It is generally assumed that Annius was quick to make use of a new Latin translation of the Greek version of the myth by Diodorus Siculus that was supplied by another fifteenth-century papal courtier, Poggio Bracciolini.

17. For one of the most thorough treatments of Annius's Egyptian myths and their artistic implications and applications in Rome, see Brian A. Curran, "Ancient Egypt and Egyptian Antiquities in Italian Renaissance Art and Culture," 2 vols. (Ph.D. diss., Princeton University, 1997), vol. 1, pp. 243–279.

18. *I cinque libri.* The history of the first Spanish kings is titled "Dei primi tempi

e di ventiquattro re di Spagna e loro antichità," ff. 286r–295r. Writing of the twentieth king, Romo, Annius constructs a fascinating relationship between Rome and Valencia and the Borgias (f. 294r).

19. For more on the ancient theology of Annius see Walter E. Stephens, "The Etruscans and the Ancient Theology in Annius of Viterbo," in *Umanesimo a Roma nel 400*, ed. Paolo Brezzi and Maristella de Panizza Lorch (Rome: Istituto di studi romani, 1984), p. 309–322. Stephens hypothesizes that the "whole meticulous reworking of Diodorus' story may be nothing more than an elaborate allegorical foreshadowing of Annius' hope for the subjugation of Italy by *Il Valentino* and Alexander" (p. 322).

20. *Annio di Viterbo,* ed. Gigliola Bonucci Caporali, volume 1 of the series *Contributi alla storia degli studi etruschi ed italiaci* (Rome: Consiglio Nazionale delle Ricerche, 1981). The second part of the volume is entitled "Annio da Viterbo Ispiratore di Cicli Pittorici," by Paola Mattiangeli, where the author pushes Annius as the inspiration for Pinturicchio (p. 269).

21. See Curran, "Ancient Egypt and Egyptian Antiquities," vol. 1, pp. 243–254, for perhaps the most concise and current artistic and historical analysis of the frescoes.

22. Mattiangeli stated this point succinctly, noting that "the identification of the Borgia bull with the divine pagan bull connected the Borgia family history with that of the Egyptian god Apis, which must therefore be interpreted as the myth of the Spanish family. With the images of the ancient Egyptian myth painted in the Sala dei Santi . . . Annio constructed a genealogy in which the pope became a direct descendant of the Egyptian Hercules, son of Isis and Osiris ("Annio da Viterbo," translation mine; p. 279).

23. Ferdinand Gregorovius, *History of the City of Rome in the Middle Ages,* trans. Annie Hamilton (London: G. Bell and Sons, 1912), vol. 8, pt. 1, p. 3, n. 2.

24. Mario Menotti, *I Borgia* (Rome: Tip. dell'Unione, 1917), vols. 1–3. A list of roughly forty notable Spaniards in Alexander VI's court is provided in an appendix in volume 3.

25. Ibid.

26. Ibid.

27. See Pastor, *History of the Popes,* vol. 5, p. 492, where he notes that in 1496 alone, Alexander appointed four new Spanish cardinals, including Juan Lopez, Bartolomeo Martini, Juan de Castro, and his son Juan de Borgia. This brought the total to nine in that year.

28. See Manuel Vaquero Pineiro, "Una realtà nazionale composita: Communità e chiese 'spagnole' a Roma," in *Roma Capitale,* ed. Segio Gensini (Pisa: Pacini editore, 1994).

29. A. Ademollo, *Alessandro VI, Giulio II, e Leone X nel Carnevale di Roma* (Florence: A. Borzi, 1967), pp. 25–26.

30. Francesco Guicciardini, *Storia d'Italia,* ed. Constantino Panigada (Bari: Laterza, 1929), vol. 2, p. 97.

31. Peter de Roo, *Materials for a History of Pope Alexander VI* (Bruges: Universal

Knowledge Foundation, 1924), vol. 3, p. 248. De Roo cites Burchard on the revenge of the Orsini against Spanish residents in Rome. Guicciardini also notes the burning of houses and warehouses belonging to Spanish courtiers and merchants (*Storia d'Italia*, vol. 2, p. 99).

32. Gregorovius, *History of the City of Rome*, vol. 8, pt. 1, p. 5.

33. Hillgarth, *Spanish Kingdoms*, vol. 2, p. 581. In a bull of 1493 Alexander VI conferred title to the Indies to the Spanish monarchs.

34. Guicciardini, *Storia d'Italia*, vol. 2, pp. 115-138. Guicciardini's account of the Spanish victory in Naples and the related demise of Cesare Borgia is still the clearest contemporary summary of these events.

35. Gregorovius, *History of the City of Rome*, vol. 8, pt. 1, p. 44. In the Treaty of Blois (1505) Louis XII renounced Naples and gave his niece Germaine de Foix to Ferdinand in marriage.

36. Jesús Manglano y Cuculo de Monfull, baron of Terrateig, *Política en Italia del Rey Católico, 1507-1516* (Madrid: Consejo Superior de Investigaciones Científicos, 1958), p. 67. The most detailed study for these years, this work is marked by an extensive use of the resources in the national archive in Simancas, the Royal Academy of History, and the Archivo Histórico Nacional. Its argument, however, is also marked by the strong nationalism of the Franco era that leads to rather amazing suspensions of historical judgment or leaps of faith. In Terrateig's view, for example, Alexander VI was probably the "uncle" of Caesar and his other children.

37. See Terrateig, *Política en Italia del Rey Católico*, vol. 1, pp. 149-175, for the most detailed account of the negotiations and stipulations of the investiture and related military alliance.

38. Letter from Ferdinand to the Spanish ambassador in Rome, dated April 14, 1507, preserved in the Archivo Histórico Nacional in Madrid. Cited by Terrateig, *Política en Italia del Rey Católico*, vol. 2, pp. 18-26.

39. Guicciardini, *Storia d'Italia*, p. 196.

40. J. Hillgarth, *Spanish Kingdoms*, vol. 2, p. 581.

41. The full letter is found in Terrateig, *Política en Italia del Rey Católico*, vol. 2, pp. 104-107.

42. For details see Pastor, *History of the Popes*, vol. 6, pp. 368-373.

43. J. Hillgarth, *Spanish Kingdoms*, vol. 2, pp. 563, 567.

44. AGS, Estado, Roma, leg. 847, unfoliated doc. 72, 1513.

45. Hillgarth, *Spanish Kingdoms*, vol. 2, p. 584.

CHAPTER 2: CHARLES V AND THE
SPANISH MYTH OF ROME

1. *Topos*, defined as both a geographical place and a common place or element of rhetoric, serves well to bring together the dual realities of Spanish Rome as a literary creation and a physical place and community.

2. For recent work on the ancient Roman period, see S. J. Keay, *Roman Spain* (Berkeley: University of California Press, 1988), and J. S. Richardson, *Hispaniae: Spain*

and the Development of Roman Imperialism, 218–82 B.C. (Cambridge: Cambridge University Press, 1987).

3. See especially Amos Parducci's review of the theatrical literature in the early modern and modern period, "Drammi spagnoli d'argomento romano," in *Italia e Spagna* (Rome, 1948), pp. 263–309. The author cites no fewer than 210 titles, the majority of which were produced in the seventeenth and eighteenth centuries.

4. Karl Brandi, *The Emperor Charles V,* trans. C. V. Wedgwood (London: Jonathan Cape, 1939), p. 77.

5. Ludwig Pastor, *History of the Popes,* ed. Ralph Francis Kerr (St. Louis: Herder, 1928), vol. 7, p. 257.

6. See Brandi, *Emperor Charles V,* pp. 152–165, for what remains the most balanced and lucid synthesis of the diplomatic details of the alliance and war against Francis I of France.

7. Ibid., p. 208.

8. See Pastor, *History of the Popes,* vol. 10, pp. 231–245, for details on the conclave.

9. Ibid., vol. 10, pp. 270–271.

10. For a fine synthesis and analysis of contemporary humanist accounts of the sack see Kenneth Gouwens, *Remembering the Renaissance: Humanist Narratives of the Sack of Rome* (Leiden: Brill, 1998). For the impact of the sack on artistic production see especially André Chastel, *The Sack of Rome, 1527* (Princeton: Princeton University Press, 1983). Good general histories include E. R. Chamberlain's, *The Sack of Rome* (London: Batsford, 1979), and Judith Hook's *The Sack of Rome* (London: Macmillan, 1972).

11. See Pastor, *History of the Popes,* vol. 9, pp. 306–386 for a detailed account of the events leading up to the sack.

12. Ibid., vol. 9, p. 398. Pastor gives a detailed description of the sack and its aftermath in chapters 11 and 12, pp. 388–467. His account, which strongly emphasizes the cruelty of the Spaniards in the sack, is marked by a clear anti-Spanish sentiment that dominates much of his history of the sixteenth and seventeenth centuries. Frequently unsubstantiated by primary sources or making selective use of those available, Pastor's account of the Spanish place in Roman history is distorted by his obvious distaste for their influence in Italy and Rome.

13. Luigi Guicciardini, *The Sack of Rome,* trans. and ed. James H. McGregor (New York: Italica, 1993). Speaking of the soldiers, this contemporary source notes, "Nor did they treat the Spaniards, Germans, and the Flemish who had lived a long time in Rome any better than any Italian courtier or clergyman" (p. 98).

14. André Chastel, *The Sack of Rome, 1527,* trans. Beth Archer (Princeton: Princeton University Press, 1977), p. 108. "The Germans were bad, the Italians worse, and the Spanish worst of all," wrote one contemporary survivor, the Augustinian prior Kilian Leib, about the invaders.

15. Ibid., p. 107.

16. Gouwens, *Remembering the Renaissance,* p. 83.

17. Marcel Bataillon, *Erasme et l'Espagne* (Paris: Droz, 1937), p. 258.

18. Brandi, *Emperor Charles V*, p. 207.

19. Hook, *Sack of Rome*, p. 282. It is symbolically appropriate that Charles V first heard news of the sack while celebrating the birth of Philip II in Valladolid. The news caused him to cease all celebrations, and it is certain that when the duke of Alba's troops were outside of Rome during Philip's war with Paul IV thirty years later the lessons of 1527 were not lost on either side.

20. Alfonso de Valdés, *Diálogo de las cosas ocurridas en Roma* (Madrid: Ediciones de "La Lectura," 1928).

21. Ibid., p. 73.

22. Ibid., p. 82.

23. Ibid., p. 83.

24. Ibid., p. 143.

25. Ibid., p. 222.

26. Bataillon, *Erasme et l'Espagne*, p. 415.

27. Ibid.

28. *"Descriptio Urbis": The Roman Census of 1527*, ed. Egmont Lee (Rome: Bulzoni, 1985), pp. 310-312. In addition to heads of households the census counted *bocche*, or mouths, which totaled 53,689. Who exactly was included under the designation *spagnolo* is not clear, but since only one head of household was identified as *catalanus* it seems reasonable to assume that at this point people from the kingdoms of both Aragon and Castile were identified as *spagnolo*.

29. AGS, Estado, Roma, leg. 848, document 29, unfoliated.

30. Pastor, *History of the Popes*, vol. 10, p. 39.

31. Brandi, *Emperor Charles V*, pp. 276-277.

32. Pastor, *History of the Popes*, vol. 10, pp. 56-57.

33. Ibid., vol. 10, p. 98.

34. Ibid.

35. Brandi, *Emperor Charles V*, pp. 369, 438.

36. Biblioteca El Escorial, MS 1.3.30-31. The document is entitled *Raggionamento di Carlo V Imperatore al Re Filippo suo Figliuolo nella consignatione del governo de suoi stati e regni dove si contiene come debba governare in tempo della pace e della guerra*, ff. 24-112r.

37. Florián de Ocampo and Ambrosio Morales, *La Crónica de España* (Zamora, 1541; Alcalá, 1574). Ocampo's history was originally intended to go through the Gothic period, but the writer died after completing the first five books, which went up only to the Roman period. These books were first published in 1541. Morales took up the task on Ocampo's death and published seventeen more books in three volumes in 1574. I have used the 1791 Madrid edition of Ocampo and Morales's *Crónica* edited by Benito Cano.

38. Antonio Palau y Dulcet, *Manual del librero hispanoamericano* (Barcelona and Oxford: Libreria Palau, 1973) vol. 2, pp. 299-300.

39. The best study on Spanish printing thus far is Clive Griffin's book on the Cromberger printing house in Seville, *The Crombergers of Seville* (Oxford: Clarendon, 1988). According to Griffin, evidence for the sixteenth century suggests that print-

ings ran as high as a thousand copies, although the average may have been closer to seven hundred.

40. Ocampo and Morales, *Crónica,* vol. 1, p. 16.

41. Ibid., vol. 1, p. 385.

42. Ibid., vol. 1, pp. i–ii.

43. In this sense, the genesis of Ocampo and Morales's work is politics, or what Hegel called the "internal vital principle" of history that he claims formed the "pragmatic basis" of all historical narrative. See Hayden White, "Narrative in Historical Theory," *History and Theory* 23, no. 1 (1984): 4.

44. See Hayden White, "The Value of Narration in the Representation of Reality," in his *The Content of the Form* (Baltimore: Johns Hopkins University Press, 1987), p. 13.

45. Ocampo and Morales, *Crónica,* vol. 1, p. ii.

46. Ibid., vol. 1, p. vii.

47. Ibid., vol. 1, p. 125.

48. See H. J. Erasmus, *The Origins of Rome in Historiography from Petrarch to Perizonius* (Assen: Van Gorcum, 1962), pp. 49–50. Erasmus assumes that Ocampo relied on Annius for the basic ancient story of the Spanish king Italus.

49. Ocampo and Morales, *Crónica,* vol. 1, p. 134.

50. Ibid., vol. 1, p. 145.

51. Ibid., vol. 1, p. 146.

52. Pastor, *History of the Popes,* vol. 11, pp. 224–231.

53. AGS, Estado, Roma, leg. 863. An unfoliated document from 1535 entitled *Memorial del subsidio* noted that 252,000 ducats were granted. In a later document from 1536, AGS, Estado, Roma, leg. 865, f. 7r, it was specified that 40,000 would come from the clergy of Aragon and the rest from the clergy of Castile.

54. AGS, Estado, Roma, leg. 865, f. 18r.

55. Brandi, *Emperor Charles V,* pp. 365–67.

56. Pastor, *History of the Popes,* vol. 11, p. 239.

57. Ibid., vol. 11, pp. 241–245.

58. Ibid., vol. 11, pp. 254–256. Paul's sons also benefited: Cardinal Alessandro was promised the bishopric of either Jaen or Monreale and Ottavio a state in Naples with an income of ten thousand ducats.

59. AGS, Estado, Roma, leg. 867, unfoliated, doc. 138. In 1538, for example, the Spanish ambassador in Rome wrote to Charles with a list of requests coming from people in the court, including one from an Italian member of the curial office of the datary who sought the *naturaleza* (a form of naturalization) from Castile so that he could receive pensions from that kingdom.

60. AGS, Estado, Roma, leg. 867, 1538, unfoliated, document 66.

61. Pastor, *History of the Popes,* vol. 11, p. 291.

62. Brandi, *Emperor Charles V,* p. 498. Margaret apparently disliked both her husband and his family a great deal and occasionally served as a spy for her father.

63. AGS, Estado, Roma, leg. 870, unfoliated, document 3. In 1541 the marquis

of Aguilar, Charles's ambassador in Rome, wrote to the emperor with one of the most detailed accounts of the Colonna crisis.

64. Ibid.

65. Leopold von Ranke, *History of the Popes,* trans. E. Fowler (New York: Colonial Press, 1901), vol. 1, p. 261.

66. AGS, Estado, Roma, leg. 872, doc. 10. The letter is entitled *Instrucion para vos Juan de Vega del nuestro consejo de lo que aveys de hazer en el cargo de nro embaxador cerca de nro muy santo padre.*

67. AGS, Estado, Roma, leg. 872, doc. 11. This is one of the first letters from Philip to Rome preserved in the national archive in Simancas, and it was a telling sign for the future that it concerned ecclesiastical finance, or, in his own words "the granting of benefices and pensions to cardinals and foreigners from those kingdoms."

68. Ranke, *History of the Popes,* vol. 1, p. 266.

69. AGS, Estado, Roma, leg. 867, unfoliated, doc. 116 and 129.

70. Biblioteca El Escorial, MS 1.3.30–31, vol. 31, f. 107r–108v.

CHAPTER 3: THE ROMAN WORLD IN THE AGE OF PHILIP II

1. Karl Brandi, *The Emperor Charles V,* trans. C. V. Wedgwood (London: Jonathan Cape, 1939), p. 632.

2. For a contemporary account of the war with Paul IV see P. Nores, *La guerra carafesca, ossia guerra degli spagnoli contro il papa Paolo IV,* Archivio Storico Italiano (Florence: Olschki, 1848), prima serie, tomo 12.

3. Vat. Lat. 13411, *Relatione delli Principi D'Italia,* ff. 234r–238v, contains a late sixteenth-century estimate, for example, that claimed the king annually received 4 million gold scudi from his Italian possessions.

4. Leopold von Ranke, *History of the Popes,* trans. E. Fowler (New York: Colonial Press, 1901), vol. 1, p. 196.

5. BAV, Urb. Lat. 849, "Trattato sopra alli disordini d'Italia al Re Felippo," f. 65r.

6. BAV, Urb. Lat. 849, "Trattato secondo al med.o delli rimedii, che converebbero alli disordine sopra detto," f. 79.

7. BAV, Vat. Lat. 13411, unfoliated. "Relatione de Roma nel tempo de Papa Pio V fatta dal Sig.r Michel Suriano l'anno 1571."

8. See especially the letters written by the duke in Grottaferrata and Ostia from October 24 to December 2, 1556: duque de Alba, *Epistolario del III Duque de Alba Don Fernando Alvarez de Toledo* (Madrid, 1952), vol. 1, 1536–1567, pp. 434–446. Among the recipients were Cardinals Pacheco, Camerlengo, Belay, Burgos, Santaflor, and Caraffa. The letter to the emperor of October 31 reveals a particularly confident posture on the part of the duke, who sees peace on his terms as being imminent (pp. 439–440).

9. See BAV, Urb. Lat. 1038, f. 266r.

10. Brandi, *Emperor Charles V,* p. 640.

11. Urb. Lat. 1038, ff. 162v–163r.

12. Urb. Lat. 1038, f. 163r.

13. BAV, Urb. Lat. 1038, f. 266r.

14. AGS, Estado, Roma, leg. 883, unfoliated.

15. For an insightful account of the function of archives in building empire see Thomas Richards, "Archive and Utopia," *Representations* 37 (1992): 105. In a point that can also be applied to both the Roman and Spanish use and functions of archives Richards writes, "These forms of universal knowledge retained a specific ideological force as a means for representing the vast and various empire as a closely organized unit," and "in a particular domain of empire a myth of knowledge was actually capable of producing what was taken for positive fact"; "the production of certain kinds of knowledge was in fact constitutive of the extension of certain forms of power."

16. Ranke summed up the point saying, "A cordial understanding with the Pope was most essential to Philip II, whose authority in Spain, being founded in a great measure on ecclesiastical interests, it was his policy to keep these carefully in his hands" (*History of the Popes,* vol. 1, p. 234).

17. The literature on the papal conclaves for the period 1559–1622 is extensive, and Pastor's *History of the Popes* remains the most thorough secondary source, providing a synthesis of the primary Italian accounts. He omits, however, substantial primary sources compiled by Spaniards and Italian subjects of the Spanish crown in Italy. These include the volumes entitled *Relaciones de los conclaves* found in the University of Salamanca Library, MSS 2156–2158, which cover the entire period in question, and the accounts kept by the Council of State, which include royal correspondence with cardinals and ambassadors. These are found in the Simancas collection in a volume entitled *Conclaves,* leg. 1870. I consulted both these sources, as well as the secondary accounts, for this study.

18. BAV, Urb. Lat. 1039, f. 106r.

19. HSA, MS HC 380/170, f. 10r. "Respuesta de Fray Melchor Cano a una consulta de Phelipe Segundo sobre hacer guerra al Papa."

20. BAV, Urb. Lat. 1039, f. 92v.

21. See John Elliott, *Imperial Spain* (London: Penguin, 1963), p. 200, where he notes that "the financial contribution of the Spanish Church to Hapsburg imperialism in the sixteenth and seventeenth centuries still awaits an adequate study, but its importance would be difficult to overestimate." A similar lacuna is true concerning Spanish contributions to Rome in this period, a lacuna which this study hopes to begin to fill.

22. BAV, Urb. Lat. 1039, f. 136r.

23. For a good history of ecclesiastical taxes, including the *subsidio, cruzada,* and *decima* in the late fifteenth and early sixteenth centuries, see Tarsicio de Azcona, "Aspectos económicos referentes al episcopado y al clero," in *Historia de la Iglesia en España,* ed. Ricardo García-Villoslada (Madrid: Edica, 1980), vol. 3, pt. 1, pp. 190–91. The papal bulls and briefs granting and renewing the cruzada and subsidio

between 1458 and 1576 can be found in AGS, Estado, Roma, legs. 19 and 20. For the later decades, the various renewals and additional concessions from Rome including the excusado are found in numerous other legajos in Simancas containing the diplomatic correspondence. They will be noted in the following pages.

24. See Elliott, *Imperial Spain*, pp. 201, 286. Elliott notes that the excusado consisted of the tithes paid on the wealthiest piece of property in each parish.

25. Vat. Lat. 13411, "Memoria di quel che fruttano al Re di Spagna un anno per altro le Bolle della Crucciata, et altre Bolle di Chiese, et Monasterii: et Giubilei che chiamano di Cura, et sussidio Ecc.o," ff. 167v–202v. The cruzada was reported to bring in 1,080,000 ducats, and of this the king received 864,000 over three years.

26. BAV, Urb. Lat. 1039, f. 138v.

27. For the most thorough treatment of the *patronato real* in both Iberia and the New World see W. Eugene Shiels, *King and Church: The Rise and Fall of the Patronato Real* (Chicago: Loyola University Press, 1961).

28. Nicolás López Martínez, "La desamortización de bienes eclesiásticos en 1574," *Hispania* 86 (1962): 238.

29. For the later figures see Quintín Aldea, "La economía en las iglesias locales," *Hispania* 26 (1973): 23.

30. The royal share of New World treasure first reached 9,060,725 ducats in the period 1581–1585. From 1561 to 1565 the total was 2,183,440. For a complete account for the period from 1503 to 1660 see Elliott, *Imperial Spain*, p. 184.

31. See ASR, camerale II, *Spogli*, buste 1. The last pages contain a list entitled "Nota delli' Arcivescovati et Vescovati di Spagna e delle entrate loro," which lists the estimated incomes in 1561 for the seven archbishoprics and forty-one bishoprics of Spain.

32. For the medieval origins of the office of collector see William E. Lunt, *Papal Revenues in the Middle Ages* (New York: Columbia University Press, 1965). Lunt notes that there were collectors in the kingdoms of Castile and Aragon as early as the thirteenth century, although the office did not become permanent until the fourteenth century (vol. 1, p. 43, and vol. 2, pp. 36–38).

33. ASR, camerale II, *Spogli,* buste 1. f. 137v. The office of the collector was often a contentious one, and the Spanish clergy and nobility alike were sensitive to its abuse. Although there were occasional calls for an abolishment of the office, it continued throughout the sixteenth and seventeenth centuries.

34. ASR, camerale II, "Conti delle entrate e dell'uscita," buste 1, f. 6r, f. 21r. By 1589 papal income from the Spanish vacancies is listed as follows: "Dalla Colletoria di Spagna—50,000"; "Dalla Colletoria di Portugallo—4,000"; "Da Cleri del Regno di Napoli—15,090." The revenue from Spanish lands was the fifth or sixth largest item on the papal register, coming after taxes from other parts of the papal states, and, together with the 8,000 escudos payment for the feudal dues from Naples, comprised roughly 5 percent of the 1,546,279 escudos papal income for 1589.

35. BAV, Urb. Lat. 1039, f. 344r.

36. BAV, Urb. Lat 1039, f. 375r.

37. The strong influence that Spanish theologians and the Spanish monarchy

exercised at Trent is analyzed in some detail in Bernardino Llorca, "Participación de España en el Concilio de Trento," in *Historia de la Iglesia en España,* vol. 3, pt. 1, pp. 453–500. For details on the large contingent of Spanish theologians and prelates at the council see C. Gutiérrez, *Españoles en Trento* (Valladolid: Instituto Jerónimo Zurita Consejo Superior de Investigaciones Científicos, 1951).

38. Ludwig Pastor, *History of the Popes,* ed. Ralph Francis Kerr (St. Louis: Herder, 1928), vol. 15, p. 192. For a good account of the reconvening of the council see chapter 5.

39. Ibid., vol. 15, p. 272. The Spanish bishops' attempt to claim divine origins for the bishops' duty of residence, for instance, was contested by the papacy since it weakened its own central power and rights to grant dispensations.

40. Ibid., vol. 15, p. 329. The emperor was ready to grant the chalice to the laity and to allow the clergy to marry, for example; and Catherine de' Medici was about to grant religious liberty to the Huguenots in France.

41. See Blas Casado Quintanilla, "La cuestión de la precedencia España-Francia en la tercera asamblea del concilio de Trento," *Hispania Sacra* 36 (1984): 195–214, for details concerning the struggle for precedence.

42. For the importance of the general issue of precedence during the reign of Philip II see his first biographer, Luís Cabrera de Córdoba, *Felipe Segundo, Rey de España* (Madrid: Aribau, 1876), vol. 1, p. 397. Writing about the conflict over precedence in Rome in 1564, Cabrera de Córdoba explains the importance of this issue to the court's self-image as the greatest European power. For Philip it was not simply a matter of local prestige in Rome or Trent but rather something that touched on the historical place and legitimacy of Spain. Cabrera de Córdoba underlines the perceived historical importance of the debate when he argues that the Spain of Philip II deserved greater privileges and honors in Rome because it had finally regained its ancient status as a united and restored kingdom. Cabrera de Córdoba claims that the traditional privileges of the crowns of Aragon, Castile, and Navarre were lesser than those of a united Spain. Moreover, he argues that because Spain had been united under the Christian Visigothic king Recared in the seventh century, before France was united under Charlemagne, the historical precedence should go to the Spanish ambassador.

43. Ibid., vol. 1, pp. 330–332.

44. The French did retain diplomatic precedence in Rome in the face of strong attempts by Philip II to usurp this traditional privilege. Historical precedent was too strong and the threat of a serious breach in relations with France too great for the pope to take this extra step.

45. AGS, Estado, Roma, leg. 2014, "Tractado de precedencia en favor de Spagna." ff. 94r–106v.

46. AGS, Estado, Roma, f. 94r.

47. AGS, Estado, Roma, 94v.

48. AGS, Estado, Roma, f. 98r–98v. The section was entitled "Li servitii del Re di Spagna."

49. See BAV, Urb. Lat. 1040, f. 161v. The *Avvisi* report stated that the Spanish

king had not tried to intervene and that his ambassador had only "spoken to the sacred college and presented the letters of His Majesty without nominating anyone in particular, and he asked them in the name of his king to choose a good pope, who would be a good pastor." Ranke also notes that contemporaries such as Carlos Borromeo had considered "religion and purity of faith" above all else (*History of the Popes*, pp. 242-243). Even Pastor believed that Philip "in spite of his many shortcomings" refused to use his great influence in the election (*History of the Popes*, vol. 17, p. 12).

50. AGS, Estado, Roma, leg. 901, unfoliated.

51. Ibid. The full text provides an excellent synthesis of Philip's views on the qualities of a pope: "And so you should know that my intention in past elections has always been, and is also now, that he [the pope] have the zeal he must for the service of the Lord and to watch out for the universal good of Christendom and its peace, both eliminating errors and dissensions that have arisen in religion . . . and at the same time that he [the pope] have as a goal to conserve the peace, unity, and conformity of Christianity, especially in Italy, where there is always war."

52. BAV, Urb. Lat. 1040, f. 183v.

53. BAV, Urb. Lat. 1040, f. 270v.

54. Pastor, *History of the Popes*, vol. 18, p. 8.

55. BAV, Urb. Lat. 1040, f. 346r.

56. BAV, Urb. Lat. 1040, f. 585r.

57. BAV, Urb. Lat. 1040, f. 355v.

58. BAV, Urb. Lat 1040, f. 349r.

59. See Ranke, *History of the Popes*, p. 254. The author points out that on one occasion when Philip II was reported ill, "the pope raised his hands to Heaven, imploring God to deliver him from that malady; the aged pontiff prayed that the Almighty would take some years from his own life and add them to that of the king, on whose existence so much more depended than on his own."

60. See Luciano Serrano, *La Liga de Lepanto* (Madrid: Impr. de archivos, 1918), vol. 1, p. 30.

61. AGS, Estado, Roma, leg. 902, unfoliated. The pope wrote to Philip with this news and emphasized that he named Pompeo Colonna commander "as a servant of Your Majesty."

62. BAV, Urb. Lat. 1041, f. 50v.

63. BAV, Urb. Lat. 1041, ff. 185r, 249r.

64. BAV, Urb. Lat. 1040, ff. 436v, 490v.

65. See Paolo Prodi, *The Papal Prince*, trans. Susan Haskins (Cambridge: Cambridge University Press, 1987), pp. 121-125, for the most sophisticated discussion to date on what the author calls the symbiosis of temporal and spiritual power in the early modern papacy.

66. See Pastor, *History of the Popes*, vol. 17, pp. 344-363, vol. 18, pp. 9-11, and Elliott, *Imperial Spain*, pp. 228-229.

67. BAV, Urb. Lat. 1040, f. 394r.

68. Pastor rather dramatically claimed that "the removal of Carranza to the Eternal City is certainly one of the most striking proofs of the great impression

which the personality of Pius V had made even upon the greatest men of his time"
(vol. 17, p. 343).

69. BAV, Urb. Lat. 1041, f. 129r.

70. BAV, Urb. Lat. 1041, f. 130r.

71. BAV, Urb. Lat. 1040, f. 593r; BAV, Urb. Lat. 1041, f. 133v.

72. For a detailed, pro-papal account of these disputes see Pastor, *History of the Popes*, vol. 18, pp. 27–71.

73. BAV, Urb. Lat. 1042, f. 5r.

74. BAV, Urb. Lat. 1042, f. 34v.

75. BAV, Urb. Lat. 1041, f. 323r.

76. See Jack Beeching, *The Galleys at Lepanto* (London: Hutchinson, 1982), p. 192, for a detailed account of the preparations for the battle. Beeching puts the number of Spanish galleys at roughly ninety and the number of men paid for by Philip II at twenty thousand. Also see Geoffrey Parker, "Lepanto (1571): The Costs of Victory," in his *Spain and the Netherlands, 1559–1659* (London: Collins, 1979), pp. 122–133, for a more detailed account of the Spanish contribution; a contribution estimated at 1.2 million escudos out of a 2 million escudos estimated total cost.

77. BAV, Urb. Lat. 1042, ff. 68v–69r.

78. BAV, Urb. Lat. 1042, f. 71r.

79. Ibid.

80. Serrano, *Correspondencia diplomática*, vol. 4, p. 498.

81. BAV, Urb. Lat. 1042, ff. 158r–159r.

82. Pastor, *History of the Popes*, vol 19, p. 13.

83. Ibid., vol. 19, p. 25. In addition to Philip's firsthand knowledge of Boncompagni, Pastor notes, the Spanish ambassador had sent the king a "highly favorable account of the good qualities" of the cardinal, who "had always borne himself well in the affairs of Spain."

84. Ricardo García-Villoslada, "Felipe II y la contrareforma católica," in *Historia de la Iglesia de España*, vol. 3, pt. 2, p. 60.

85. AGS, Estado, Roma, leg. 924, unfoliated.

86. Ibid.

87. Ibid.

88. Ibid.

89. Ibid.

90. Acknowledging the positive, cooperative side of papal-Spanish relations in this period provides a necessary corrective to much of the previous historiography on both the papacy and Philip II, which emphasizes the conflict and tensions between the two powers. While it is true that in matters of ecclesiastical jurisdiction tensions remained high throughout the period—so much so that at times it may have appeared, in the words of John Elliott, that "there existed between the two a kind of undeclared war" (*Imperial Spain*, p. 230)—these disputes took second place to the larger areas of common concern. I do not wish to diminish the tensions between monarchy and papacy, especially in matters of ecclesiastical jurisdiction in Spain, Naples, and Sicily, but I do view them as generally subordinated to the over-

whelmingly cooperative and mutually beneficial foreign-policy concerns of the two powers.

91. BAV, Urb. Lat. 1047, f. 195r. The pope, for instance, told Cardinal Granvelle that he must try to dissuade the king from pursuing his designs in Portugal and from "the continued extortion that is done with little shame."

92. Pastor notes that the papal nuncio to Madrid, Monsignor Sega, described the king and pope as being like two merchants who in spite of all their juridical disagreements would never break off their mutual relations because of the interwoven interests (vol. 18, p. 366).

93. BAV, Urb. Lat. 1047, f. 167r.

94. BAV, Urb. Lat. 1046, ff. 132v, 144r.

95. AGS, Estado, Roma, leg. 905, unfoliated.

96. BAV, Urb. Lat. 1048, f. 246r.

97. BAV, Urb. Lat. 1050, f. 210r.

98. BAV, Urb. Lat. 1051, f. 258r.

99. BAV, Urb. Lat. 1051, f. 258r.

100. Pastor, *History of the Popes*, vol. 19, p. 370.

101. Ibid., vol. 19, pp. 513–39. Pastor gives details on the problems of banditry but completely omits the Spanish role in containing disgruntled vassals.

102. BAV, Urb. Lat. 1051, f. 335r.

103. BAV, Urb. Lat. 1051, f. 520r.

104. For a succinct analysis of papal finances in this period see Peter Partner, "Papal Financial Policy in the Renaissance and Counter-Reformation," *Past and Present* 88 (1980): 17–62. Partner supports my basic thesis about Spanish military dominance in Rome when he notes, "From the time of the signature of the treaty of Cateau-Cambresis in 1559 the Habsburgs were in effect bearing a large part of the true defence of the Papal State" (52).

105. Ibid., pp. 50–52.

106. BAV, Urb. Lat. 1046, f. 260r.

107. Ibid.

108. BAV, Urb. Lat. 1045, f. 444r.

109. ASR, Camerale II, "Conti delle entrate e dell'uscita," buste 1, f. 21r. These major papal registers give primary debits and credits. They include the papal income from taxes on all ecclesiastical states as well as the "spiritual spoils" from sources such as the Spanish vacancies.

110. BAV, Urb. Lat. 1045, f. 440r.

111. BAV, Urb. Lat. 1046, f. 21r.

112. BAV, Urb. Lat. 1047, f. 26r.

113. BAV, Urb. Lat. 1046, f. 377r.

114. BAV, Urb. Lat. 1047, f. 372r.

115. Florián de Ocampo and Ambrosio Morales, *La Crónica de España* (Madrid: Benito Cano, 1791), vol. 3, p. 21. See pp. 1–72 for a detailed account of Morales's professional life and work.

116. This task led to a manuscript entitled "Viaje a los reinos de León, Galicia,

y Principado de Asturias," originally composed in 1572, and published in a contemporary edition by Biblioteca Popular Asturiana (Oviedo, 1977).

117. Ocampo and Morales, *Crónica,* vol. 3, pp. xxv–lx.

118. Ibid., vol. 3, p. xlix.

119. Ibid., vol. 3, p. 31.

120. Ibid., vol. 3, p. 90.

121. Ibid., vol. 3, p. 91.

122. Ibid., vol. 4, p. 1.

123. Ibid., vol. 4, p. 39.

124. Ibid., vol. 4, p. 24.

125. Helmut G. Koenigsberger, *The Practice of Empire* (Ithaca: Cornell University Press, 1969), p. 47.

126. See especially Marie Tanner, *The Last Descendant of Aeneas* (New Haven: Yale University Press, 1992), for an eloquent analysis of this process. Also see Francis A. Yates, *Astraea: The Imperial Theme in the Sixteenth Century* (London: Routledge and Kegan Paul, 1975) for the broader European manifestations of this same theme.

127. Tzvetan Todorov. *The Semiotic Conquest of America* (New Orleans: Graduate School of Tulane University, 1982), p. 13.

128. *Enciclopedia cattolica* (Florence, 1951), vol. 3, p. 1368.

129. Alejandro Recio, *La 'Historica Descriptio Urbis Romae,' obra manuscrita de Fr. Alonso Chacón* (Rome, 1968), p. 60.

130. Ibid., p. 55.

131. See ibid., pp. 65–69, for a complete list of Chacón's works.

132. Ibid., p. 77. The list of Chacón's books is preserved, albeit in a confused state, in the Vatican library, MS Vat. Lat. 8185.

133. Alfonso Chacón, *Historia Ceu Verissima a Columniis multorum vindicata* (Rome, 1576), p. 1r.

134. Ibid., p. 1v.

135. Ibid., pp. 4–12.

136. Ibid., p. 33.

137. Giovanni Pietro Bellori and Pietro Santi Bartoli, *Colonna Traiano* (Rome: Rossi, 1673).

138. Pastor, *History of the Popes,* vol. 21, p. 42.

139. BAV, Urb. Lat. 1053, f. 328v.

140. BAV, Urb. Lat. 1053, f. 290r.

141. BAV, Urb. Lat. 1053, f. 356r.

142. AGS, Estado, Roma, leg. 946, unfoliated, an excellent summation of the amounts received from the three gracias from 1560 to 1585. The general sum of 2 million ducats is also noted in Pastor, *History of the Popes,* vol. 21, p. 264.

143. BAV, Urb. Lat. 1054, f. 207r.

144. BAV, Urb. Lat. 1054, f. 430r.

145. For the definitive study of the grain supply in early modern Rome and the Papal State see Volker Reinhardt, *Überleben in der frühneuzeitlichen Stadt: Annona und Getreideversorgung in Rom, 1563–1797* (Tübingen: Niemeyer, 1991).

146. For the best description of the complicated system of Italian weights and measures see Ronald E. Zupko, *Italian Weights and Measures from the Middle Ages to the Nineteenth Century* (Philadelphia: American Philosophical Society, 1981). According to Zupko, a rubbio of grain fluctuated between roughly 8 and 9 kilograms in this period (p. 234). What further complicates the matter is that in many of the Roman documents, such as the Avvisi, the measure used for grain was the salma. See pp. 241–252 for variations in the salma.

147. Reinhardt, *Uberleben in der frühneuzeitlichen Stadt*, p. 131.

148. Ibid., pp. 130–133. These figures are taken from the more expansive chart on all grain imports.

149. BAV, Urb. Lat. 1054, f. 164r.

150. BAV, Urb. Lat. 1054, f. 396v.

151. See García-Villoslada, "Felipe II y la contrareforma católica," pp. 70–71, for a succinct description of the *Pragmática de las cortesías* and the reaction of Rome.

152. See Philip II's angry letter to Sixtus, quoted in full in Pastor, *History of the Popes*, vol. 21, p. 366, in which the king accuses the pope of actually having "allowed heresy to take root in France."

153. BAV, Urb. Lat. 1058, f. 107v.

154. For more details on the conflict and negotiations involving French affairs Pastor, *History of the Popes*, vol. 21, pp. 340–369; Ranke, *History of the Popes*, vol. 2, pp. 141–149.

155. Pastor, *History of the Popes*, vol. 21, p. 366.

156. BAV, Urb. Lat. 1058, f. 453v.

157. BAV, Urb. Lat. 1058, f. 485r.

158. BAV, Urb. Lat. 1058, f. 523r.

159. Ranke, *History of the Popes*, vol. 2, p. 153.

160. Ibid.

161. Jean Delumeau, *Vie économique et sociale de Rome* (Paris: Bibliothèque des écoles français d'Athènes et de Rome, 1957), vol. 2, p. 619.

162. Urb. Lat. 1059, f. 7r.

163. Urb. Lat. 1058, f. 606r and 606v.

164. BAV, Urb. Lat. 1059, f. 28r. A report from the nuncio in Spain claimed that the king had ordered 10,000 rubbi of grain be sent to Rome from Sicily each year.

165. BAV, Urb. Lat. 1059, f. 77r.

166. BAV, Urb. Lat. 1059, f. 95v.

167. BAV, Urb. Lat. 1059, f. 136v.

168. Delumeau, *Vie économique*, vol. 2, p. 857.

169. BAV, Urb. Lat. 1059, f. 138r.

170. BAV, Urb. Lat. 1059, f. 188r.

171. BAV, Urb. Lat. 1059, f. 381v. From the beginning of the fourteenth century to the mid-fifteenth century, in what became known as the Avignon Captivity, the papacy was located in Avignon, enabling the French monarchy to dominate papal affairs.

172. Ranke, *History of the Popes*, vol. 2, p. 157.

173. BAV, Urb. Lat. 1059, f .361v.

174. BAV, Urb. Lat. 1059, f. 376r.

175. BAV, Urb. Lat. 1059, f. 357r.

176. BAV, Urb. Lat. 1060, f. 107v.

177. BAV, Urb. Lat. 1060, f. 421v.

178. BAV, Urb. Lat. 1060, f. 167v.

179. See table 1.

180. AGS, Estado, Roma, leg. 959, unfoliated.

181. BAV, Urb. Lat. 1061, f. 71v.

182. BAV, Urb. Lat. 1061, f. 609r.

183. BAV, Urb. Lat. 1060, f. 174r.

184. BAV, Urb. Lat. 1060, f. 305v.

185. BAV, Urb. Lat. 1060, f. 388r.

186. BAV, Urb. Lat. 1060, f. 307r.

187. Most Roman affairs were handled by the king personally during the reign of Philip II, but in his later years and during much of the reign of Philip III this council, which included former ambassadors Olivares and Sessa, took on more importance. It is indicative of the centrality of Roman affairs in the politics of Imperial Spain that it is in the "State" section of the Simancas archive that the bulk of Rome-related documents can be found. This is in contrast with the other Italian territories, which were supervised by the less powerful Council of Italy. For a succinct introduction to the history of the Council of Italy see Manuel Rivero Rodríguez, "La fundación del consejo de Italia," in *Instituciones y elites de poder en la monarquía hispana durante el Siglo XVI,* ed. José Martínez Millan (Madrid: Ediciones de la Universidad Antónoma de Madrid, 1992).

188. BAV, Urb. Lat. 1061, f. 480v.

189. BAV, Urb. Lat. 1061, f. 480v.

190. AGS, Estado, Roma, leg. 959, unfoliated.

191. BAV, Urb. Lat. 1063, ff. 494r and 545r.

192. BAV, Urb. Lat. 1062, f. 490r.

193. AGS, Estado, Roma, leg. 965, unfoliated.

194. Pastor, *History of the Popes,* vol. 23, p. 267.

195. BAV, Urb. Lat. 1062, f. 542r, 580r.

196. BAV, Urb. Lat. 1062, f. 493v.

197. BAV, Urb. Lat. 1063, f. 336v.

198. Pastor, *History of the Popes,* vol. 23, p. 134. For details on negotiations leading up to the absolution, Spanish opposition, and the event itself see pp. 100–146.

199. AGS, Estado, Roma, leg. 968, unfoliated.

200. Philip's health was closely watched in Rome, and it was known that he was very sick as early as 1596.

201. The nature of Philip II's patron-client relationships, which ranged from the horizontal relationship of equals that he had with the pope to the more complex webs of clients whom he cultivated among cardinals and other Roman nobility, will be analyzed in more detail in the following chapter.

202. BAV, Urb. Lat. 1063, f. 568v.

203. BAV, Urb. Lat. 1064, f. 52r.

204. Ranke, *History of the Popes*, vol. 2, pp. 186–89.

205. Ibid., p. 192.

206. Pastor, *History of the Popes*, vol. 23, p. 212.

207. BAV, Urb. Lat. 1067, f. 558r.

208. BAV, Urb. Lat. 1067, f. 579v.

209. BAV, Urb. Lat. 1068, f. 182r.

210. AGS, Estado, Roma, leg. 1856, unfoliated.

211. Ibid.

212. Pastor, *History of the Popes*, vol. 23, p. 207.

213. See especially Pastor, *History of the Popes*, vol. 23, pp. 248–258, for details on the cardinals created by Clement VIII.

214. BAV, Urb. Lat. 1071, f. 15r.

215. BAV, Urb. Lat. 1071, f. 15v.

216. Jerónimo Gracián, *Trattato del giubileo dell'anno santo* (Rome, 1599).

217. *Enciclopedia cattòlica*, vol. 6, p. 666.

218. Gracián, *Trattato*, p. 20.

219. Ibid., pp. 97–99.

220. Ibid., p. 99.

221. Miguel de Cervantes, *The Trials of Persiles and Sigismunda*, trans. Celia Weller and Clark Colahan (Berkeley: University of California Press, 1989).

222. Ibid., p. 127.

223. Ibid., p. 312.

224. BAV, Urb. Lat. 1073, f. 114r.

225. See Pastor, *History of the Popes*, vol. 25, pp. 1–27, for details on the conclave.

226. BAV, Urb. Lat. 1073, f. 216r.

227. Pastor, *History of the Popes*, vol. 25, p. 38.

228. BAV, Urb. Lat. 1073, f. 290r.

229. Pastor, *History of the Popes*, vol. 25, p. 42.

230. AGS, Estado, Roma, leg. 1858, unfoliated, doc. 45.

231. BAV, Urb. Lat. 1073, f. 542r.

232. See BAV, Urb. Lat. 1073, where it is reported that the pope had sent his nephew to Palermo to seek grain (f. 480r), and that he had been successful in his negotiations (f. 606r).

233. BAV, Urb. Lat. 1074, f. 37r.

234. BAV, Urb. Lat. 1074, f. f. 394r.

235. See Ranke, *History of the Popes*, vol. 2, pp. 224–242, for what remains one of the best concise accounts of the disputes. Pastor also devotes two chapters to the conflict in *History of the Popes*, vol. 25, pp. 111–216. See also William Bouwsma, "The Venetian Interdict and the Problem of Order," in his *A Usable Past* (Berkeley: University of California Press, 1990), pp. 97–111, for an insightful analysis of the conflict.

236. Ranke, *History of the Popes*, vol. 2, p. 237, and Pastor, *History of the Popes*, vol. 25, pp. 158–161.

237. BAV, Urb. Lat. 1074, f. 484v.
238. Pastor, *History of the Popes,* vol. 25, p. 162.
239. BAV, Urb. Lat. 1075, f.61v.
240. BAV, Urb. Lat. 1075, f. 128r.
241. Pastor, *History of the Popes,* vol. 25, p. 162.
242. BAV, Urb. Lat. 1075, f. 235r.
243. BAV, Urb. Lat. 1076, f. 513v.
244. BAV, Urb. Lat. 1077, f. 313r.
245. ASR, Camerale II, "Conti delle entrate e dell'uscita," buste 4, f. 92v.
246. AGS, Estado, Roma, leg. 1865, unfoliated.
247. Ibid.
248. Ibid.
249. ASR, Camerale II, Buste 1. The main register from the *depositeria generale* records the income from the papal collectors in Spanish realms in 1609 as 67,000 scudi. Total revenues were 1,790,521 in that year.
250. AGS, Estado, Roma, leg. 1860, unfoliated. A report from the Spanish ambassador in 1608 which gave detailed notes of cardinals' revenues calculated that close to 60,000 ducats from churches in Spanish realms were being given to twenty-three cardinals.
251. AGS, Estado, Roma, leg. 1868, unfoliated. In 1620 the Council of State in Spain complained about the many benefices that were distributed to *non-naturali,* said to total 22,000 ducats.
252. Ibid.
253. For details on the conclave see especially Pastor, *History of the Popes,* vol. 27, pp. 29–41. BAV, Urb. Lat. 1086, f.403r, notes that Cardinal Ludovisi received an 800-ducat pension from Spain, while Pastor wrote that he received 1,500 ducats total: *History of the Popes,* vol. 27, p. 47.
254. BAV, Urb. Lat. 1090, f. 65.
255. BAV, Urb. Lat. 1091, f. 71r.
256. AGS, Estado, Roma, leg. 3138, unfoliated. The printed treatise is entitled *Oratio ad Beatiss. in Christo Patrem ac s.d.n. Gregorium Decimumquintum Philippi IIII. Hispaniarum et Indiarum Regis Catholici Nomine, Obedientiam praestante Illustrissimo, et Excellentissimo Viro D. Emanuele a Zuniga, et Fonseca* (Rome, 1617).
257. Ibid.

CHAPTER 4: THE PEOPLE OF SPANISH ROME

1. Girolamo Accolti, *La festa et ordine belissimo che tiene la natione di Spagna nel far la processione del santissimo sacramento, la Domenica di Resurretione, nel aurora in Roma, intorno a Piazza Navona, 1596* (the treatise was dedicated to the duke of Sessa, Philip II's ambassador to Rome) (Rome, 1596).
2. Ibid.; BAV, Urb. Lat. 1064, f. 244r.
3. AOP, leg. 1115, ff. 79r–80v. The charity registers for the confraternity note that more than 700 scudi were spent on various forms of charity in 1596 for hun-

dreds of Spaniards. These included friars in need of a habit, pilgrims begging for food, orphans who were given monthly support, some women from Navarre who were given medicine, poor soldiers looking for a meal, and prisoners who needed food.

4. Loren Partridge and Randolph Starn, "Triumphalism in the Sala Regia in the Vatican," in *Triumphal Celebrations and the Rituals of Statecraft*, ed. Barbara Wisch and Susan Scott Munshover (University Park: Pennsylvania State University Press, 1990), p. 24.

5. Ferdinand Braudel, "L'Italia fuori d'Italia: Due secoli e tre Italie," in *Storia d'Italia*, vol. 2: *Dalla caduta dell'Impero romano al secolo XVIII*, ed. Giulio Einaudi (Turin: Einaudi, 1974), p. 2156. Braudel proposes that "three Italies" existed between 1450 and 1650 and that the third, roughly spanning the century after 1559 and the Peace of Cateau Cambresis, was defined above all else by the influence and domination of Spain, what he calls the *pax hispanica*. Italy during this century was characterized as being "pacifica, libera di vivere a suo modo per molto tempo," with the Spaniards playing the role of generally benevolent, if exploitative, lords. Similarly, Romolo Quazza referred to the period from 1559 to 1631 as that of the "preponderanza spagnola" "Spagna e Italia dal 1559 al 1631," *Italia e Spagna*, ed. A. Pavolini (Florence: F. Le Monnier, 1941), 165–192. He explained that he chose those chronological boundaries for the following reason: "Il 1559, perché segna il riconoscimento di ampi possessi territoriali della Spagna nella nostra penisola, e il 1631, perché la cessione di Pinerolo alla Francia da parte di Vittorio Amedeo I attesta materialmente la rinnovata potenza della rivale sul suolo d'Italia."

6. Carla Hesse and Thomas Laquer, "Introduction," *Representations* 47 (Summer 1994): 1.

7. See I. A. A. Thompson, "Castile, Spain, and the Monarchy: The political community from *patria natural* to *patria national*," in *Spain, Europe, and the Atlantic World*, ed. Richard L. Kagan and Geoffrey Parker (Cambridge: Cambridge University Press, 1995), pp. 137–138, for a discussion of hispanization in the second half of the sixteenth century.

8. Ibid., pp. 138–139. Thompson leans toward Armando Represa's terminology of "the immersion of the Castilian into the Spanish" to describe Hispanicization and also points out that H. G. Koenigsberger's suggestion that identification with Spain was a result of Castilian imperialism is undermined by the fact that this was a view from outside Castile and certainly not the perception of the Castilians themselves. See H. G. Koenigsberger, "Spain," in *National Consciousness, History, and Political Culture in Early-Modern Europe*, ed. Orest Ranum (Baltimore: Johns Hopkins University Press, 1975).

9. Edward Muir, *Civic Ritual in Renaissance Venice* (Princeton: Princeton University Press, 1981), p. 221.

10. Accolti, *Festa et ordine belissimo*, ff. 2r–4v.

11. BAV, Urb. Lat. 1041, 1570, f. 249.

12. AOP, leg. 71, f. 77r.

13. Carl H. Landé, "The Dyadic Basis of Clientelism," in *Friends, Followers,*

and Factions, ed. Steffen Schmidt, Laura Guasti, Carl H. Landé (Berkeley: University of California Press, 1977), p. xix. Landé describes the corporate group as "a discrete, multi-member aggregate having property, aims and duties which inhere in the group as such, and are distinct from those of its individual members. Each member has rights and duties with respect to the group. All members are bound together by virtue of their shared membership in the group and by their common obligation to protect its interests and fulfill its obligations. Some examples are families, lineages, clans, tribes, guilds, and in the modern world organized interest groups, political parties and nation states."

14. Benedict Anderson, *Imagined Communities* (London: Verso, 1983), p. 54. "Nothing more impresses one about Western Christendom in its heyday than the uncoerced flow of faithful seekers from all over Europe, through the celebrated 'regional centres' of monastic learning, to Rome. These great Latin-speaking institutions drew together what today we would perhaps regard as Irishmen, Danes, Portuguese, Germans, and so forth, in communities whose sacred meaning was every day deciphered from their members' otherwise inexplicable juxtaposition in the refectory." While Anderson points out the role that pilgrimage had in building the religious sense of community among the different peoples of Europe, he omits the central role that pilgrimage centers also had in emphasizing and defining the major national identities of Europe.

15. Peter Sahlins, *Boundaries* (Berkeley: University of California Press, 1989), p. 113.

16. For the best survey to date on Italian confraternities see Christopher Black, *Italian Confraternities in the Sixteenth Century* (Cambridge: Cambridge University Press, 1989).

17. AOP, leg. 71, f. 2r. From the first major register of the confraternity, dated 1603. The subtitle of this section is "Origen de la Archicofradia."

18. AOP, leg. 517. It was not until 1603, when Spanish immigration to the city was actually decreasing, that the confraternity began to keep a membership roster, and the number of members in the early decades is thus left obscure. The roster, which is arranged alphabetically according to the members' first names, unfortunately provides little additional information about them.

19. AOP, MSS 240, unfoliated.

20. See, for example, Orest Ranum, "Spain," in *National Consciousness,* pp. 163–165.

21. John H. Elliott, "A Europe of Composite Monarchies," *Past and Present* 137 (1992): 57–58.

22. Ibid., p. 58.

23. Ibid., p. 57.

24. See Jean Delumeau, *Vie économique et sociale de Rome* (Paris: Bibliothèque des écoles français d'Athènes et de Rome, 1957), pp. 37–51, for a good description of the Spanish courier system.

25. Luís Cabrera de Córdoba, *Felipe Segundo, Rey de España,* (Madrid: Benito Luna, 1876), p. 399.

26. BAV, Urb. Lat. 1050, f. 204r.

27. Pio Pecchiai, *Roma nel cinquecento* (Bologna: Cappelli, 1948), p. 447. Pecchiai puts the population of Rome in 1591 at 116,690 based on a description of the population found in Vatican manuscript Cod. Vat. Ottob. 2434, f. 856, which I also consulted. Since this manuscript is little more than a fragment, without any specific census records or detail, the numbers it provides must be taken as estimates. See also F. Cerasoli, "Censimento della populazione di Roma dall'anno 1600 al 1739," *Studie e documenti di storia e diritto* (Rome, 1891), p. 8. The author puts the population of Rome in 1600 at 109,729.

28. A succinct, if somewhat narrow, working definition of patronage in this period is provided by Robert Harding, "Corruption and the Moral Boundaries of Patronage in the Renaissance," in *Patronage in the Renaissance,* ed. Guy Fitch Lytle and Stephen Orgel (Princeton: Princeton University Press, 1981), p. 50. Harding describes the patronage system as "a method and set of criteria for appointment to public offices and ecclesiastical benefices, and for the award of titles, honors, certain privileges, fiscal exemptions, money, gifts, lands, and pensions."

29. See Linda Levy Peck, "Court Patronage and Government Policy: The Jacobean Dilemma," in *Patronage in the Renaissance,* p. 27. Although Renaissance historians such as Peck have often noted that "patronage provided both the essential means by which Renaissance rulers gained the allegiance of the politically important and the primary method by which they integrated regional governments and elites into the state," few have analyzed how this same system was used by foreign rulers to gain political power in another monarch's realm.

30. Important works on the papal court in the sixteenth century like John D'Amico's *Renaissance Humanism in Papal Rome* (Baltimore: Johns Hopkins University Press, 1983) and Charles Stinger's *The Renaissance in Rome* (Bloomington: Indiana University Press, 1985), serve well to illuminate papal patronage of humanist authors, or, in the case of Paolo Prodi's *The Papal Prince* (Cambridge: Cambridge University Press, 1987) provide a sophisticated analysis of the development of the political theory and structures of papal absolutism; but they stop short of a closer analysis of competing patronage networks in Rome. For the seventeenth century, two important recent studies that have furthered our knowledge in this area are Mario Biagioli, *Galileo, Courtier* (Chicago: University of Chicago Press, 1993), and Frederick Hammond, *Music and Spectacle in Baroque Rome* (New Haven: Yale University Press, 1994). For a more detailed study of patron-client systems in eighteenth-century Rome see Renata Ago, "Burocrazia, 'nazioni' e parentele nella Roma del Settecento," *Quaderni Storici* 67 (1988): 73–98, and her book *Carriere e clientele nella Roma barocca* (Rome: Laterza, 1990).

31. Sharon Kettering, *Patrons, Brokers, and Clients in Seventeenth-Century France* (New York: Oxford University Press, 1986).

32. Although the literature on patronage and the arts in the early modern period is vast, work that focuses on the broader political implications, as well as specific functionings, of patronage in different political contexts is much less developed. Besides Kettering, important exceptions to this rule include the collection *Patronage*

in the Renaissance; Ronald Weissman, "Taking Patronage Seriously: Mediterranean Values and Renaissance Society," in *Patronage, Art, and Society in Renaissance Italy,* ed. F. W. Kent, Patricia Simons, and J. C. Eade (Oxford: Oxford University Press, 1987); and the review article by Robert Shephard, "Court Factions in Early Modern England," *Journal of Modern History* 64, no. 4 (1992): 721–745. Two of the best collections of anthropological essays on patron-client systems are *Patrons and Clients in Mediterranean Societies,* ed. Ernest Gellner and John Waterbury (London: Duckworth, 1977), and *Friends, Followers, and Factions,* ed. Steffen Schmidt, Laura Guasti, Carl H. Landé and James Scott (Berkeley: University of California Press, 1977).

33. See Landé, "Dyadic Basis of Clientelism," p. xiv. Landé defines a dyadic alliance as "a voluntary agreement between individuals to exchange favors and to come to each other's aid in time of need." He also notes that horizontal dyadic alliances are based on exchange of favors between essentially equal partners and can also be called implicit contracts.

34. Ibid., p. xvii. Drawing heavily on George Foster, Landé points out that dyadic alliances and explicit contractual alliances often complement one another and together help explain the way a community works. Formal contracts alone do not provide for all the needs of a community or its individuals, and must often be "enlivened" by the personal relationships of the dyadic alliance.

35. AGS, Estado, Roma, leg. 924, unfoliated.

36. Ibid.

37. ASR, Tesoreria Segreta, buste 1299, f. 2r.

38. Landé, "Dyadic Basis of Clientelism," p. xxxii. The author goes on to point out that the term *faction* "is used today to denote groups which compete for dominance within the confines of a political party. Both 'factions' of the pre-party and intra-party type tend to be characterized by unstable membership, uncertain duration, personalistic leadership, a lack of formal organization, and by a greater concern with power and spoils than with ideology or policy."

39. Ibid., p. xx. To quote Landé, "It is common for clienteles to be pyramided upon each other so that several patrons, each with their own sets of clients, are in turn the clients of a higher patron who in turn is the client of a patron even higher than himself. In such a pyramid, an individual may be both a patron and a client."

40. Ibid. Landé sums up the importance of intermediaries in the following way: "A final consequence of the directly interpersonal nature of linkage in dyadic non-corporate groups is the important place occupied by intermediaries. In order to obtain the aid of other members of the group — or persons outside the group — with whom an individual has no direct personal ties, he may work through an intermediary aid-giver or aid-givers, thereby creating a dyadic chain."

41. The expanding importance of the sixteenth-century Spanish ambassador as a political figure has been acknowledged by such historians as Antonio Domínguez Ortiz who describes the ambassador generally as "not just the personal representative of the king who sent him, but an active agent for gathering information and weaving intrigue." This author also astutely notes that "perhaps the most important embassy was that of Rome, not just for the delicate negotiations it involved

but for its incomparable value as an international listening-post." See *The Golden Age of Spain, 1516–1659*, trans. James Casey (New York: Basic, 1971), pp. 43–44.

42. Laurie Nussdorfer, *Civic Politics in the Rome of Urban VIII* (Princeton: Princeton University Press, 1992), pp. 39–40.

43. AGS, Estado, Roma, leg. 883, unfoliated.

44. Ibid.

45. AGS, Estado, Roma, leg. 902, unfoliated.

46. BAV, Urb. Lat. 1040, f. 255r. The Avvisi writer notes that a "Hebreo literato" and his wife were baptized in Santo Apostolo and the "Comendatore di Castiglia" was there along with the Signora Donna Giovanna d'Aragona; and that the wife of Michiel Ghislero became Christian in the temple of Minerva sponsored by the ambassador of Spain and Signora Hersilla (f. 282r).

47. BAV, Urb. Lat. f. 349r. It was also noted by the Avvisi writer that the pope gave 10,000 scudi to the catechumens so that they could do good works for the poor.

48. BAV, Urb. Lat. 1040, f. 283r.

49. BAV, Urb. Lat. 1040, f. 346r.

50. BAV, Urb. Lat. 1040, f. 479r.

51. BAV, Urb. Lat. 1041, f. 40r.

52. BAV, Urb. Lat. 1041, f. 95r.

53. Kettering, *Patrons, Brokers, and Clients*, p. 7.

54. BAV, Urb. Lat. 1049, f. 204r.

55. This figure is taken from John Elliott, *Imperial Spain* (London: Penguin, 1963), p. 313.

56. BAV, Urb. Lat. 1064, ff. 7v–8r. The Avvisi reports from 1596 include a list of pensions paid to the major commanders of the Order of Santiago, which notes that of the twenty-five major commanders, the highest pension, 14,000 ducats, went to the Comendador of Castile, the office held by ambassadors Requeséns and Zúñiga.

57. BAV, Urb. Lat. 1064, f. 437v.

58. ASC, Notai, vol. 866, f. 96r.

59. ASC, Notai, vol. 870, f. 285v.

60. ASC, Notai, vol. 870, ff. 288v, 289r.

61. BAV, Urb. Lat. 1045, f. 293r.

62. Urb. Lat. 1047, f. 29r.

63. AGS, Estado, Roma, leg. 938, unfoliated.

64. BAV, Urb. Lat. 1046, f. 260r.

65. BAV, Urb. Lat. 1051, f. 482r. Also see AGS, Estado, Roma, leg. 938, unfoliated, for the letter to the king from Ludovico Bianchetti requesting the habit for his brother.

66. AGS, Estado, Roma, leg. 961, unfoliated.

67. AGS, Estado, Roma, leg. 965, unfoliated.

68. Ibid.

69. Ibid.

70. Ibid.

71. AGS, Estado, Roma, leg. 961, unfoliated.

72. Ibid.

73. AGS, Estado, Roma, leg. 978, unfoliated.

74. AGS, Estado, Roma, leg. 901, unfoliated.

75. Barbara McClung Hallman, *Italian Cardinals, Reform, and the Church as Property* (Berkeley: University of California Press, 1985), p. 9. This book is the best work to date on economic details about the College of Cardinals in the sixteenth century; it provides a wealth of information about administrative offices and their function in the papal court and broader Roman society during the first half of the century.

76. The extremely complex and tangled relationships between cardinals were marked by a wide array of personal conflicts, grudges, debts, and family obligations that often affected their decisions, regardless of loyalty to any foreign prince. This was especially apparent during conclaves, such as the one of 1559. Ludwig Pastor's lengthy account of that election serves as a good example of the shifting alliances and complicated exchanges between cardinals that made it difficult for the Spanish party to elect their first candidates or to rely on many of the cardinals for consistent support (*History of the Popes*, ed. Ralph Francis Kerr [St. Louis: Herder, 1928], vol. 15, pp. 1–65).

77. AGS, Estado, Roma, leg. 911, unfoliated.

78. Ibid.

79. BAV, Urb. Lat. 1040, f. 428r.

80. BAV, Urb. Lat. 1042, f. 92v.

81. ASC, Notai, vol. 858, f. 43r. This cleric, who also counted the goodly sum of 1,000 ducats of gold among his estate, is typical of the many Spanish courtiers living off of Spanish benefices in Rome while serving a Spanish or Italian patron.

82. ASC, Notai, vol. 858, f. 87r.

83. ASC, Notai, vol. 861, f. 166r.

84. BAV, Urb. Lat. 1041, f. 220v; Urb. Lat. 1045, f. 440r. Among Granvelle's income was a reported 6,000 ducats in pension from Seville in 1569, and 6,000 more from Toledo in 1576.

85. BAV. Urb. Lat. 1041, f. 185r.

86. AGS, Estado, Roma, leg. 910, unfoliated.

87. Giovanni de' Medici was created cardinal in 1560 at the age of seventeen by Pope Pius IV. See Pastor, *History of the Popes*, vol. 15, p. 98.

88. AGS, Estado, Roma, leg. 946, unfoliated.

89. Not to be confused with his more famous cousin of the same name, Cardinal Marcantonio Colonna was the former archbishop of Taranto who was made cardinal in 1565 in part as a reward for his good work at Trent. Pastor, *History of the Popes*, vol. 16, p. 394.

90. BAV, Urb. Lat. 1040, f. 526v.

91. AGS, Estado, Roma, leg. 911, unfoliated.

92. AGS, Estado, Roma, leg. 910, unfoliated.

93. AGS, Estado, Roma, leg. 911, unfoliated.

94. AGS, Estado, Roma, leg. 924, unfoliated.

95. BAV, Urb. Lat. 1042, f. 155v.

96. BAV, Urb. Lat. 1045, f. 276v.

97. BAV, Urb. Lat. 1046, f. 21r.

98. BAV, Urb. Lat. 1050, f. 54r.

99. Cardinal Aragona, born Innico Avalos d'Aragona in the Kingdom of Naples, was a good example of an Italian of Iberian ancestry who inclined toward Philip II. Aragona had earlier been a knight of the order of Santiago, and so a vassal of the Spanish king, and his long term as a cardinal, 1561–1600, made him a valuable member of the faction.

100. AGS, Estado, Roma, leg. 3138, unfoliated.

101. AGS, Estado, Roma, leg. 950, unfoliated. A letter from the ambassador in 1588 noted that the congregation overseeing the Inquisition included Deza, Madruzzo, San Severina, Santi Quatro Coronati, and Marcellis, all in the Spanish faction.

102. BAV, Urb. Lat. 1052, f. 228r.

103. BAV, Urb. Lat. 1054, f. 306r. The consistory reports noted that Deza was to get 45,000 of the 60,000-ducat pension from Zaragoza.

104. Ibid.

105. ASC, Notai, 1619, unfoliated.

106. Guido Bentivoglio, *Memorie, overo diario del Cardinal Bentivoglio* (Amsterdam, 1648), pp. 67–68. Cardinal Bentivoglio wrote in his memoirs that Deza was one of the most highly regarded of the cardinals of his time.

107. AGS, Estado, Roma, leg. 1870, unfoliated.

108. BAV, Urb. Lat. 1058, f. 135r–135v. The report named Como and Gesualdo "come primi della fattione spagnola," and twenty-one others, including San Giorgio, Aragona, Marcantonio Colonna, Paleotto, Como, Alessandrino, Madruccio, Santi Quatro Coronati, Deza, Lancillotto, Rusticucci, Pinelli, Salviati, Sforza, Mattei, Aldobrandino, Ascanio Colonna, Montalto, Santa Severina, Caraffa, and San Marcello.

109. BAV, Urb. Lat. 1058, f. 485r.

110. BAV, Urb. Lat. 1059, f. 7r.

111. BAV, Urb. Lat. 1059, f. 105r.

112. BAV, Urb. Lat. 1059, f. 152r.

113. BAV, Urb. Lat. 1060, f. 3r.

114. AGS, Estado, Roma, leg. 964, unfoliated.

115. Ibid.

116. AGS, Estado, Roma, leg. 965, unfoliated. The official letter from the king listed the recipients as Aldobrandino, 3,000 ducats; San Jorge, 3,000; Santi Quatro Coronati, 1,500; Toledo, 1,500; Pinto, Paravillino, and Aquaviva, 1,000; and Pistoza, 800.

117. AGS, Estado, Roma, leg. 968, unfoliated.

118. AGS, Estado, Roma, leg. 972, unfoliated.

119. Ibid.

120. AGS, Estado, Roma, leg. 1870, unfoliated.

121. AGS, Estado, Roma, leg. 1857, unfoliated, doc. 52.

122. AGS, Estado, Roma, leg. 1860, unfoliated.

123. Ibid.

124. BAV, Urb. Lat. 1094, f. 158r.

125. Among a sample group of a hundred Spaniards who left wills in Rome between 1559 and 1624, roughly 20 percent identified themselves as clergy. It is impossible to know with any great precision the exact percentage of clergy among long-term Spanish residents in Rome because of the lack of a database that would allow a detailed breakdown of the general Spanish population.

126. Records in the church of Santiago show that Constantino Castillo had a will drawn up first in 1551 and amended later in 1566 shortly before he died. He was thus in Rome at least fifteen years, although I was unable to find the exact date of his arrival. For the original will see AOP, leg. 2192, unfoliated. For a copy of the later will see AOP, leg. 60, ff. 250v–258r.

127. For details on the evolution of the office see Niccolò Del Re, *La curia romana* (Vatican City: Libreria editrice Vaticana, 1998), pp. 227–230.

128. AOP, leg. 2192, unfoliated. In 1551, when the will was first written, the income of the houses was thirty-four gold escudos per year. More details on the dowries will be given in the following pages.

129. Ibid.

130. Ibid. Like many Spanish clerics, Castillo also had relations in the city, including a cousin, Estevan de Castillo, who was a Franciscan friar in the community attached to the church of Santa Maria in Aracoeli, and who acted as one of the executors and heirs of his will. Other executors included Julio Orandino, an auditor of the Rota, and the bishop of Bagnara.

131. Ibid.

132. AOP, leg. 60, f. 327v. He identifies himself as "Licenciado Pedro de Foix Montoya, Referendario de las signaturas de gracia y justicia de Su Santidad."

133. AOP, leg. 1, f. 383.

134. ARSI, Rom. vol. 152a, "Catalogo dei Superiori e Professori del Collegio Romano, 1551–1773." Francisco Toledo is listed as a "lettore santissima Logica" in 1560, and again as a "lettore santissima Teologia" from 1564 to 1569 (pp. 64–65).

135. *Bibliothèque de la Compagnie de Jesus*, ed. Carlos Sommervogel (Louvain: Editions de la Bibliothèque S.J., Collège philosophique et théologique, 1960), vol. 8, pp. 64–82.

136. BAV, Urb. Lat. 1053, f. 550v.

137. BAV, Urb. Lat. 1060, f. 425v.

138. BAV, Urb. Lat. 1063, f. 480v.

139. BAV, Urb. Lat. 1063, f. 480r.

140. *Bibliothèque*, vol. 8, p. 84.

141. ASC, Notai, vol. 619, unfoliated.

142. AGS, Estado, Roma, leg. 959, unfoliated.

143. AGS, Estado, Roma, leg. 966, unfoliated. Peña described the duke of Sessa as the person in Rome "que me governar," and asked the king to keep him "a su real servicio mientras tuviere vida."

144. ASC, Notai, vol. 619, unfoliated.

145. Ibid.

146. ASC, Notai, 864, ff. 25-38. While Manríquez was not as wealthy as Castillo, he was prosperous enough even as a friar to collect a substantial personal library (more than two hundred volumes) and such luxury items as silver platters, sets of crystal, and paintings.

147. Del Re, *Curia romana,* pp. 328, 357.

148. BAV, Urb. Lat. 1040, f. 342v; Urb. Lat. 1045, f. 241r.

149. BAV, Urb. Lat. 1042, f. 25r. Also see BAV, Urb. Lat. 1058, f. 495r, where the death of "Señor Ferrante Torres uno degli Agenti del Re di Spagna cortegiano vecchio" is noted in 1590.

150. AOP, leg. 71, ff. 63r-67v.

151. Ibid.

152. Ibid. The *juro* (tax privilege) was worth 8,672 gold ducats per year.

153. ASC, Notai, vol. 858, f. 53r. A notarized document identifying Gaspar de la Peña, cleric from Avila, as a *scriptor Apostòlico.*

154. BAV, Urb. Lat. 1049, f. 391r.

155. ASC, Notai, vol. 859, f. 252.

156. ASC, Notai, vol. 868, f. 180r.

157. BAV, Urb. Lat. 1046, f. 514r.

158. AOP, leg. 60, f. 238r.

159. ASC, Notai, vol. 857, f. 136r.

160. ASRI, Rom. 152a, p. 64, "Catalogo dei superiori e professori del Collegio Romano, 1551-1773."

161. *Bibliothèque,* vol. 4, pp. 1648-1651.

162. ASRI, Rom. 152a, pp. 64-80.

163. *Bibliothèque,* vol. 7, pp. 1663-1685.

164. Ibid., vol. 8, p. 513.

165. BAV, Urb. Lat. 1064, f. 536r. The Avvisi reporter noted that "Angelo Paz Spagnolo" had lived in Rome since the days of Sixtus V and had lived with "a very good reputation for sanctity." When he died "suddenly, many people" went "to see him," and during two days of exposition three habits were "stripped by the people as relics."

166. BAV, Urb. Lat. 1064, f. 547v. Although the Spanish friar was never canonized, the Franciscans of San Pietro in Montorio evidently believed in his sanctity, for they placed his body under the high altar where saints' relics were typically found. His tomb remained there until late in the twentieth century, and visitors to the church can still find a plaque to the left of the high altar commemorating his life.

167. ASC, Notai, vol. 857, ff. 4v, 56r.

168. ASC, Notai, vol. 857, f. 13v.

169. ASC, Notai, vol. 857, f. 134v.

170. ASC, Notai, vol. 858, f. 237r.

171. ASC, Notai, vol. 858, f. 149r.

172. ASC, Notai, vol. 866, f. 289v.

173. ASC, Notai, vol. 868, f. 231r.

174. ASC, Notai, vol. 870, f. 106r.

175. ASC, Notai, vol. 872, f. 416r.

176. ASC, Notai, vol. 605, f. 120.

177. Ibid.

178. ASC, Notai, vol. 1619, unfoliated.

179. See Ronald Weissman, "The Importance of Being Ambiguous: Social Relations, Individualism, and Identity in Renaissance Florence," in *Urban Life in the Renaissance,* ed. Susan Zimmerman and Ronald Weissman (London: Associated University Presses, 1989), pp. 269–280. One could easily apply Weissman's description of social relations in Renaissance Florence to those of Rome when he describes the city as "a socially complex society, characterized by overlapping, conflicting, mutual committments to kin, neighbors, friends, clients, patrons, and business associates. Thus, social relations were usually mutually supportive, but on occasion, they were also quite competitive" (p. 271).

180. BAV, Urb. Lat. 1040, f. 318r.

181. MS 5801, Don Juan Chumacero y Carillo and Don Fr. Domingo Pimentel, *Memorial sobre los excessos, que se cometen en Roma, contra los Naturales de estos Reynos de España* (1633), p. 96.

182. Ibid., p. 39.

183. MSS 1323, Juan Pablo Frances, *Informe y consulta a V. Magestad, en razon de los memoriales dados en nombre de los Reynos y diversas Iglesias, acerca de algunos despachos, y negocios de Roma* (1629), f. 101r.

184. ASC, Notai, vol. 872, f. 108. In a notarized document from 1581 Antonio Fonseca established as his official procuradores in Spain: Gaspar de Santestevan, a cathedral canon from Valladolid; Bernardino Vizcarrezo, a regidor in Valladolid; Francisco de Cuevas in Burgos; Ruy Gómez in Medina del Campo; and his brother Manuel Fonseca, who then resided in Madrid. This particular document empowered the said procuradores to collect the insurance money on merchandise originally purchased in various Iberian cities that had been lost in a shipwreck on its way to Italy.

185. Ferruccio Lombardi, *Roma: Palazzi, Palazzetti, Case* (Rome: Edilstampa, 1991), p. 396. I have been unable to find an exact date for the palace's construction.

186. ASC, Notai, vol. 866, f. 203. The notarial records have Jerónimo Fonseca in Rome from at least 1575, when he had a document drawn up granting to his brothers Antonio, Manuel, and Francisco in Portugal the rights to settle his deceased parents' estate.

187. AOP, leg. 71, f. 44r.

188. AOP, leg. 2192, unfoliated. Found in the original will of Antonio Fonseca from 1587.

189. AOP, leg. 71, f. 41v.

190. AOP, legs. 2192, 71.

191. AGS, leg. 3138, unfoliated. The printed treatise is entitled *Oratio ad Beatiss. in Christo Patrem ac s.d.n. Gregorium Decimumquintum Philippi IIII. Hispaniarum et In-*

diarum Regis Catholici Nomine, Obedientiam praestante Illustrissimo, et Excellentissimo Viro D. Emanuele a Zuniga, et Fonseca.

192. AOP, leg. 2192, f. 4r.

193. AOP, leg. 2192, unfoliated. This version of the will is dated 1602, while another, later copy found in AOP, leg. 1, ff. 282r–289v, is dated 1601.

194. AOP, leg. 2192, unfoliated.

195. ASC, Notai, vol. 607, f. 32r. A 1595 loan agreement between the duke of Sessa and the bank in which he agreed to pay the latter the balance of 20,330 scudi owed from the total of 44,849 borrowed since 1592.

196. ASC, Notai, vol. 871, ff. 1r–13v. The inventory of his goods can be found in the same volume, ff. 35r–40v.

197. ASC, Notai, vol. 861, f. 49r.

198. Ibid., ff. 50r–60v.

199. ASC, Notai, vol. 872, f. 239r. The will is entitled, "Memoria di ultima volunta di Domenico Trizeno pittore spagnolo natural de Valladolid."

200. Ibid.

201. ASC, Notai, vol. 858, f. 1567.

202. AOP, leg. 60, ff. 241v–243r.

203. ASC, Notai, volumes 857–876 cover the years 1562 to 1586. The Spaniard Jerónimo Rabassa, appears to have taken over the bulk of Avila's business after 1586.

204. AOP, leg. 60, f. 243r.

205. AOP, leg. 60, f. 170v.

206. AOP, leg. 60, f. 171r.

207. AOP, leg. 60, ff. 175r–176r.

208. ASC, Notai, vol. 876, ff. 269r–275v. The last testament of Isabel Perez de Peramato is accompanied by a notarized letter in which she explains in great detail why she is excluding her husband from her will. It is from this letter that we learn of her marital history and problems.

209. ASC, Notai, vol. 876, f. 270r.

210. ASC, Notai, vol. 876, f. 270v.

211. ASC, Notai, vol. 876, f. 272r.

212. Among the sample group of a hundred Spaniards who left wills between 1559 and 1624, roughly 25 percent were women.

213. ASC, Notai, vol. 874, f. 138r.

214. ASC, Notai, ff. 140r–141v.

215. AOP, leg. 60, ff. 200v–202v.

216. AOP, leg. 601, unfoliated.

CHAPTER 5: THE PIETY OF SPANISH ROME

1. The definition of *pietas* in the *Oxford Latin Dictionary* (Oxford: Oxford University Press, 1982), p. 1378, is, "An attitude of dutiful respect towards those to whom one is bound by ties of religion, consanguinity, etc."

NOTES TO PAGES 161–165

2. BAV, Urb. Lat. 1041, f. 125v.

3. BAV, Urb. Lat. 1041. The amount of the endowment when the will was originally drawn up was 34 gold scudi. Initially this provided roughly three dowries per year. AOP, leg. 2192, unfoliated. By 1611, however, the income from the endowment had grown enough to provide fifteen women with dowries or roughly half of all those distributed. AOP, leg. 1277, ff. 202–206.

4. See especially Samuel Cohn, *Death and Property in Siena, 1205–1800: Strategies for the Afterlife* (Baltimore: Johns Hopkins University Press, 1988).

5. The wills used for this section were found in the archives of the Confraternity of the Most Holy Resurrection and of churches in Rome, and the archive of the Capitoline in Rome. While they represent only a fraction of the total number, they were the most detailed and extensive of the wills preserved. More specifically, all of the wills used in this sample had estates worth at least 50 silver scudi and all the people involved died in Rome. This sample does not pretend to offer a comprehensive analysis of every Spaniard who left a will in Rome since such a task exceeds the boundaries of this work. Moreover, the fact that most Spaniards who surfaced in other documents, such as the Avvisi, Spanish church and confraternity records, and royal correspondence, also appear in the records of the Spanish notaries whom I did consult indicated that a search through the hundreds of other Italian notaries would have yielded a small number of Spanish wills for the time invested.

6. AOP, leg. 53, unfoliated. Of the ninety-seven houses noted in 1585, twenty-four had been acquired since 1562, when the record begins.

7. AOP, leg. 1, ff. 167r–169v.

8. AOP, leg. 1, ff. 177r–178v.

9. AOP, leg. 1, f. 264r.

10. AOP, leg. 1, f. 198r.

11. AOP, leg. 1, f. 214r.

12. AOP, leg. 1, f. 221r.

13. AOP, leg. 1, f. 271r.

14. AOP, leg. 1, ff. 282r–289v.

15. AOP, leg. 1, ff. 305v–306r.

16. AOP, leg. 1, ff. 183r–185v.

17. AOP, leg. 1, f. 292r.

18. AOP, leg. 1, f. 313r.

19. AOP, leg. 1, f. 316r.

20. AOP, leg. 1, f. 331r.

21. William A. Christian, Jr., *Local Religion in Sixteenth-Century Spain* (Princeton: Princeton University Press, 1981), p. 182. Christian points out that in the baroque period devotion to the saints declined while Marian devotion remained at a high level and votive devotion to Christ increased greatly. This generally mirrors the situation in Rome, and it is likely that the many priests who traveled to or lived in Rome for a time played a significant role in this shift, just as they had previously been central players in the importation of relics and indulgences from Rome that built up the local devotion to saints. See especially p. 137, where the author cites the promi-

nent role of Roman relics in the devotional life of sixteenth-century Spain, especially at the court of Philip II, and p. 147, where he notes three instances of priests who returned from Rome in the years 1569–1575 with both relics and indulgences.

22. Peter R. Brown, *The Cult of the Saints* (Chicago: University of Chicago Press, 1981), p. 65. Not unlike the late fourth-century Christian world, the late sixteenth-century Catholic world continued to be preoccupied with sin and its remission. Although there were more means by which to erase sin in the later period, most noticeably confession and a plethora of indulgences, the importance of the saint as heavenly patron and intercessor remained strong.

23. BAV, Urb. Lat. 1060, f. 492v.

24. BAV, Urb. Lat. 1060, f. 536r.

25. See Elizabeth Cohen, "Honor and Gender in the Streets of Early Modern Rome," *Journal of Interdisciplinary History* 22 (1992): 612, where it is noted that the Spanish prostitute Francesca d'Avila was involved in a legal dispute over an attack on her house in 1607.

26. BAV, Urb. Lat. 1054, f. 389v. In 1586 Sixtus V established an endowment for sixty dowries and entrusted the charity to the Confraternity of the Gonfalone.

27. For details on the Roman Confraternity of the Annunciation see M. D'Amelia, "Economia familiare e sussidi dotali: La politica della Confraternita dell'Annunziata a Roma," in *La donna e l'economia: Atti della XXII settimana di studi dell'Istituto di Storia Economica,* ed. F. Datini (Prato: Le Monnier, 1990).

28. BAV, Urb. Lat. 1048, f.133r.

29. BNM, MSS 2392, *Las Iglesias de Roma,* Por El Doctor Francisco De Cabrera Morales, Acolytho de la Santidad de N. Senor Clemente VIII, Con Privilegio del Papa Sixto V, En Roma, Por Luis Zannetti, A instancia de Gio. Antonio Franzini librero ala ensena de la Fuente, I heredero de Jeronimo Franzini ano 1600, ff. 72v–73r.

30. AOP, leg. 1277. The information is taken from a register entitled *Escutrinos de Donzellas desde el Año de 1567 hasta el Año de 1645.*

31. Ibid. For the high and low total figures of 1602 and 988 scudi see ff. 255 and 295, respectively.

32. AOP, leg. 60, ff. 250r–258v.

33. AOP, leg. 1, f. 150r.

34. AOP, leg. 71, f. 44r.

35. AOP, leg. 60, ff. 175r–176v.

36. ASC, Notai, vol. 860, f. 12r.

37. AOP, leg. 1, f. 214r.

38. ASC, Notai, vol. 874, ff. 138r–141v.

39. AOP, leg. 2192, unfoliated.

40. AOP, leg. 60, ff. 327r–330v.

41. AOP, leg. 1, ff. 339r–344v.

42. AOP, leg. 71, ff. 159r–161r. The list of rules for visitors preserved in the *Libro Maestro* of the confraternity is entitled "Instrucción y forma que se ha de guardar en el casamiento de las donzellas."

43. AOP, leg. 71, f. 160r. From a section entitled "Calidades y requisitos de

256

Donzellas." In the 1560s and 1570s, when the Spanish immigrant population was just beginning to grow, a high percentage of the women receiving dowries were from Burgundy, Flanders, and Germany. By 1600, however, the great majority of women were daughters of immigrant Spaniards, and by the 1620s, the majority were granddaughters of Spaniards, reflecting the rise and fall of the immigration pattern generally.

44. Ibid.

45. AOP, leg. 611, unfoliated. From the document entitled *Libro de Instrumentos e Dotes.*

46. André Vauchez, *La Sainteté en occident aux derniers siècles du moyen age* (Rome: Ecole française de Rome, 1981).

47. Ibid., p. 308.

48. Ibid., p. 318.

49. See Peter Burke, "How to Be a Counter Reformation Saint," in his *The Historical Anthropology of Early Modern Italy* (Cambridge: Cambridge University Press, 1987), pp. 48–62.

50. Unlike most other canonizations both before and after, the records, or *processi,* for the canonization of Diego of Alcalá are not preserved in the Vatican Secret Archive or, for that matter, in the National Library in Paris, where a variety of other *processi* including that of Saint Ignatius of Loyola, can be found. What has been preserved, however, are two printed texts by Francisco Peña, the auditor of the Rota, and the apostolic notary, Pietro Gallesini. Both these works recount in great detail the life, miracles, and canonization of the saint and generally serve as neatly compiled, if abbreviated, *processi.*

51. See Pierre Delooz, *Sociologie et canonisations* (Liège: Faculté de droit, 1969) p. 127. The canonization of Diego of Alcalá was the last to occur before Sixtus V officially established the Congregation of Rites to regularize and oversee the process. The establishment of this congregation is pointed to by Delooz and others as a critical turning point in the process of canonization that increased official scrutiny of candidates and further centralized power in the growing Roman bureaucracy. In the case of Diego, however, it can already be seen that there was a heightened concern in Rome with the collection of "official" testimony, and that the auditors of the Rota and committees of cardinals were overseeing the cause. When Sixtus V established the congregation as the guardian of the canonization process, then, he was simply institutionalizing and refining the procedure that had evolved during the long process of Diego of Alcalá.

52. Francisco Peña, *De Vita Miraculis et Actis Canonizationis Sancti Didaci* (Rome, 1589), p. 120.

53. Pietro Gallesini, *La vita, i miracoli, et la canonizatione di San Diego d'Alcala de Henares,* trans. Francesco Avanzi (Rome, 1589), p. 166.

54. Ibid., pp. 138–139.

55. Peña, *Vita Miraculis et Actis,* p. 123.

56. Ibid., p. 123. This same letter was sent again to Pius V in 1565. See AGS, Estado, Roma, leg. 901, unfoliated.

57. See Eric Waldram Kemp, *Canonization and Authority in the Western Church* (London: Oxford University Press, 1948), p. 143.

58. A copy of the letter can be found in *Opúsculos Castellanos de Ambrosio Morales,* ed. Francisco Valerio Cifuentes and Benito Cano (Madrid, 1793), vol. 3, p. 201.

59. Ibid., p. 202. Morales, it should be remembered, was also the author of the *Crónica de España* who so capably presented Spain as the rightful heir of the Roman Empire. Not surprisingly, Philip II also called on him to help document the sacred geography of his realms, and the king eventually sent him on a journey throughout the kingdoms of Asturias, León, and Galicia to collect information about the relics of holy men and women venerated in the cities and towns of those provinces. See Ambrosio Morales, *Viage de Ambrosio Morales por orden de D. Phelipe II a los reynos de León, y Galicia, y principado de Asturias,* ed. Antonio Marin (Madrid, 1765).

60. Gallesini, *Vita,* p. 155.

61. Ibid., pp. 206–211.

62. Gallesini, *Vita,* p. 95. Gallesini, like Peña, attributes 130 miracles to the saints but recounts only those he considers most important.

63. Gallesini, *Vita,* p. 95.

64. Ibid., p. 95.

65. Ibid., pp. 95–135.

66. Ibid., p. 94.

67. AGS, Estado, Roma, leg. 947, unfoliated. See, for example, the letter from 1586 in which Sixtus pointed out the difficulties of the expedition but nonetheless urged Philip to prepare for it.

68. Gallesini, *Vita,* p. 170.

69. Ibid., p. 171.

70. Ibid., pp. 201–207.

71. Ibid., p. 221.

72. AGS, Estado, Roma, leg. 947, unfoliated. Among the correspondence sent from the ambassador in Rome to the king was a document entitled "Memoria de lo que costa una Canonización." The itemized bill included 180 ducats for the papal vestments; 500 ducats for the cardinals who sat on the commission that oversaw the canonization; 300 ducats for the master of ceremonies; 200 ducats for the procurator and advocado of the cause; 300 ducats each to the three auditors of the Rota who oversaw the cause; 300 ducats for the standards; 500 ducats for the painting of the saint; 600 ducats for the publication of the bull of canonization, and 1,500 ducats for new clothes for the ambassador and his household specifically for the event. In a separate letter concerning the canonization also found in legajo 947, it was noted that the money for the event would come from the Kingdom of Naples.

73. Francisco Peña, *Canonizatione di S. Diego di Alcala di Henares* (Rome, 1588), p. A2.

74. BAV, Urb. Lat. 1064, f. 411r.

75. Delooz, *Sociologie et canonisations,* p. 252.

76. Vauchez, *Sainteté en occident aux derniers siècles du moyen age,* p. 318.

77. See ASV, Riti, vol. 4153 and vol. 220. Sixteenth-century copies of the four-

teenth-century process, as well as one copy from the fourteenth century, are preserved in the records of the Congregation of Rites. In 1577 the old process, in the
form of a sixty-folio account preserved in the Dominican archives of Barcelona, was
resurrected and copied by the public notary, Pedro Ferres, but it was not until the
1590s that the cause was again considered by Rome.

78. See AGS, Estado, Roma, leg. 965, and ASV, Riti, vol. 220, f. 8v, for a copy
of the king's letter.

79. Girolamo Cecotti da Cotognola, *Alcuni miracoli di S. Raimundo confessore*
(Rome, 1601), ff. 270r–273v.

80. Ibid.

81. ASV, Riti, vol. 220, f. 1r.

82. BAV, Vat. Lat. 14091, f. 4r. A written account of the canonization procedure
presented to the pope by the Congregation of Rites named Francisco Peña among
the auditors of the Rota who reviewed and recommended the case.

83. Ludwig Pastor, *History of the Popes,* ed. Ralph Francis Kerr (St. Louis: Herder, 1928), vol. 23, pp. 238–241.

84. BAV, Urb. Lat. 1069, f. 273r.

85. BAV, Urb. Lat 1069, f. 244v.

86. ASV, Riti, vol. 3192, unfoliated. The early pages of the process note that
Philip II appointed the Dominican priest Juan Guitierrez, *predicatore Regis,* as his
official procurator to push the cause of Isidore in Rome.

87. Ibid.

88. ASV, Riti, vol. 3156, unfoliated. Philip II's letter came in 1597, just a year
before his death, and would be the last letter he wrote urging the cause of a saint.

89. Ibid.

90. Ibid.

91. Ibid.

92. Ibid.

93. Ibid.

94. Ibid.

95. Ibid.

96. Francesco Maria Bourbon, *Relatio facta in consistorio secreto super vita, sanc-
titate, actis canonizationis, et miraculii Beati Ignatii* (Paris, 1644), p. 27.

97. Nacelle Zambeccari, *Oratio in publico Consistorio supplicantis pro beatii Ig-
natio Loiola Fundatore Societatis Jesu, eiusque Socio Francisco Xaverio* (Rome, 1622),
p. 11.

98. Bourbon, *Relatio,* p. 28.

99. Pastor, *History of the Popes,* vol. 23, p. 47.

100. Ibid. pp. 119–121.

101. Ibid., p. 121.

102. See Giacinto Gigli, *Diario romano,* ed. Giuseppe Ricciotti (Rome: Tumminelli, 1958), pp. 57–62.

103. Ibid., p. 59.

104. Ibid., pp. 60-61.

105. Ibid., p. 57. Although Ignatius, Francis Xavier, and Teresa were closely associated with their religious orders, contemporaries such as Giacinto Gigli also emphasized their Spanish origins. Gigli describes the four Iberian saints in the following way: "Isidoro Agricoltore della villa de Madrid Spagnolo, il Beato Ignazio Lojola Spagnolo fondatore della Compagnia di Gesu, il Beato Francesco Xaviero Spagnolo Apostolo dell'Indie, . . . la Beata Teresa Spagnola fondatrice delle monache, et frati Carmelitani."

106. Mutio Dansa di Penna, *Nella canonizatione de cinque gloriosissimi santi* (Rome, 1622), p. 3.

107. Ibid., p. 6. This poem was dedicated to Don Diego Bario Nova, a knight of Santiago, who is described as the "fido ministro del gran Giove Hispano."

CHAPTER 6: URBAN VIII AND THE
DECLINE OF SPANISH ROME

1. Giacinto Gigli, *Diario romano,* ed. Giuseppe Ricciotti (Rome: Tumminelli, 1958), p. 83.

2. For details on the election see Ludwig Pastor, *History of the Popes,* ed. Ralph Francis Kerr (St. Louis: Herder, 1928), vol. 28, pp. 1-26. The author notes that "in Paris, where people had excellent recollections of him as nuncio, Urban VIII's election was hailed with delight; Madrid, on the other hand, was greatly perturbed because it was feared it would not be possible to get from him as much as had been obtained from Gregory XV" (pp. 25-26).

3. See ibid., pp. 69-74, for a description of the events leading up to the French occupation of the Valtelline.

4. Gigli, *Diario romano,* p. 85.

5. Ibid., p. 73.

6. Ibid., p. 283.

7. BAV, Urb. Lat., 1095, ff. 215v-216r.

8. Leopold von Ranke, *History of the Popes,* trans. E. Fowler (New York: Colonial Press, 1901), vol. 2, p. 560.

9. Gigli, *Diario romano,* p. 87.

10. Pastor, *History of the Popes,* vol. 28, p. 97. The Treaty of Monzon, signed on March 5, placed the Valtelline under the joint protection of Spain and France and ensured the free passage of Spanish troops through the region.

11. Urb. Lat 1101, f. 12r. An avviso dated December 28, 1630 noted that during the last consistory of 1630, the pope responded to Cardinal Borgia's defense of Father Innocenzo.

12. Urb. Lat 1101, f. 12v.

13. Urb. Lat 1101, f. 56r.

14. BNM, MS 10882. *Protesta que hizo el Em.o señor Cardenal de Borja al Papa Urbano VIII,* ff. 3r-8v.

15. BNM, MS 978. *Discorso curioso fatto dall'Abbate Giulio Cesare Braccini intorno alla Protettione di Francia data dal Re Christ.o al Card. Antonio Barberino,* May 10, 1633, f. 165v–66r.

16. Gigli, *Diario romano,* p. 150. Gigli claimed that the bull was aimed particularly at Borgia.

17. Ibid., p. 154.

18. BNM, MS 2890, ff. 77–163. "Relatione, ó sia memoria curiosa de casi, e contese gravi con Cardinali, Ambasciatori, et altri Prencipi, e de delitti seguiti in Roma dalli 18 de Gennaro 1635 per tutto li 18 di deciembre 1643. scritta da Mons.r Giov. Batt.a Spada Lucchese Gov.re di detta Città nel d.o tempo, e che poi da Innocentio X.o fù creato Cardinale, chiamato di Sta. Susanna con una piena notitia de tratati temperamenti, gratie, e castighi usati circa le dette materie." Appointed governor of Rome by Urban VIII in 1635, Giovanni Battista Spada was responsible for keeping civic order and overseeing the papal police. The memoirs from his nine years in power provide one of the most detailed records of social disturbances in Rome between 1634 and 1643. They are particularly valuable for what they reveal about the rising level of violence in the city in these years and the corresponding rise in the prominence of the French and their conflict with the Spanish faction. This conflict and the contest for Rome, in fact, dominated the legal record the whole time Spada was governor, and the constant appearance in the record of Spanish and French feuds sets the tone for the entire report and also constitutes the most violent episode in the entire period. f. 82r.

19. BNM, MS 2890, f. 83r.

20. BNM, MS 2890, f. 93r. Gigli also provides an account of the incident (*Diario romano,* p. 162.)

21. BNM, MS 8541, ff. 117r–175r. An untitled treatise signed by Diego de Zúñiga, a resident in Rome, dated August 23, 1637. The letter was a lament concerning the actions against Spaniards taken in Rome by Urban VIII, particularly those of 1637. Folios 122v–125r give a detailed account of the events that transpired after the pope fell ill.

22. BNM, MS 8541, f. 126v.

23. For the festival life of Rome in the time of Urban VIII see especially Frederick Hammond, *Music and Spectacle in Baroque Rome* (New Haven: Yale University Press, 1994), and *L'effimero barocco: Strutture della festa nella Roma del seicento,* ed. Maurizio Fagiolo dell'Arco and Silvia Carandini, 2 vols. (Rome: Bulzoni, 1977–78).

24. Pastor, *History of the Popes,* vol. 28, pp. 409–413. Pastor notes that d'Estrées had been sent to Rome particularly because of his "domineering character," which must have been quite satisfied with the dominating spectacle of the cavalcata.

25. BCR, vol. misc. 586, Ludovico Grignani, *Descrittione delle feste fatte in Roma per la Nascita del Delfino hora Ludovico XIV* (Rome, 1643), p. viii.

26. Ibid.

27. For more details on the festivities surrounding the birth of the dauphin see Frederick Hammond, *Music and Spectacle in Baroque Rome* (New Haven: Yale University Press, 1994), pp. 228–231. Hammond also locates the celebrations in the context

of the international contest for power between France and Spain. The two early modern powers had been formally at war again since 1635.

28. My thanks to Fred Hammond, who provided me with the information concerning the rental arrangement between the Barberini brothers.

29. BCR, vol. misc. 586.

30. Ibid., p. xxxii.

31. BNM, MS 2890, ff. 131r–135v.

32. BNM, MS 2890, ff. 134v–139r.

33. BNM, MS 2890, f. 154v.

34. BCR, MS 1570, ff. 298v–299r.

35. BCR, MS 1570, f. 302v.

36. BNM, MS 2890, f. 154v.

37. BNM, MS 2890, ff. 154v–158r. Gigli also has a lengthy description of the battle with slightly different details from those in the governor's reports (*Diario romano*).

38. BNM, MS 2890, ff. 159r–163v. These pages provide an abbreviated account of the trial. Among the conclusions were the following: the Spanish ambassador had shown ill will against Lamego by saying publicly that he wanted him dead or alive, and ten people testified to this. It was also shown that the ambassador had brought soldiers from Naples to aid in the capture and that he dressed them up as *palafrenieri,* or doormen, and went around the city with them. The Spanish were the first to put their hands to the sword and had approached the carriage of Lamego shouting at him to get out and fight.

39. For the most recent and succinct description of the War of Castro and its consequences for Urban VIII, see Laurie Nussdorfer, *Civic Politics in the Rome of Urban VIII* (Princeton: Princeton University Press, 1992), pp. 205–227.

40. Ibid., pp. 213–215.

41. See Pastor, *History of the Popes,* vol. 30, pp. 14–30, for details of the conclave.

42. Ibid., p. 59.

43. Gigli, *Diario Romano.*

44. See Justo Fernandez Alonso, "Santiago de los Españoles y la Archicofradía de la Santíssima Resurrección de Roma hasta 1754," in *Antholigica Annua* (Rome: Instituto Español de Historia Ecclesiastica, 1960), vol. 8, p. 314. He notes that in 1754 the confraternity was dissolved and its property incorporated into the church of Santiago.

45. BCR, MS 1570, *Instruttione all Ecc.mo Signore Ambasciatore Cattolico per la sua venuta in Roma. Come si deve diportare nel suo negotione con tutti.* ff. 36r.

CHAPTER 7: SPANISH REVIVAL AND RESILIENCE, 1650–1700

1. AOP, leg. 622, *Relación de las fiestas que el ecelentissimo señor D. Luis de Guzmán, Ponze de León, Embaxador Ordinario de la Magestad Catholica a la Santidad de Alexandro VII. Pontifice Maximo. Hizo en Roma por el nacimiento de le Serenisimo, y Alti-*

simo Principe de las Españas D. Carlos Felipe de Austria, escrita por D. Enrique de Sevilla. Y dedicada al Eminentiss. y Reverendiss. Senor Cardenal D. Pasqual de Aragon (Rome, 1662).

2. Ibid.

3. AOP, leg. 622, f. 10r.

4. BNM, MS 2378, ff. 479–481, a report from Rome dated April 13, 1647.

5. Urb. Lat. 1100. ff. 33r–35r.

6. Giacinto Gigli, *Diario romano,* ed. Giuseppe Ricciotti (Rome: Tumminelli, 1958), pp. 274–75.

7. For the details on the papal response to the revolt of Masaniello see Ludwig Pastor, *History of the Popes,* ed. Ralph Francis Kerr (St. Louis: Herder, 1928), vol. 30, pp. 78–88.

8. AMEE, AEESS, leg. 91, unfoliated. From a group of documents entitled *Ceremonial desde el año 1646 hasta 1696.* A letter dated September 21, 1652, from the king to Cardinal Tribulcio expressed his enthusiastic approval of the presentation of chinea that year by Prince Camillo Pamphili, nephew of the pope.

9. AMEE, AEESS, leg. 90, ff. 206–207.

10. AMEE, AEESS, leg. 90, ff. 229r–229v.

11. Urb. Lat. 1100, f. 210r, 276r.

12. AMEE, AEESS, leg. 61, ff. 93r–97v. A report from the ambassador to the king from 1651 included a list of roughly twenty-five Catalans, predominantly clerics in the Curia, who inclined toward the French. Juan dela Casa, for example, was a courtier of the French ambassador and of one of the Barberini cardinals, who procured for him a pension from the cathedral in Barcelona. Men in the Curia included Juan Torres, Jayme Pasqual, Thomas Parigi, and Joseph Soler.

13. AMEE, AEESS, leg. 62, f. 98r.

14. AMEE, AEESS, leg. 62, f. 134r; the letter is dated April 6, 1655.

15. AMEE, AEESS, leg. 62, ff. 136r–136v.

16. AMEE, AEESS, leg. 62, f. 90r.

17. AMEE, AEESS, leg. 62, f. 143r.

18. AMEE, AEESS, leg. 62, 141r.

19. AMEE, AEESS, leg. 62, ff. 243r–252v.

20. AMEE, AEESS, leg. 62, ff. 253v–251r.

21. AMEE, AEESS, leg. 91, unfoliated. The volume is entitled *Ceremonial desde el año 1646 hasta 1696,* and the first letter about the queen of Sweden is dated March 30, 1656.

22. AMEE, AEESS, leg. 63, f. 1r.

23. AMEE, AEESS, leg. 70, f. 1r.

24. Richard Krautheimer, *The Rome of Alexander VII* (Princeton: Princeton University Press, 1985), pp. 99–100.

25. AMEE, AEESS, leg. 70, ff. 103r–187r. A detailed account of the events by the Venetian ambassador, Cardinal Pietro Rasadonna, is entitled *Il Famoso Fatto de Corsi successo in Roma nel Pontificato d'Alessandro Settimo.* This was the account sent

to Philip IV by his ambassador, and it included on the first page the judgment that the event had "altered if not changed the temperament" of the pope. The main change was that the French were increasingly seen as a threat to the Papal State. For another account of the conflict between Créqui and Alexander VII see especially Pastor, *History of the Popes,* vol. 31, pp. 91–103.

26. Marcantonio Nobili, *Descrittione del Nobile Corteggio e Maestosa Pompa con la quale l'Eccellentissimo Signore D. Maffeo Barberino Prencipe di Palestrina & Ambasciatore straordinario della Maestà Cattolica uscì dal Real Palazzo di Spagna la Vigilia di San Pietro à presentare la Chinea alla Santità Alessandro VII* (Rome, 1663).

27. AMEE, AEESS, leg. 71. The queen wrote personally to announce the death of the king in September 1667 (f. 134r). The marquis of Astorga had been named the new ambassador in May 1666 but had not yet gone to Rome, and Cardinal Sforza was named temporary ambassador by the queen (ff. 284r). Cardinal Hesse was named protector of Aragon (f. 331r).

28. AMEE, AEESS, leg. 71, f. 317r, 349r. The queen wrote to the ambassador in early 1667 urging that attention be paid to the creation of cardinals, and shortly thereafter wrote again to her ambassador about the factions then active among the cardinals.

29. In a number of instances the chinea and Easter processions were again notable enough to rate descriptive and laudatory treatises. See, for example the 1671 anonymous treatise, *Lettera si descrive en essa la relazione dela celebre, e pomposissima cavalcata fatta dall' Illustrissimo D. Antonio Pietro Alvarez Osorio* (Rome, 1671), pp. 1–14, which described the presentation of the chinea; and the 1675 treatise by Dionisio Torres, *Relatione delle feste fatte in Piazza Navona dala Ven. Archiconfratenita dela Sanctissima Resurretione* (Rome, 1675), pp. 1–8.

30. For details of the canonization ceremony see *Relatione delle Cerimonie and Apparato fatto nella Basilica di San Pietro nella Canonizatione de Cinque Santi* (Rome, 1671), pp. 1–7.

31. Pastor, *History of the Popes,* vol. 31, p. 468.

32. AMEE, AEESS, leg. 72, f. 1r. A letter from the queen dated January 1670 expressed anger over an incident in which the Spanish captain Don Joseph de Zúñiga had to chase a band of two hundred bandits who were aided by five hundred men from the Papal State, presumably under the pay of the French. Captain Joseph Artus was killed along with four men of his squadron. The queen wanted the pope to do everything necessary to remedy such a grave offense.

33. AMEE, AEESS, leg. 73, ff. 23r–38r. In a letter of June 26, 1675, the queen protested against the entry the French had been granted to the port of Civitavecchia.

34. AMEE, AEESS, leg. 73, f. 29r.

35. AMEE, AEESS, leg. 74, ff. 133r–137r.

36. AMEE, AEESS, leg. 75, an unfoliated letter from March of 1683 contains the king's protest.

37. BNM, MS 414, *Tratatti della Regalia di Francia,* ff. 303r–313r. The *Lettre du Roy á Mons. le Cardinal d'Estrées* was dated September 6, 1688.

38. AMEE, AEESS, leg. 79, ff. 1r, 107r.

39. AMEE, AEESS, leg. 79, ff. 32r, 84r: letters of support for the Colonna and Orsini families, respectively.

40. AMEE, AEESS, leg. 79, f. 24r.

41. AMEE, AEESS, leg. 80, ff. 99r–99v, 104r, and 123r.

42. Leopold von Ranke, *History of the Popes,* trans. E. Fowler (New York: Colonial Press, 1901), vol. 3, p. 186.

INDEX